D0324242

KING LEOPOLD'S
DREAM

Also by Jeremy Gavron

Darkness in Eden: The Murder of Julie Ward

KING
LEOPOLD'S
DREAM

Travels in the Shadow of the
African Elephant

JEREMY GAVRON

Pantheon Books   New York

Library of Congress Cataloging-in-Publication Data

Gavron, Jeremy, 1961–
King Leopold's dream : travels in the shadow of the
African elephant / Jeremy Gavron.
p.   cm.
ISBN 0-679-41998-5
1. Africa—Description and travel—1977–
2. Gavron, Jeremy, 1961–   —Journeys—Africa.
3. Elephants—Africa—Ecology. I. Title.
DT12.25.G39   1993
916.04'327—dc20   92-27118

Book design by Guenet Abraham

First Edition

FOR MARY AND TOSCO

CONTENTS

ACKNOWLEDGMENTS

Many people helped me along my elephant paths. Some have become characters in the text. For this I offer my thanks and apologies. But a few people gave me aid and hospitality beyond the call of duty. My special thanks to Geoff Creswell in Burundi, Soila Sayialel in Amboseli, Phil Hunsicker and Denise Stromme in the Central African Republic, Eve Abe in Uganda, Chris Munnion in South Africa, Clive Stockil in Zimbabwe, Kes and Fraser Smith and Kamate in Garamba, Stephen Cobb in Oxford and, in particular, the Mathews clan, Terry, Jeanne, Lorne, Dennis, Richard and Philip.

INTRODUCTION

In the late 1980s, I spent two years working as a newspaper correspondent in Africa, based briefly in Johannesburg and then in Nairobi. If I learned anything during this time, it was that Africa does not readily yield its heart, its intentions, its secrets. Africans are among the most friendly and welcoming people on earth. But they are also among the least forthcoming and the most personally reserved. In Africa a direct question seldom produces an honest answer. Africans prefer to work around a subject, teasing, and hiding. Africa as a whole is the same. In order to understand anything at all of Africa, I realized, it is necessary to approach the continent indirectly, from aslant—left-handed, you might say.

This book is written in the spirit of this understanding. It tells of a return to Africa for several months' travel around the continent on the trail of elephants and elephant people— the hunters, poachers, rangers, scientists, smugglers and elephant foster parents who live in the shadow of the great beasts. The result is a book about elephants that is, I hope, both more and less than an elephant book.

Less because I am not an elephant expert, simply a journalist. My idea grew out of the crisis of elephant poaching, but I never intended to write a straightforward account of this crisis or to restrict myself to this subject matter. I have been fascinated by African wildlife and the people who live in the African bush since stowing away as a boy on board books of adventure like *King Solomon's Mines, Born Free* and Gerald Durrell's *The Bafut Beagles*. When I came to write my own book, my intention was, in part, simply to indulge this enthusiasm. I would take elephants as my theme, set off around Africa, and rely on happenstance and impulse. And although this is not a journey of personal or inner exploration—whenever possible I have tried to keep myself in the background—it is still a personal journey. The trails and stories I have followed are the ones that have most interested me. An elephant expert would probably not have taken the sidetrack to the last elephant in Burundi or delved into the history of gomphotheres or tracked the lopsided dreams of a nineteenth-century Belgian king.

At the same time, this book is, I venture to suggest, a little bit more than an elephant book. Although elephants are for the most part the subject, they are also a symbol, an example. At this moment, Africa is going through perhaps the greatest upheaval of any region on earth at any time in history. No continent has ever had to change as dramatically as Africa in the twentieth century. One hundred years ago, most Africans lived in the Iron Age. Now many live in the computer age. The most fundamental conflict in Africa remains that between the old indigenous ways and the new imported ways. And the elephant is an important representative of the old Africa.

Before the arrival of the white man, the lives of Africans and elephants were deeply entangled. Both species lived all across the continent, from desert to swamp, mountain to coast. Elephant feet tramped out the paths that men followed and elephant tusks dug the water holes that sustained men in drought. Elephants provided meat for the hunter and ornaments, in the form of ivory, for chiefs. For many tribes, the elephant was the greatest god. After independence, the first instinct of Africans was to turn around and wipe out their elephant populations: not merely to use the ivory to buy modern material goods; but also, it seems to me, to destroy their world's wildness and danger, to erase what many Africans regard as a primitive and shaming past.

That instinct is slowly being curtailed. Africans (and outsiders working in Africa) are coming to realize that an Africa bereft of its own heritage and traditions would sit in an uneasy limbo, and that the continent's future depends as much on harnessing its own past as on grabbing something of the outside world's alluring present. In a small way, the fate of Africa is wrapped up in the fate of the African elephant.

So, indirectly, coming from aslant, I have tried in this book, both through the subject matter and in diversions along the way, to reveal a little not only about elephants and elephant people, but also about what I have learned of Africa itself.

KING LEOPOLD'S
DREAM

Chapter One

THE LAST ELEPHANT IN BURUNDI

The last elephant skulked behind the last tree like a shamefaced old drunk. Its eyes were sunken shadows. Its trunk was a fat maggot. It had a knobbly forehead and stubby tusks. The tree was a lone beam in a field of stumps.

The cartoon, by Jeff Mac Nelly of the *Chicago Tribune*, had arrived in the mail that morning. I cut it out and stuck it to the pinboard in my London kitchen. The drawing was a caricature, a parody. But its lone bashful elephant disturbed the dust on a memory. As I stared at it, my thoughts began to drift back to a warm afternoon in Africa and a conversation about another last elephant, a real last elephant.

"Hang on," I could hear myself asking, "Burundi has only one elephant?"

"That's right," replied Esmund Bradley Martin.

"How come?"

"All the rest were killed."

"But not this one?"

"No, not this one."

"So when did all this happen?" I pressed. "When were all the other elephants killed? How long has this one been the last elephant in Burundi?"

"Oh," said Esmund. "Years. Years and years."

We were sitting on the porch of Esmund's house on the outskirts of Nairobi. Esmund was a gangling American with a sheep's belly of white hair on his head. His large, sprawling garden was erupting with crimson flame trees and apricot bougainvillea blossoms. In the pastel blue sky, creamy clouds were drifting by like wraiths.

I was living in Nairobi too, sending stories about Africa back home to a British newspaper. I had come to talk to Esmund about elephant poaching and ivory. His particular interest was the ivory. He had spent much of his recent life tracking elephant tusks from the cheeks where they had started life to the billiard balls, piano keys, Japanese seals and pornographic Chinese carvings where they ended up. The way Esmund saw it, Burundi's last elephant was interesting only as an ironic totem, a conservationist's black joke.

His reason was Burundi's central role in Africa's illegal ivory trade. All around Burundi, in Zaire, Tanzania, Zambia and Kenya, elephants were being poached. The ivory was then sent to carving factories in Japan, China and Hong Kong before reaching the main ivory markets in Europe, America and Japan. The killing was easy. Exporting the tusks from Africa was also easy. But smuggling illegal, and therefore unlicensed, ivory through customs in Asia and the West was harder. It entailed large expense and regular losses. So the Burundi government had come up with a solution. It would sell official licenses for any ivory shipped out of Burundi. All the ivory traders had to do was sneak their tusks across the border into Burundi.

As a result, through much of the 1980s, Burundi was exporting tens of thousands of tusks a month. All of them carried licenses declaring them to have come from domestically culled elephants. And all the time Burundi had only one elephant. Big conservation joke.

While Esmund sniggered dryly, I shifted dreamily in my chair and wondered about this curious country, fifteen hundred miles away in the heart of the continent. What did I know of Burundi? That it was one of Africa's smallest nations. That on the map it nestled like a dozing cat around the northern tip of Lake Tanganyika. That it had once been a Belgian protectorate. That it was prone to terrible tribal massacres. That it was very densely populated.

I tried to imagine where and how a last elephant might live, but all I could come up with was an image like Mac Nelly's cartoon: a baleful creature wandering in decreasing circles around a diminishing patch of ragged forest.

Esmund wasn't much help either.

"I think it lives on an island," he said.

"An island, in a landlocked country?"

"An island in a river, maybe."

"But definitely in the wild. It's not a pet elephant?"

"Oh, no." Esmund shook his head.

For the rest of my posting in Africa, I tried to find an excuse to visit Burundi. But every time I booked a flight, I found myself having to rush off to cover some more pressing story for my newspaper: fighting and famine in Ethiopia; terrible floods in Khartoum; rebellion in Uganda.

So I had to make do with asking any wildlife experts I ran into around Africa about the elephant. Most simply shook their heads in ignorance. One gave me a computer print-out of continent-wide elephant numbers. Every country south of the Sahara and north of the Limpopo River had an elephant population—except the Gambia and Burundi. Officially, Burundi had had no elephants since the early 1970s. When I did finally find a mention of an elephant in Burundi, in a United Nations publication, it said the animal lived in a zoo. But Burundi had no zoo.

Now, years later, back in London, this drawing had rekindled my curiosity. I looked again at the cartoon elephant. There were times, I knew, when my own reporting of Africa had been scarcely less caricaturish than this. As a journalist, I had rushed from story to story, seldom able to concentrate on any one topic or even one country for more than a few days. But in my time in Africa, I had collected a mental scrapbook of clues and ideas about the continent. And ever since I had left Africa, I had been wanting to go back, to devote some time to just one of these ideas, hoping by delving deeply in one place to find out something more about the continent as a whole.

And why not delve into the elephant? These beasts were more than simply the largest animals in Africa. They were as much a part of Africa as the African people. Over thousands of years of living side by side with people, elephants had become interwoven into the tapestry of the continent's history and culture. Moreover, in recent years, because of the ivory poaching, elephants had also become a flesh-and-blood symbol of what I considered to be the most important question of all for Africa: the struggle of ancient traditions and resources to survive and contribute in the modern African world.

I had little idea where such exploration into elephants would lead. But I knew where it could begin: in Burundi. If, that is, the last elephant was still alive.

I picked up the telephone and dialed Esmund Bradley Martin in Nairobi.

"What about this last elephant?" I asked.

"I don't know. I think I heard it died."

"Oh."

"But don't take my word," he softened. "Call the British embassy in Bujumbura. They'll know."

Britain had no embassy in Bujumbura, Burundi's capital. There had once been an honorary consul, a character out of Graham Greene, fond of tea and gin-and-tonics but not of the few British tourists who knocked on his door hoping for help with visas. But even this honorary consul was now dead. So I tried the American embassy. When I mentioned elephants, I was put through to a woman named Mimi Brian.

"I'm the unofficial wildlife expert," she explained.

"Do you know about the elephant?"

"Sure, it's still around. It hadn't been seen for a while and we were worried that it was gone. But it's resurfaced."

"Have you seen it?"

"I haven't myself. But I know someone who spotted it just recently. A Frenchman called Yves Gaugris. If you want to find it, you'd better come soon. The rainy season starts at the end of September, and then it's impossible to get out there."

Mimi Brian lived in a damp bungalow with peeling whitewashed walls on a hillside above Bujumbura. Green trees and iron roofs glimmered dully below. Beyond, the waters of Lake Tanganyika stretched into the distance, a sleepy, wine-colored sea.

Mimi was a peppy southerner. She had red glasses and strong white teeth. Her accent was Deep South: when she talked, her vowel sounds swilled around her mouth.

"Come into the garden and say haah to my friends Poco and Socrateees," she drawled.

I followed her onto the patchy back lawn. In the middle was a huge cage and inside were a pair of chimpanzees. Mimi pushed a hand between the bars and the chimps loped over.

They were a sleazy duo. They had patchy fur, sloping shoulders and shifty eyes. They looked like a couple of lounge lizards. Mimi tickled their fingers and they squatted beside the bars, crooning dreamily and grunting through pursed lips.

Mimi was only temporarily fostering Poco and Socrates. Eventually, they would be released into a forest sanctuary. Both had been born in the wild. The hunters who captured them had probably killed and eaten their mothers. The babies had been sold as pets and kept until the wildlife authorities had recently confiscated them.

"Oh, not again," Mimi shrieked. "Why do they always have to do this when I have guests."

I looked down. The finger tickling had been too much. Both chimps had developed bright pink erections. Mimi pulled her hand away and went to collect the chimps' food. She spread a square of canvas on the grass in front of the cage and laid out carrots, fruit and rice. The chimps poked their arms through and fed themselves, tipping their heads back and dropping the food into their mouths like Romans eating grapes.

While we stood in the garden, the world had darkened. I looked up at the sky. Overripe clouds hung low above. They were the color of charcoal. The effect was like a watercolor washed in layers of grey and black and ash.

"Has it rained yet?" I asked.

"It's been spitting," Mimi said. "It's never completely dry here. But it can threaten for weeks before the real rains come. You should have a few days yet to find the elephant."

"And where exactly is the elephant?"

"It lives up along the banks of the Rusizi River, which runs north out of Lake Tanganyika. The river is the border between Burundi and Zaire. There's a particular spot, some twenty or thirty miles up the river, where the elephant is usually seen."

Unfortunately, Mimi did not know exactly where this spot was. And her French friend Yves Gaugris, the only person she was sure did know, was out of the country. So Mimi suggested I talk to another conservationist, an American named Peter Trenchard. He worked for Burundi's wildlife department and lived at Gitega, a couple of hours east of Bujumbura.

"There's a party in Gitega tonight," Mimi said. "Given by a Peace Corps worker who lives up there. Peter will be there. I've taken the liberty of arranging you a ride."

Gitega lay in the center of Burundi, beyond the hills that rose out of Lake Tanganyika. As we drove away from Bujumbura, the road wound up toward the clouds. We saw no towns along the way, but the land was still densely populated. Burundi was home to 5 million people, and most of them lived as subsistence farmers in the countryside, growing cassava, plantain and sweet potato.

Looking out of the window, I could see hundreds of tiny plots. Every inch of land seemed to be tended. Patches of cultivation nestled together in the valley bottoms. Bands of crops ran along the roads. Yellow and brown fields clung to the rounded hills like the mottled markings on giant tortoise shells. These hills had once been covered in forest, but now only a few trees remained: the odd rearguard copse or ancient sentinel sheltering a cluster of mud huts. It was hard to imagine even a last elephant finding cover here.

The land was also sprinkled with people. Dark shapes tilled the land and jinked along narrow paths. More people were walking along the road, goods from town slung on their backs or balanced on their heads. Apart from a few Pygmies, Burundi's population was made up of two tribes: the Hutu and the Tutsi. They looked quite different. The Tutsi were tall and slender, the Hutu short and squat. The Hutu were the majority and the original inhabitants of what had become the neighboring states of Rwanda and Burundi. The minority Tutsi had come from the north a few hundred years ago. They had quickly subjugated the Hutu masses in both Rwanda and Burundi.

This subjugation still continued in Burundi. But in Rwanda, European colonialism and then independence had brought new ideas. Stirred to action, the Hutu had overthrown their overlords, slaughtering 100,000 Tutsi in the process. A Hutu was now president of Rwanda. In Burundi, the Tutsi had watched this killing in horror. Their reaction was to pre-empt any such occurrence in their own country, so the predominantly Tutsi army was ordered to massacre every Hutu who could read and write or had any influence or power. In the space of three months, 200,000 Hutu died, shot or chopped to pieces.

This was nearly twenty years ago. But a couple of years before my visit, a local dispute between Hutu and Tutsi had provoked further widespread carnage. The Tutsi had killed 30,000 more Hutu. The Akanyaru River in the north of the country where the killing took place had literally run red with blood.

I looked out of the window. Tall and short men walked side by side. They talked, shouted and laughed. I could see no sign of ill feelings.

We reached Gitega shortly after dusk and drove through a sprawl of dusty streets and chipped cement houses. The party had been going all day. A bottle of beer was thrust into my hands, and I talked to Peace Corps volunteers with names like Leif and Matt and Marla. Then, as the token Englishman, I was roped into a game of darts. When the players decided that the dartboard was too small and that the point was to make the darts stick to the wall, I opted out and went to look for Peter Trenchard.

I found him standing alone behind the house. He was a stocky man with strong limbs and a pleasant, chubby face. He was drinking beer from the bottle and there was a line of foam on his mustache. When I mentioned elephants, he shook his head sadly.

"You've got the wrong country," he said, giving me a pitying look. "Try Kenya. Loads of elephants there. All over the place."

I said I would see him in the morning. I was suddenly exhausted, so I found the car which had brought me here and climbed inside to try to sleep. The gear stick jammed into my back, and every few minutes there was a roar of triumph as a dart stuck fast in the cement wall of the house. Much later, it grew cold and quiet and I fell asleep dreaming of tall chimpanzees slaughtering small ones because they could not keep their penises under control.

In the morning, I had breakfast with Peter Trenchard, his pretty African wife and their fat, wide-eyed baby.

"I know about the elephant," Trenchard said. "But I've never seen it. I've never seen any elephants here. They were all gone by the time I arrived in this country. I have seen elephant bones, though, up in the Kibira forest."

"Where's that?"

"It's a narrow ridge of forest at the northern end of the Zaire-Nile divide—the hills you drove over on the way up here. There were elephants there until the mid-1970s, but they were all hunted down in the end."

"By who?"

"By the local people."

They had hunted with spears. The hills in the Kibira were steep and the paths narrow. The hunters had planted their spears at the bottom of the paths, sharp points facing up.

They had then waited for an elephant to come along and chased it down the path. The elephant would tumble belly first onto the spears. When it fell, the men would rush forward and slice the tendons in its legs. Then they would poke out its eyes. When it was dead, they would cut off the tip of its trunk and throw it into the bushes for luck.

Trenchard had found these bones while looking for chimpanzees. He had come to Burundi as a Peace Corps worker but was now working with the government, identifying the remnants of Burundi's wildlife. There were more than four hundred chimpanzees left in Burundi, as well as leopards, hippos, colobus monkeys, and a few species of smaller antelopes. But most of the other large species had disappeared. Lion, cheetah, rhino, zebra, eland, bongo, impala and waterbuck were all gone.

"This country's so crowded with people," Trenchard said. "There are cows all over the savannas and the forests have shrunk to almost nothing. The Kibira and a few other tiny patches of forest where the chimps live are all that remain. There's scarcely any room for the animals."

The cutting down of the forests had also created problems for the farmers. It was the tree roots that bound the soil to the steep hillsides. Without the trees, soil was washed away in huge layers whenever it rained. Millions of tons of this precious topsoil was ending up on the bottom of Lake Tanganyika every rainy season. The land was becoming less fertile. Landslides were common, and sometimes deadly. The local expression for the end of the world was: "when the hills meet."

"But your elephant doesn't live in the forest," Trenchard said. "It's out on the Rusizi plains."

"That's what I've heard," I said.

Trenchard did not know exactly where the elephant could

be found. But he had a suggestion. There was an old missionary by the name of Carl Johnson who had been in Burundi since shortly after the war. He was interested in wildlife. I should look him up.

"Just ask for *le vieux* Johnson," Trenchard said. "Every taxi driver will know him."

On the way back to Bujumbura, I stopped off at the southern edge of the Kibira forest. Leif, a Peace Corps worker I had met at the party, lived in a simple wooden cabin here. He offered to take me for a walk in the forest.

We climbed a rocky, grassy slope and followed a path into the trees. It was late and the world was a muted grey. The sounds were also muffled. Only the smell of the forest, damp and fecund, came unbroken to my senses. As we walked, I squinted my eyes and peered into the darkness. I saw a looming rounded shape. It was the ghost of an elephant that dissolved, after a moment, into a rock.

All these paths had originally been made by elephants. Now they had been taken over by a French judge who worked as a legal advisor to the Burundi government. In his spare time, the judge was marking the paths as walking trails. Every Sunday, he would head out into the countryside with a pail of paint in either hand and daub landmarks along the paths with directional red and white stripes. He had been doing this for years, and had mapped out nearly one hundred miles of trail.

Leif pointed out a marker. There were two adjacent strips, red and white. But in the gloom, I fancied I could see a third stripe, a blue one alongside. Up here, it did not seem so unlikely. I could just imagine the French judge, a pipe in his mouth and a sack of soft cheese and red wine on his shoulder, striding each Sunday across Burundi, claiming all the rocks and trees along the way with the three stripes of the Tricolor.

The Johnson mission lay at the end of a dirt road, on the north side of Bujumbura. When I arrived, an old man emerged from the open door of a simple red brick house. He had a leathery face, with pink patches on the dome of his head where the skin had peeled in the sun. A flourish of white hair lay like a furry caterpillar on his upper lip.

"Mr. Johnson?" I asked.

"Call me Carl," he said. "If you call me Mr. Johnson, I'll think you're talking about my father."

His denim eyes danced at the joke: he was seventy-five if a day. He gripped my hand in his mottled frontiersman's paw.

"Come on in," he said.

The house was furnished with practical asceticism: hard wooden chairs, plastic tablecloth and plates, a bath molded from cement. Dozens of long-forgotten volumes of theological debate lined the makeshift shelves. In the corner stood an ancient radio. Mr. Johnson sat straight on his wooden chair, back upright, chin aloft.

"So you want to know about elephants," he said. "Well, as for myself, I've never seen a single pachyderm here in Burundi, though my wife has. Oh, she used to see them all the time when she went out onto the plains to her women's Bible classes. But that was way back, must have been nearly thirty years ago."

"You've never seen any elephants?"

"Why, of course I have. Up in the Congo, they were everywhere."

Mr. Johnson and his wife had been in Africa for forty-five years. Most of this time had been spent here in Bujumbura, where they ran several church schools, including one for the deaf and blind. But they had first lived in the Belgian Congo, at Bunia, near Lake Albert—eager young Protestant missionaries in a land where animist beliefs came first, Catholicism a poor second, and Protestantism a distant third.

"We used to have elephants raiding the crops every night," Mr. Johnson said. "I knew a man who shot more than a hundred. I must have shot a dozen myself. Had an old German Mauser eight-millimeter rifle. I remember one elephant was causing a whole heck of trouble in the fields. I shot her one day and she tumbled over onto her head and broke a tusk, but she was back up in a second and off into the bush. We set up an ambush and got her a few days later."

His eyes sparkled with the memory.

"Boy," he said. "Were those people glad to see the back of her. One man came up and slapped her and said, 'You ate all my corn.' It was true: her belly was full of it. Almost before she was dead, they were cutting her up. For the first time in their lives the little boys had all they wanted to eat. They roasted the meat on sticks and their stomachs blew up like drums."

Mrs. Johnson poked her head out from the kitchen.

"He's asking about a living elephant, dear, and you're telling him about killing them," she said.

"I know, Mama," the old man grumbled.

"If you're really interested in this one that lives out on the plains, then you should talk to my son Harry," he said. "He's the expert. He might even be able to take you out there."

It was afternoon before Harry appeared. He was a quiet man, with restless eyes and straw-colored hair that fell flat in a circle from the top of his head, like a monk without the bald spot. He was born here in Burundi and had married the missionary girl with whom he had played as a child in the African dust. His life had been devoted to human good works, but he had also kept up a keen interest in wildlife. He had seen the elephant a couple of times and knew where it could sometimes be found.

"You want to go and have a look now?" he asked.

"Sure."

We drove north out of the city. To our right, we passed the airport and came out onto a flat, dry scrub plain. Large brown cattle with loose skin on their necks and magnificent long curved horns scuffed along in the dust.

"There used to be elephants all around here," Harry said.

"What happened to them?"

"There were several hundred up until the mid-1950s. My mother used to see herds of them when she came out here to give Bible classes. You see, this had been tsetse country. You know the tsetse fly? Sleeping sickness? Most people preferred to live up in the hills. It was more healthy up there."

"But somebody must have been living on the plains for your mother to be giving Bible classes."

"Yes. The Belgians were settling people there. There had always been a few hunters camping on the plains, but at the start of the 1950s the Belgians decided to grow cotton on the plains. They wiped out the tsetse fly and brought people down from the hills. They set up plantations and villages, which my mother visited. For a while, there were elephants and people, but it was not long before the elephants were causing trouble—raiding plots and wandering through villages at night. So the Belgians said anyone could shoot the elephants. Pretty soon they were all gone."

"Except one," I said.

"I'm not so sure. I don't think this elephant was around then. The last elephants out here were shot at the end of the 1950s. This one wasn't seen until the mid-1970s."

"Where did it come from then?"

"That I don't know," Harry smiled. It was his first smile and it only lasted for a moment.

We were now twenty miles out of town. Harry slowed down and we dropped off the road and turned westward into the scrub. In the distance was a mountain range, a grainy blue smudge against the horizon. There was no track. Harry aimed for one of the peaks, and we drove slowly over the dry, sandy earth and through patches of thorny bush. Long white thorns screeched against the sides of the vehicle.

The scrub grew steadily thicker until Harry stopped the car. We walked the last few yards, ducking under bushes and short, stumpy trees. I pushed away a final branch and found myself standing at the edge of a high escarpment.

The land we had driven across was dry and brown and brittle. But below was a different world: a scene of abundant fertility. The Rusizi River, the border between Burundi and Zaire, was a slow, chocolate-colored frontier. The banks on either side were a bright lush green. On the far side, fertile fields stretched all the way to the shadowy mountains.

In the soft afternoon light, there was something almost primeval about this land. A forest of palms, the wavering fronds a burnished white, ran down to the bank to our left. On the right, just below us, in a crook in the river, was a headland of brushed elephant grass. Three sparse, flat-topped acacia trees sat like sentinels above the blades. It was here that on previous occasions Harry Johnson had seen the elephant.

We scanned the grass with binoculars. A herd of brown and white cattle were nosing into the open, a hundred yards or so from the trees. Farther up the river, a group of bare-chested fishermen were unloading a boat. But we could see no sign of the elephant: no flapping ears, no glint of tusk.

We waited until the sun slipped behind the mountains, and then drove back to the city in the dark.

Harry Johnson knew an old man who had lived out on the plains before the cotton growers. His name was Muzeduke. Harry said he had hunted with a spear and bow and arrows until he had been wounded by a charging buffalo. Now he was crippled. One morning, Harry took me out to see him.

We drove across the plains again. This time we turned eastward from the road and jangled along a rutted track to a settlement of scattered mud huts.

"This was a cotton village," Harry said. "It's called Gihanga, which means 'Big Skull.' The village was established at the time of the elephant killing. There were skeletons all over the plains. For a long while, they had a couple of large elephant skulls in the village square."

We found Muzeduke squatting on his haunches in the shade of a frangipani tree, rolling a yellow blossom in his fingers. He was a shriveled, wrinkly old man with a wizened head and skinny limbs that protruded from an oversized pink seersucker jacket and stained, torn white shorts. When he struggled to his feet to greet us, his crouched position hardly changed. He was permanently bent double at the waist. The effect of the buffalo, I thought.

Despite the wrinkles and the faded, yellowy eyes, Muzeduke's face was still handsome and full of character. He gave me a gummy grin and crushed my hand in his bony grip.

A handful of the other village elders had now arrived. Children were sent off to find chairs, and we were led into a low dark musty hut. One of the old men winked at me, and when I smiled, he winked again and laughed.

Through Harry, Muzeduke began to tell his story.

"He says he is ninety years old," Harry said. "He says he remembers the German defeat by the Belgians in 1916."

"You don't think he's that old?"

"No, he can't be more than late sixties."

Whenever it was, Muzeduke had begun hunting while the plains were still empty of people and rich with game. Muzeduke had hunted dozens of bushbuck, buffalo and bush-pig. And he had speared two leopards and six elephants.

"How did you hunt elephants?"

"We had dogs."

The dogs tracked the elephants and then distracted them by barking and snapping at their heels while the hunters crept up on the blind side to throw their spears. Muzeduke held up his arm and patted his armpit to show the best spot.

A dozen boys were now gathered outside the hut, peering in and giggling. Muzeduke called out to them. A few minutes later, one of the boys reappeared with a spear. It was a long, crafted length of wood, capped with a heavy iron head. Muzeduke ran his hands lovingly along the smooth shaft.

"Once I threw my spear and it stuck right in the forehead of an elephant," he said. "Between the eyes. It lifted its trunk and pulled the spear out and threw it back at me. I grabbed the spear and threw it again, and others also threw their spears. Eventually, we killed it."

"Did any of the hunters ever get hurt?" I asked.

The elders began to chatter and laugh. Muzeduke caught my eyes and smiled bashfully.

"What are they saying?" I asked Harry.

"The old man is embarrassed," he said. "They used charms. They are saying something about a Pygmy witch doctor in the forest. When they were going on a particularly dangerous hunt, they would go and see him and he would give them medicine. They thought it protected them. But now they say they don't believe in those things."

"What about his accident with the buffalo?"

Harry's translation of my question prompted more snorts of laughter and rapid conversation.

"It wasn't a buffalo, it was a bushpig," Harry said. The joke was that the pig had wounded him in the groin. The back trouble had come much later, from old age or disease.

"How many elephants were there out on the plains when you were young?" I asked Muzeduke.

"Nobody can tell, but there were more elephants than people. We would always hear them in the bush, their bellies rumbling."

"What happened to them all?"

"Some went up to the forest."

"Were many killed?"

"Many. There was a chief who had a gun, he killed some. The missionaries killed some too. I was a tracker for some of them. I helped to catch two baby elephants for the Belgians."

"What about the last elephant?"

"It came down from the hills," Muzeduke said.

"Why has nobody killed it?"

"Now we are not even allowed to hunt partridges," the old man said in disgust. "Anyway, we would prefer to find another one to live with it. It is lonely. Elephants can have loneliness just like people. It's not good to be by itself. Elephants like company, they joke and play like men."

"I will tell you what to do," said James Gordon Bennett, son of the publisher of the *New York Herald*, to Henry Morton Stanley one morning in Paris in 1869. "Draw £1,000 now, and when you have gone through that, draw another £1,000, and when you have finished that draw another, and so on: *but find Livingstone.*"

Two years later, on November 10, 1871, Stanley strode into the town of Ujiji, on the eastern shore of Lake Tanganyika. Stanley knew that Dr. Livingstone was here. He also knew what it meant for his own career and reputation to have found the old man. He was so excited that he wanted to jump a somersault or bite his hand. But instead he calmed himself down, and as he strode through town toward his meeting with Livingstone, he prepared his famous line of greeting.

It was thirty years since Livingstone had arrived in Africa. He had spent most of this time on the continent, racked by fever and dysentery. He was not well and within a year he would be dead. But before he died, there were certain things he wanted to do. The most pressing was to investigate an idea he had about the true source of the Nile. Stanley's arrival was a blessing. The two men quickly became friends. With Stanley's help, Livingstone could make one final journey.

Some weeks after Stanley's arrival, he and Livingstone set off northward up Lake Tanganyika in a canoe big enough, as Stanley wrote, to carry "3,500 lbs. of ivory." After four days, they arrived at "Nyabigma, a sandy island in Urundi." This was the southern tip of the land that later became Burundi: Stanley and Livingstone were its first white visitors.

Stanley had little to say about the people of Burundi, other than that they were "very civil, if profound starers." But he was delighted by the countryside. The verdant hills rolling down to picturesque settlements in the shade of plantain trees on the lakeshore was the nineteenth-century romantic ideal: "by far lovelier" than anything back in America, Stanley's adopted home.

Livingstone, however, was disappointed. A decade earlier, John Hanning Speke had proclaimed Lake Victoria to be the source of the Nile. Livingstone was not convinced. He had heard that a river ran north out of Lake Tanganyika and up toward Lake Victoria. If this were true, then Lake Tanganyika would be the true source of the Nile. But when Stanley and Livingstone reached the top of the lake, they found that the brown waters of the Rusizi River ran gently southward into—and not northward out from—the lake. The only remarkable fact about the Rusizi was that it abounded in crocodiles.

But on their journey, Stanley and Livingstone did hear something intriguing. It was a fable, told to them by their chief boatman, an old fisherman named Ruango.

Lake Tanganyika, so the story went, had once been a great fertile plain on which had stood a large city. Two of the inhabitants of this city were a man and wife who owned a magic well, which was always full of fresh water and delicious fish. This well had been passed down from generation to generation within the family. The only rule of the well was that it remain the family's secret.

One year, the wife took a lover. Sometimes, when she went to visit him, she carried him fresh fish from the well. The fish was so good that the lover begged to know its source. But the wife refused to tell him. Then, one day, the husband left the town for a time. While he was away, the lover persuaded the wife to show him the well.

She took him to her house and gave him palm wine to drink and fish to eat. Then she led him to a secret enclosure. The man was delighted. The water was as clear as the air. The fish leaped and glinted in the light. Joyously, he reached out his hand. A fish jumped and brushed against him.

Immediately, there was a great and terrible sound. The world had cracked open. The city swiftly sank into the chasm. The waters flowed out of the well. When the husband returned, he saw the entire plain flooded beneath the waters of the well.

Looking back, there is a curious prescience to this tale. Recast, with Stanley and Livingstone as the lover and Burundi's natural resources as the well, it was the story of Burundi's future. From the moment that Stanley and Livingstone touched the fish—saw and lived to tell about the abundance and beauty of the land—Burundi's forests and wildlife were doomed.

By the time Stanley found Livingstone, much of Africa was already undergoing devastating changes. South of Ujiji, Stanley had encountered a bull elephant: a "colossal monster, the incarnation of might and the African world." But this was already a rare sight. Elsewhere, Stanley saw few elephants. In many places, there were no elephants at all.

The assault on Africa's wildlife—and its old ways—had actually begun four hundred years earlier, when the first European ship, a Portuguese schooner, anchored off the shores of West Africa. For most of the intervening period, fearful of malaria, parasites and fierce tribes, Europeans had steadfastly refused to venture inland from the coast. But their influence had extended far ahead of them. Through the sixteenth, seventeenth and eighteenth centuries, European goods, including guns and whisky, spread into the continent. And African goods came back out. These included gold, black gold—slaves—and white gold—ivory.

The ivory trade was the subject of Joseph Conrad's *Heart of Darkness*, his tale of the meeting of the old and the new in Africa. Conrad himself had skippered ivory boats down tributaries of the Congo River. And Kurtz, his man of darkness, was an ivory dealer. "Strings of dusty niggers with splayed feet arrived and departed," Conrad wrote in the novel. "A stream of manufactured goods, rubbish cottons, beads and brass wire sent into the depths of darkness, and in return came a precious trickle of ivory."

This European greed for Africa's wealth transformed the continent. Tribes became territorial. They acquired guns. They learned to prey on their habitats and on each other.

And when first Swahili Arabs and then Europeans themselves, prompted by the discovery of quinine as a cure for malaria, began to explore and loot the continent in the nineteenth century, this transformation quickened.

By this time, the slave trade was in decline. Britain had abolished the trade in 1791 and slavery in 1834. But the warring and killing for ivory continued apace. "Every pound of ivory has cost the life of a man, woman or child," Stanley later wrote. "For every five pounds, a hut has been burned. For every two tusks a village has been destroyed." And of course, the elephants suffered too. In fifty years, as many as 5 million elephants were slaughtered for their tusks. By the start of the twentieth century, elephants were extinct in large parts of the continent.

The kingdom of Urundi held out against the Arabs, Europeans, slavery and the ivory trade longer than most. It was a structured society and its Tutsi rulers were fierce fighters. Livingstone and Stanley were greeted cordially, but later visitors were not so lucky. The first Arab caravan was slaughtered by a Tutsi war party. The same fate befell the first Catholic fathers, who set up a mission near Rumonge, halfway between Ujiji and Bujumbura in 1879.

But Burundi's natural wealth, the secret of the well, had been revealed. Following the Berlin Conference of 1884–85, Burundi became a German colony. Explorers were followed by hunters and then settlers. Later, after the Second World War, Burundi was handed over to the Belgians and the white invasion continued. The Belgians hunted and farmed. Their medicines transformed African life expectancy. Soon the forests were being cut down, the wildlife was diminishing, and the human population was exploding.

The cotton-growing scheme Harry Johnson had told me about brought the end of elephants on the Rusizi. The cutting down of the forests wiped out most of the herds in the mountains. The few that were left in the Kibira were hunted down and eaten. Out on the Ruvubu plains, in the east of the country, the last elephant herds were killed in the early 1970s by Burundi's first president, Michel Micombero, who liked to hunt with automatic weapons from a flying helicopter.

In 1975, during a culling operation in neighboring Rwanda, three or four elephants escaped across the border into Burundi. One morning, a farmer woke up and found them eating his crops. He complained to the police and the elephants were found and shot. That, it was generally assumed, was the end of elephants in Burundi.

I had arranged to meet George at 7 P.M. at the Dallas, a popular bar in downtown Bujumbura. Saleh, George's friend who had set up the appointment, said I would recognize George immediately. "He is big," Saleh said. "A lot of muscle."

Some minutes after 8 P.M., George bounded up the stairs. He was built like a buffalo, six and a half feet high and wrapped in muscle. His hair was cropped flat against his huge head, and there was a hint of Oriental slant in his eyes. He was wearing tight trousers and a Hawaiian shirt: he looked like a Caribbean assassin from a James Bond movie. There was a scuffed black briefcase in his hand.

"Sorry I'm late," he smiled. Saleh had said George was Ghanaian, but he spoke like a Londoner.

"Can you change this for me?" he said, holding up a crumpled 5,000-franc note. "I've got to pay the taxi."

I pulled out five 1,000-franc notes and swapped them for his money. He leaped down the stairs, four at a time, and bowled across the road to the taxi stand. I watched him for a while wandering from taxi to taxi, waving one of the notes I had given him in the air. Then I walked over.

"Can you change a thousand?" he said. "I can't get anyone to change it. None of these blokes speaks a word of English."

A wedding party had just arrived at the Dallas, so George suggested we go to another bar. The Las Vegas was a few dingy tables and chairs in a concrete car park. George said he knew the owner. A waiter with a droopy face showed us to a table and rearranged the swirls of muck with a dirty rag.

"Drink?" said George. "I'm having Coke. I only drink champagne, and I can't afford that any more."

The waiter brought a couple of Cokes. George still had one of the small notes I had given him. He insisted on paying.

George was indeed Ghanaian: from a leading Ashanti family. "Not quite royal," as he put it. "Though you could say I'm a prince." His father had been an officer in the British army, and George had grown up in England. After attending a couple of minor public schools, he had dabbled in various businesses in England, including a summer season supplying bouncers for parties on riverboats on the Thames.

"If anyone gave us trouble, we just threw 'em in the river," he explained. "But I wanted a piece of the big time, you know. So I got into the import-export business."

"Like James Bond," I said.

"What? Yeah, James Bond." George liked the comparison.

"So I was buying and selling. Anything. Commodities. Then I met this guy who said there were three hundred tons of ivory in Bujumbura. I'd never heard of Bujumbura and neither had the guy at British Airways who sold me the ticket. I ended up in Uganda. It didn't really matter, though, because I made a quick deal in beans before I left."

George eventually made it to Burundi and found his contact. He was taken to see the stored ivory. It was in a warehouse: elephant tusks, dusty and yellow, some still stained with blood, piled from floor to ceiling.

"It was great," George said. "The ivory was from all over

Africa, but it all had Burundi licenses. All I had to do was find a market. By the end of '87, coming in on short trips, I had got a hundred tons out to the Far East."

"How much did you make, George?" I asked.

"My share was a million."

"What? Burundi francs?"

"Pounds." George grinned.

"A million pounds?"

George bared his teeth like a delighted baby. He was a dreamer, a romantic, a fantasist. But this was Africa. Here dreams were as good a currency as reality. And George had the papers to prove his story. He opened his briefcase and pulled out sheaves of papers: faxes from Hong Kong, letters from the president's office, bills for tens of thousands of pounds from the local hotels.

He reeled off a telephone number.

"The president's office," he said. He slammed his huge hand on the table with pleasure. "Those were the days."

Then, at the end of 1987, President Jean-Baptiste Bagaza flew off to attend a summit of Francophone heads of state, in Quebec. In his absence, he was deposed. The new president, Major Pierre Buyoya, keen to win international approval and aid, cracked down on various shady activities—including Burundi's role in Africa's illegal ivory trade.

But there remained a problem. Burundi still possessed eighty-four tons of ivory. These tusks had clearly been poached. But most of them were owned by influential men: cabinet ministers, army officers, wealthy businessmen. The ivory was worth some £8 million. There was pressure on President Buyoya to allow one more sale.

"Enter me," George said. "I had agreed on a price. I had people who wanted to buy and people who wanted to sell. I flew in to Bujumbura expecting to stay no more than ten days. Ten days, then I'd be gone."

A year later, George was still here. Within days of his
arrival, a far more serious snag had arisen. The world community had voted to ban the international trade in ivory.
Burundi's ivory was now, legally at least, stranded. But
George just couldn't leave it. For months, he tried the black
markets in China, Japan, Hong Kong, even Korea. Finally,
after spending £50,000 on room, telephone and champagne
at the Hotel Source du Nil, his money had begun to run
short. So he gave up the champagne and moved into a cheaper
residence.

"It's terrible, all this waiting," he said. "I can't stand this
bloody place. Bloody Africa. I can't even speak French. The
only thing I can say is '*Voulez-vous coucher avec moi?*' and
every time I say that, it costs me fifty quid."

"Why don't you go home?" I asked.

"The investment. I've put too much money into this deal.
And anyway, I only need one more month. There are still
people who want ivory. I'll be here a maximum of one more
month, then the deal will be finished."

"One month? Really, George?"

"I'm serious," he said. "I'm almost there."

"Then what?"

"Then I can wear my elephant T-shirt."

"What T-shirt?"

"You know the one: it says ONLY ELEPHANTS SHOULD WEAR
IVORY."

He laughed again, in pure delight. Then he saw my raised
eyebrows.

"Look, I don't kill the elephants," he said. "When the ivory
gets here, they're already dead. I'll tell you, the problem is
the African countries themselves." His voice rose in indignation. "You know who's doing the poaching? The rangers!
If these countries just got a grip on things, they could stop
the poaching."

"Then you'd be out of a job."

"This is just one deal, it's the last ivory deal. I'd be pleased. I like elephants. I'm all for saving them. But business is business."

I saw George one more time. He was leaning against a car outside an auto repair shop, dressed in jeans and a torn T-shirt. We started talking, and then a black limousine drove past and George took off after it, shouting until it stopped. A tinted window opened and a fist, decorated in gold bands, stretched languidly forward and shook George's hand. After a minute, the car pulled away and George loped back across the road.

"Next week," he grinned. "Next week it's all over, and then I'm getting out of here. Just one more week."

Some months later, back in London, I received a letter from Burundi. George had been thrown in jail for failing to pay a £5,000 phone bill at his new residence. He had eventually produced the money and freed himself, but he was running out of patience with Burundi. Iraq had recently invaded Kuwait and George was talking about the money to be made in sanction busting. He had heard there was a demand for tea in Baghdad.

Yves Gaugris, Mimi's elephant expert, had finally returned from vacation in France. One evening I went round to see him. Gaugris looked like a peasant. He had the figure of a prize French bull. He was short and square, with a huge head that emerged without a neck from a massive pair of shoulders. But his most treasured feature was his belly: huge and firm, a labor of love.

It was a warm evening and we sat outside, drinking whisky and eating chocolates from France, while the mosquitoes shrieked in our ears.

"You are interested in elephants?" Gaugris said. "But there is only one elephant in Burundi."

"I know. I've been looking for it. I thought you might know something about it."

"But of course, it was me who found him."

This was not strictly true: the local Africans had found the elephant. But Gaugris was the first white man to see it.

This was back in 1974. Gaugris had recently arrived in Burundi and heard stories about the solitary beast. He persuaded a member of the Burundi flying club to take him up one Sunday for a spin along the course of the Rusizi River. They found the elephant in the long grass, not far from where I had been looking with Harry. At the time, Gaugris reckoned from the size of its tusks that it was an adolescent male.

Over the years, Gaugris had seen the elephant many more times. Sometimes he took his family for picnics on the escarpment above the elephant's bend in the river. He had even used his 600-mm lens to take a distant picture of the beast. Only once had he seen the elephant close up. He was in a boat on the river, and the elephant suddenly appeared from one bank. It slipped into the waters only a few meters away.

"It was magnificent," Gaugris recalled. "He swam across and then rose out of the river, dripping with water, and disappeared. We heard his belly rumbling."

I asked Gaugris where the elephant had come from.

He gave a Gallic shrug. There was no reasonable answer. The last elephants had been killed in the Rusizi by 1960. There had been no reports of elephants in the area for a decade and a half. When Gaugris had first seen the elephant, in 1974, it had been around fifteen years old. It could not possibly have survived on its own since infancy. It must therefore have come from outside.

"But from where?" I asked.

"Yes," Gaugris pouted. "From where? The elephant is

surrounded on all sides. There are people all around. The nearest surviving elephant population is in the Kahuzi–Biega National Park in Zaire. That is more than eighty miles away."

Then I remembered Muzeduke's idea, that this elephant had come down from the Kibira forest to escape the hunters there. What about this possibility?

"Boffff," Gaugris said. "*Peut-être*. But the nearest part of the Kibira is thirty miles from the Rusizi. By 1970 the new airport road had been built. Livestock had arrived on the plains in huge numbers. Fences had been constructed. Settlements had multiplied. Certainly, an elephant can walk thirty miles in a night, but the chances of a lone adolescent doing so without meeting people, without being diverted or turned back or killed, these are very slight. In my view, there is only one solution. He must have come in by parachute."

We sat in silence on the porch for a few moments, contemplating this puzzle. Gaugris took a chocolate.

"It is a mystery," he said. "But it is not the only mystery. The other is why it has not been killed, like all the rest."

"Yes," I said. "Why?"

"Well, I have given the matter a good deal of thought. There is no rational reason. It is true the people in Burundi do not like elephant meat. But they like the tusks. And the Zairois adore elephant meat. The Zairois soldiers are often shooting hippos in the Rusizi. Why not shoot the elephant?"

Gaugris paused to pick out another choice chocolate. I waited, like a pupil with a master storyteller.

"So I have come up with this answer," Gaugris continued. "These people who live down by the river are animist. They believe in nature. They think wild animals are their own ancestors reincarnated. This does not stop them killing the individual animals. But if an entire species disappears, it is different. Then perhaps they lose a fragment of their own belief system."

"So they won't kill this last elephant because it would destroy their own heritage? It would wipe away their past?"

"*Voilà.*"

At the very point of extinction, old Africa had resurfaced.

"And you know that the Burundi army feeds this elephant," Gaugris said.

"No?"

"Yes, sometimes an army helicopter goes out there and drops stale bread for the beast. I haven't seen this, but I imagine it runs away. Maybe it thinks it's being bombed."

M y   t i m e   i n   B u r u n d i was coming to an end. I wanted to make another trip down to the Rusizi to try to find the elephant, but Gaugris was too busy to go with me, so I persuaded an American named Geoff Creswell who had a Jeep to take me. The rains had held off since the morning of my arrival, but as we drove out of the city, I looked westward. A bank of dark, swollen clouds was gathering over the mountains in Zaire.

Geoff Creswell was a rangy, long-limbed Kansan with large features and a ponytail. He had a slow, sonorous way of talking and a fondness for expressions like: "In the great universal library of conservation, Burundi is a comic book in the children's section." He kept a catalogue in his head of great lines from movies and used them to throw meaning on life like a preacher uses quotes from the Bible.

Geoff was looking after a dozen chimpanzees lodged around Bujumbura like Poco and Socrates with Mimi. But he was really an elephant man. Until recently, he had been an elephant keeper at the "World Famous Topeka Zoo" in Topeka, Kansas, and as he drove he told me about zoo elephants. In his view, elephant keeping was a brutal job. He spoke with great relish about keepers he had known who had been gored to death by their elephants, or trampled on, or tossed twenty feet, or simply squashed lazily against a wall until they burst.

"It's psychological warfare," Geoff said. "The only way you can maintain control over a ten-ton elephant is by fooling the animal into thinking that you are stronger."

One keeper whom Geoff particularly revered had survived an extraordinary attack. His elephant had advanced on him without warning one morning and thrown him twenty feet against the bars of its cage. The elephant had pummeled the keeper with its tusks and stamped on him a few times. Finally, the keeper was rescued by a colleague pulling him out under the bars. The keeper had a broken arm, a broken collarbone, broken ribs, a fractured skull and internal bleeding. But knowing that if he failed to restore his dominance immediately he never would, he walked back into the cage and stared at the elephant until it lifted its trunk sheepishly and looked away. Then he was rushed to the hospital.

"Of course, it was a love-hate relationship," Geoff said. "All the elephant really wanted was to have its tongue scratched."

We turned off the road at the twenty-five-kilometer mark and followed the tracks Harry Johnson had made. We parked the Suzuki in the shade of a thorn tree and walked to the edge of the escarpment. It was a Sunday, and the valley beneath us was absolutely still and silent. Not a cow or fisherman in sight. We scanned the grass, but saw no sign of the elephant. Even the air, hot and heavy, seemed lethargic.

"Let's go down to the river," I said.

We clambered over a pile of rocks and slid down a bank of dry, loose soil. Thick, tangled bushes dangled their thorns like daggers in our path. The only sound was the occasional clatter of palm fronds, moved as much by the heat as any breeze. As we descended, the vegetation became softer and

greener, and the ground almost damp. Eventually, I reached
a high bank over the river. A monitor lizard was warming
itself on a ledge halfway down to the water. It took fright
and bounced away, sliding over the mud and finally leaping
into the river, its scales glistening emerald and gold for a
moment before it disappeared.

Geoff arrived and we sat on the bank. The river was about
fifty yards across and a thick, sluggish brown. Only the occasional banana leaf, spiraling past in a lazy eddy, disturbed
the languor of the surface. All we could see on the far side
was the ridge of high, green grass above the bank.

Eventually, we heard the sound of bells clanking. We
pulled ourselves up and walked downstream for a few
hundred yards. We reached a clearing on the bank and saw
the first cows emerge from the grass across the river and slide
nervously down to the water. More cattle arrived, and before
long there were two or three dozen standing in the river,
some of them belly-deep, lapping at the cool waters. Behind
them, a couple of men appeared and stood at the water's
edge, making sure the cows drank their fill.

"Hello," we called across.

The men looked up, startled.

"*Wapi ndofu?*" we shouted. "Where is the elephant?"

It was hard to hear above the snorts and splashing of the
cattle, so I beckoned the men to swim across. They hesitated,
but eventually one slipped off his clothes and tiptoed into the
icy river. He made his way upstream in the shallows, flailing
his arms and high-stepping to escape the drag of the water,
his body wet and glistening like polished ebony in the sunlight. Then he struck out, heading for a point above us. He
had estimated the strength of the current perfectly. He swam
lazily across and ended up a few feet from where we were
standing on the bank. He sat smiling at us from the shallows
and then climbed onto a rock. He had a patchy goatee beard

and was wearing only a skimpy pair of purple silk under-drawers. His body was small, dark and lithe, like a black cat or a mongoose.

Geoff asked him whether there were crocodiles in the river.

"Yes, many," he said.

"Wasn't he afraid?"

"No, this grass is magic. We throw some on the river when we come down and then the crocodiles cannot harm us or the cows."

He smiled and wiped his face.

"What about the elephant?" I asked.

"Yes, he's here. I saw him just a few minutes ago," he said. "Over there." He waved his arms back across the river.

"On the Zaire side?"

"Yes, he swims back and forth," he said. "Sometimes he's in Burundi, sometimes in Zaire."

"Is he friendly?"

"When he first came, he was angry, but now he is not. He runs away from us, but he does not attack us. When we come down with the cattle, we always check to see where he is."

"Is he always in the same place?"

"Yes, always around here. Just near this spot."

"How many elephants are there?"

"Just one, always just one."

"What happened to the others?"

"Gone, killed."

"Why has this one not been killed?"

By this time, a young boy had appeared from the Burundi side and had walked over to the rock. The Zairian man looked at the boy and laughed.

"We don't kill him. It is bad."

"Why?"

"Everyone knows that it is bad."

"Is it spirits? Are the spirits of people in animals?"
Both the man and boy laughed again.
"No, it's just bad," he said.
"Do you hunt any other animals?" I asked.
"We hunt," the man said.
"Would you eat elephant meat?"
"We eat."
"So why not eat this one?"
The man shrugged. His friend was calling him from across
the river. It was time to go.

Geoff and I thanked him and he slipped back into the river.
The clouds were now moving swiftly toward us from the
west, and it had suddenly grown colder. A wind was whipping up tiny waves on the water and swaying the palm trees,
which clattered in response. We began to climb up the steep
earthen slopes of the escarpment.

Halfway to the top, something made me turn. The men
were driving their cattle away from the water toward a patch
of long grass. As the first cow nuzzled its way between the
high blades, the vegetation on the other side shook and a
grey shape emerged, twice the size of the cows. It was the
elephant.

He was big, though not huge. He had a good pair of tusks
that shone white against the green. He stood belly-high in
the shorter grass and twisted his head from side to side in
annoyance at the disturbance, like a dog shaking water out
of its ears. Then he ambled away toward some longer, more
protective grass. I thought he was about to disappear. But at
the last moment, he stopped and turned around again. He
looked back toward the cattle. Then he lifted his trunk and
raised his head, and above the wind I thought I heard a call,
high and sad and lonely. Then the grass parted and he was
gone.

In the distance, the sky had turned the color of night. We

clung to the slope and stared at the grass until a claw of lightning flashed across the darkness. A moment later, the thunder came, a long, low rumble against the far mountains.

That night, the first real rains fell. I lay in my bed and watched the rain pound against the window, beating ceaselessly and without effect on the black glass until morning came.

Chapter Two

ELEPHANTS ARE NOT
BEETLES

I was six years old when an elephant first tumbled into my consciousness. Her name was Dicksie, she was from Africa, and she also tumbled (leaning forward to grab a sticky bun) into the concrete moat surrounding the elephant house at London Zoo.

The fall left Dicksie wedged on her back at the bottom of the narrow moat. A crane was brought in to haul her to her feet. But in the original tumble, Dicksie had cracked one of her huge femurs. When the crane heaved her upright, the broken leg crumpled and she toppled back down again. Elephants are so heavy that if they get in the wrong position, they can crush themselves to death. This is what happened to Dicksie. That night, surrounded by her keepers, she died.

I must have seen Dicksie on television or in the newspapers, because I can still recall pictures of her trapped upside down in the moat. Her legs were sticking up helplessly into the air. Her trunk was twitching along the concrete like a snake with a broken spine. Her head and neck were cruelly bound with ropes and metal coils. But it was her eyes, or rather her one visible eye, that I remember most. It was tiny in proportion to the rest of her head: an oily button in a sea of grey wrinkles. And in one shot it was captured looking directly into the camera. As I took it, Dicksie was looking straight at me.

I was delighted. And I was spellbound by what I saw in the eye. Even at that age, I had worked out that eyes were windows to the mind. And in Dicksie's eye I found—or imagined I found—unexpected depths of wisdom and un-derstanding, sadness and resignation. From that point on, I took it into my head that there was more to the animals of the zoo than any adult appeared prepared to admit.

London Zoo became my favorite outing. And the elephant house was the Mecca of the zoo. As soon as I arrived, my father would lift me up so I could look over the wall and down into the moat where Dicksie had died. Then I would run into the dark yellow interior of the elephant house. I can still remember the mixture of thrill and horror I always felt at the first musty draft of urine, dung and sweat. And then, as my eyes became accustomed to the darkness, there were the elephants themselves, huge slow wonders, with their strange trunks, curious round feet, and wet, flickering eyes.

Nearly a quarter of a century later, leaning forward in my seat on the flight from Bujumbura to Nairobi, I stared out of the window. The old Boeing was hauling itself into the air north from the airport. Down below was the road out to Gihanga. To the left were the plains. And as we climbed, I caught a glimpse of the Rusizi River, wriggling gently across the valley, irrigating the grassy banks where a lone elephant still lived.

In my mind, this elephant and Dicksie were two of a kind. It was not only their shared isolation: Dicksie dying alone in a concrete moat; the Burundi elephant living out its days cut off from the rest of its kind. It was something more, something I thought I had felt in both creatures. These elephants were not merely sad and lonely. They seemed to understand that they were sad and lonely.

As the plane rose higher, clouds closed around. I drew away from the cold window and shook myself out of this reverie. How could I possibly know what these elephants were thinking? Even with language, it was hard enough for one human to know the mind of another human. It suddenly felt foolish to suggest that elephants could understand such matters. Wasn't I simply imposing my own human reactions onto these beasts? I had no answers. But I knew some people who might: a group of women working with elephants in Kenya, led by an American named Cynthia Moss.

The plane landed with a thump at Nairobi Airport, and as soon as the doors opened, the warm, fresh, familiar smell of Kenya swept into the plane. When I had checked into a hotel, I put a call through to Cynthia Moss. Her elephants lived in Amboseli National Park, a land of dry salt pans and oozing swamps a hundred miles south of the capital. Cynthia spent much of her time there, but she also had a house in Nairobi.

A servant answered the telephone. Cynthia was out. But she was in Nairobi. I left a message and went out for a walk.

It had been several years since I had lived in Nairobi. In my absence, it had grown dirtier and more crowded. But there was still something appealing about this town. It was a world in transition and it sparkled with wild confusion and endearing fantasies. Shoeshine boys offered to buy your shoes. Strangers stopped you in the street to tell you their dreams. Everybody talked of riches and happiness. Words, words. The city already had all the language of success. It was only the realization of these words and dreams that had yet to catch up.

A hawker sidled up beside me. He had a squint that made his eyes look in different directions. He held up a bracelet.

"Real elephant hair," he said.

"Plastic," I said. "I don't want elephant hair, but I might buy it if it's plastic."

"Yes, Bwana," he said, and winked his bad eye shut. For a moment he looked fine. Then the wink ended and the shiftiness returned. "You are very clever man. It is plastic. Now you want it?"

I shook my head and walked on down Kenyatta Avenue. Nairobi's most deformed beggar had always sat on the pavement on this road. He was a handsome man with deep-set eyes and a neat mustache. His deformity was his feet, medicine-ball–sized messes of scabs, lumps and bloody pink flesh. I had thought these feet would have killed him by now. But I was wrong. He was still sitting in his usual place, outside the ice-cream stall, his feet stretched out in front of him. I dropped a few shillings into his hand, avoided his eyes and quickened my step.

When I returned to the hotel, there was a message from Cynthia Moss. She was back home. I called her again.

"I'm tied up in Nairobi," she said. "I won't be going down to Amboseli for a while. Why don't you go down and visit Norah and Soila and come over to see me when you get back?"

It was midday on the salt pans of Amboseli and the sun was sizzling in the blue canvas of the sky. In the distance, the snowy summit of Mount Kilimanjaro floated above a silver choker of cloud. I waited while a Jeep maneuvered slowly along a rutted track, throwing up a trailer of pale dust. When it approached, I flagged it down and introduced myself.

Soila Sayialel and Norah Njirane were cousins. They came from the dusty border town of Loitokitok. Soila was the pretty one. She had a round, chubby face and frizzy hair. A dark scar ran like a careless gash of purple lipstick out of the right side of her mouth. She had pink polish on her nails and shiny shaven legs beneath her cotton skirt.

Norah was darker and more serious. Her long face and flared nostrils gave her the look of a black horse or a zebra. Her frizzy hair was combed straight up from the top of her head. She was dressed all in turquoise.

"Climb in," said Soila.

We followed the track through a forest of date palms. There were signs of elephants everywhere. Half-stripped branches dangled from wounded trees. Dried droppings carpeted the earth like sawdust in a butcher's shop. Dappled footprints crossed and recrossed the track. Finally, around a bend, we found some elephants: a group of five old bulls hanging out together in the white dust. We rolled toward them and stopped ten feet away.

The bulls stood in a loose huddle, their haunches facing inward and their tusks scything out at the world. They looked like a group of musketeers who had drawn their swords to make a gallant last stand, and then fallen asleep while waiting. One had his back legs crossed, like a man leaning against a bar. Another's trunk rested lazily on his tusks. They opened their eyes and blinked at us. Then they went back to sleep, swaying slightly, their breaths vibrating noisily.

"You see the big one?" asked Soila.

I looked. The bull was huge. He had long, thick tusks, one of them chipped at the end.

"That's Dionysus. He's the biggest bull in the park."

"How old is he?"

"In his forties. The one behind is Patrick."

"How can you tell?"

"You can tell by the face. Like I can tell you from other *mzungus*, from other white people. It's not so hard to learn."

"What are the distinctive features?" I said.

"Look there. The marks on the ears. The notches. The tusks. The shape of their bodies. The way they stand."

Dionysus had heard our whispers. He opened one eye and reached out his trunk, uncurling it slowly toward us like a hand delivering an offering. The tip of the trunk was pink dotted with grey. It looked like a pig's nose.

"What's he doing?"

"Smelling."

"Smelling what?"

"You."

Dionysus had no need to sniff at Norah and Soila. He had grown used to the soapy, oily scent of the two Masai women. They had been working as research assistants to Cynthia Moss for the past five years and they spent almost every day out here on the Amboseli plains, among the elephants.

Even after all this time, it was still a job that roused a certain bafflement among their African friends. Norah and Soila were town Africans. They had grown up in an urban habitat. Their teenage concerns had been discos, clothes, and boys. They had never seen an elephant. The few miles that separated Loitokitok from the bush could have been the Indian Ocean. If they had thought about elephants at all, it was with shivers of fear.

"When we first got these jobs, we were quite frightened," Norah said. "Even our parents thought we would surely be killed. We didn't like these elephants. We thought they were too strong."

"You thought they'd be aggressive?" I said.

Norah opened her eyes wide in agreement.

"And they're not?"

I looked up at the snoozing Dionysus, just a few feet away.

"Ah, they can be," Norah said. "But so can you, I think. You just have to know when they are getting angry and not provoke them."

"So you like the elephants now?"

"We like them so much. You know, they are so intelligent. I think sometimes they are more intelligent than people."

"And they are interesting," Soila said. "If you watch buffalo, they don't do anything. They just stand and stare at you. Elephants are always up to something. They are always talking or worrying. They make us laugh so much. You can never get bored."

Norah and Soila were mothers. They each had young sons, back in Loitokitok with their grandparents. But neither was married. They were fed up with men, they said. They preferred elephants. Each had a favorite bull—a "boyfriend." They had photographs of the two beasts up on their walls.

I told them about the last elephant in Burundi.

"So do you think he would be lonely?" I asked.

"I think he is," Soila said. "Even these males are very social animals. They don't stay with the herd for life like the females, but they still like to be around other elephants. Bulls have their own society, like you men going out to drink beer. Most of the time the bulls are with other bulls. I think they like the company."

"And they like the females, too," Norah added. "If there are no females, then how are the males going to breed? What does this elephant do when he comes into musth? I think he must be very frustrated."

The car erupted into giggles. Dionysus opened his eyes at the noise and shook his head and ears in annoyance. White dust puffed up from his loose skin like vapor, enshrouding him in a pale floating mist.

"Yes," Soila said. "Your bull must be lonely."

The next day, Norah took the bus to Loitokitok to see her son. In the afternoon, I went out with Soila to find some female herds. We skirted the edge of the Ol Tukai Orok palm forest and turned eastward onto the white pans. The grass was eaten flat down to the ground. A couple of wildebeests were digging into the soil with their front teeth.

In the distance, under Observation Hill, a solitary blip in the flat landscape, was a lone bull. I watched him as we drove past. He was standing out in the open, on his own, doing nothing. Farther on, we spotted a family walking toward us. Soila stopped the car and we sat waiting.

"Three Holes and Iris," Soila said as they came closer. "See, this one has three holes in her ear."

Three Holes was in the lead. She was the matriarch. The calves and younger adults walked behind. Iris, another old female, brought up the rear. As they plodded closer, Three Holes came over for a sniff. She marched right up to the car, periscoping and dipping her trunk. Suddenly, she was so close that all I could see was her saggy belly and the loose folds of skin at the top of her legs. I breathed in. The smell was familiar; the same warm, dungy odor that had filled the cave of the London Zoo elephant house.

Three Holes was also sniffing and she soon caught my scent. Like the bulls the day before, she was confused by the new smell in Soila's car. She snorted and peeled away. Her calf, which had been snuffling at her heels, skidded after her. The family rumbled and shook their heads. They were still making throaty noises as they disappeared into a clutch of trees.

We drove on until we reached the edge of the Enkongo
Narok swamp. These waters and their rich vegetation were
the lifeblood of the dry park. The contrast between the arid
white plains and the deep green and blue of the grass and
swamp was dazzling. We rolled to a halt. In the mud and
water in front of us were the rounded, blackened backs of
twenty or so elephants. The soft breeze carried the noise of
squelching, splashing, munching and rumbling toward us.

"AAs," said Soila. "That is Wart Ear, the matriarch. I like
her. She is a good old lady."

There were fifty-two female herds in Amboseli and Norah
and Soila knew them all by name. The members of each herd
usually had names beginning with the same letter. In the AAs
were Abigail, Agatha, Alison, Amy, Amelia, Audrey, Astrid. Wart Ear, the matriarch, had been named before the
lettering system had been adopted.

The AAs were the first Amboseli herd Cynthia Moss had
identified. Their history was well documented. In 1976, when
drought brought the elephants into conflict over water with
the local Masai and their cattle, Wart Ear, Alison and Amy
had all been speared by young Masai warriors, the *moran*. All
three had survived, but both Amy and Alison had lost their
calves.

Just recently, there had been more drama in the AAs.

"You see that one there?" Soila said, pointing to a shiny
back in the swamp.

"Yes."

"That is Astrid, Alison's calf. A few weeks ago, she had
her own first baby. It was stillborn."

Astrid had been seen behaving strangely one morning. She
had been rolling on the ground, getting up, sitting down,
dribbling urine. The researchers had come to watch, and late
in the afternoon, Astrid had given birth.

"All the cows were very excited," Soila said. "They rumbled and pushed forward to have a look. It was long grass so we could not see at first that something was wrong. But the calf did not get to its feet. Alison and Astrid pulled it up, but it collapsed and then we realized it was dead."

The herd stayed with the body until dusk, standing disconsolately around. Then they moved on. But Astrid refused to leave her calf. The next morning, she was still guarding the carcass. She had spent the night driving away hyenas. It was only when the rest of the herd returned that Astrid reluctantly left her dead calf to the scavengers.

The AAs were still in the swamp. We waited as the afternoon drew on. The sun slipped downward, throwing long soft pink beams onto the snow on Mount Kilimanjaro. The colors of the earth and trees and grass softened and grew more subtle. The air cooled. It was a delicious hour.

The elephants were now ready to head off to their sleeping places among the trees. The older females emerged first, pulling themselves up out of the swamp with loud plops, like the sound of boots being retrieved from mud.

The younger elephants followed. One calf struggled at the edge of the swamp, slipping on the steep, moist bank. An adolescent female with stubby white tusks ambled slowly through the mud behind the calf, swinging her head from side to side. When she came up, she lowered her forehead and nudged the little one up the bank. At the top, the calf gathered itself and then turned and squeaked indignantly at the swamp, shaking its head and trunk and flapping its ears.

"This little one is too proud," Soila said.

We watched for a few more minutes as the herd gathered on the dry land. The elephants that had been separated in the swamp all day greeted each other with rumbles and by urinating and touching trunks and tusks. Then, with Wart Ear out in front, they set off for the trees, a column of mud-caked water beasts trudging ponderously across the white pan into the deepening violet dusk.

When I returned to Nairobi, I went to see Cynthia Moss. Her house lay in a quiet leafy suburb. A pair of grand jacaranda trees spread their boughs over her driveway, and their petals lay on the ground like a fresh fall of lilac-tinged snow. I carved a path through the blossom and parked in the shade.

An old servant answered the door. He showed me into a sitting room of soft cushions and colorful Indian and African cloth. There were elephant prints on the walls, elephant sculptures on the bookshelves, and an elephant tea cozy on the table. An Abyssinian cat lay sprawled royally on the couch.

After a few minutes, Cynthia breezed into the room. The servant brought tea and we sat and chatted.

"How was Amboseli?" Cynthia asked. "You saw lots of elephants? No problems?"

"No problems. It was great. I didn't want to leave."

"Oh, good," she said. "I feel the same way. Even if I'm away for only a few days, I start to get itchy to return to Amboseli."

"Really? Even after all these years?"

"Sure. I hate not knowing what's happening with the elephants. Once you get involved with their lives and society, it's like watching a soap opera. You get hooked and you don't want to miss an episode. And there's always something new going on. Just the other day I saw a mother carrying her dead calf around for several days."

"It wasn't Astrid?"

"No, no. It was another mother with a dead calf. I've seen behavior like Astrid's before. But this was new. I still want to find out why the elephant was doing it. What was going on."

Cynthia was small and pixielike. Her cheeks were as plump as apples and her grin was ready and wry. But there was also a toughness in her skin and bright blue eyes: physical and mental weathering from the years in the bush.

It was almost twenty years ago that Cynthia had begun watching her Amboseli elephant soap opera. She had first come to Africa on vacation a few years earlier, in the late 1960s. On that trip, she had visited Lake Manyara National Park in Tanzania and there met a young Scotsman named Iain Douglas-Hamilton, who was studying elephants. Cynthia was intrigued by the animals and the fieldwork. She hung around Manyara and was soon "hooked." She canceled the rest of her travels and stayed at Manyara for eight months.

Afterward, Cynthia returned to the United States. But over the next few years, she came back to Manyara several more times. And in 1972 she moved up to Amboseli to start her own elephant research project. It was later that year, while nipping around the park in an old Renault sedan, that she first met Wart Ear and the rest of the AAs.

Back then, zoologists still had only a sketchy knowledge of elephant society. Men had observed and domesticated elephants for thousands of years. As early as the fourth century B.C., Aristotle had written a long essay on elephant biology in his *Historia Animalium*. But Aristotle's account was a mixture of fact and myth. He was only two months off with his estimation that elephant pregnancies lasted two years. But he was a little further from the truth when he claimed that elephants lived for three hundred years and suffered from only one disease, flatulence.

Elephant information remained similarly anecdotal far into the twentieth century. As late as 1960, scientific journals were still publishing articles about elephant graveyards and flatulence—"the intestinal rumblings, which never seem to cease," as the naturalist and ranger A. B. Percival put it. The graveyards were a myth. And while elephants are flatulent, the "intestinal rumblings" are usually communication rumbles, produced in the throat. It was not until 1965 that the first serious study of African elephants in the wild began, and this was Iain Douglas-Hamilton's work in Lake Manyara Park.

In Amboseli, Cynthia had the benefit of Douglas-Hamilton's pioneering work. But there was still much to learn. When Cynthia began collecting data in Amboseli, it was like trying to put together a jigsaw puzzle that had never before been assembled. The pieces were the six hundred elephants in the park and Cynthia's first task was to identify them by photographing their distinguishing features: their ears, whose unique patterns of veins, notches, warts, holes and tears made them elephant versions of fingerprints. As Cynthia built up her elephant ear gallery, the pieces of the jigsaw began to fall into place and the overall picture of the elephant society in the park became clearer.

At the heart of this society were some fifty herds. Elephants are matriarchal and these herds were all led by mature females. Each herd numbered between five and twenty individuals and was generally made up of an extended family. The two or three old females in a herd were usually sisters or cousins. The rest were their calves and grandcalves.

Calves were always born into these safe families. The females would often remain in the same herd for life. Males left when they reached sexual maturity, in their late teens. They then led a more nomadic existence. They would often make friends with other males or spend time with females— but their bonds with other elephants were seldom as tight as those within a female herd.

Over the years, Cynthia had witnessed the entire life and

culture and society of the Amboseli elephants unfold. She had seen calves being born and old elephants dying. She had watched how the herds dealt with drought and poaching. She had noted how they reacted to the changes in their world: more tourists, more cattle, more aircraft flying above. She had come to know the character and place in the society of almost every elephant in the park.

Like several other pioneering animal watchers, such as Jane Goodall and Dian Fossey, Cynthia Moss was not a trained scientist. Before coming to Africa, she had been a journalist, working for *Newsweek*. Because of this, she had taken special care to carry out all the conventional scientific studies. She collected data on population dynamics, breeding patterns, social status, feeding habits and so on. And she sought to explain everything the elephants did by the prevalent conventional theory of animal behavior: survival logic.

Survival logic is a simple Darwinian idea. It says that all animals have one aim in life: to promote the survival of their genes. Animals choose the best mate to have the strongest babies. They protect their offspring to ensure the continuation of their line. They even cooperate in hunting and gathering because this is the best way to secure food for their young, their gene carriers. Survival logic could explain all actions by all animals: lions, slugs or elephants.

But alongside such a conventional scientific approach to her elephants, Cynthia developed other ideas. Her lack of scientific training meant she had had to work hard to be taken seriously by the establishment. But it also meant that she was not loaded down with zoological preconceptions. Like Jane Goodall in her chimpanzee studies, Cynthia could view the behavior of her elephants without bias or blinkers.

When Cynthia first began working in Amboseli, most scientific studies still approached animals as though each species was made up of so many identical individuals. Every elephant

52 KING LEOPOLD'S DREAM

was an archetypal elephant. But Cynthia soon realized that this was not true. Like pet dogs, elephants were all different. Some had happy dispositions, others were more sullen. Some were trusting, others by nature suspicious. Theodora, for instance, was "playful and flamboyant." Tuskless was "smart, inventive, brave and gutsy, and one of the sweetest-natured animals I have ever known."

In Amboseli, I had seen the members of the AA herd greet each other with rumbles and trunk twirling when they met up after a day in the Enkongo Narok swamp. According to survival logic, this greeting was simply an instinctive social interaction designed to improve the survival chances of the herd's genes. The greeting tightened the bonds of the herd. And a strong herd created a safer environment for the calves.

But when Cynthia watched elephants greeting, she saw something else, something more akin to what happened when human friends met. "The sounds of the greeting rent the air," she had written in her book *Elephant Memories*, "as over and over again they gave forth rich rumbles and piercing trumpets of joy."

Elephant feelings. This was what I had sensed in Dicksie and the Burundi elephant. This was the beginning of what I was trying to understand.

"So elephants really do experience joy?" I asked.

"Of course they do."

"But isn't joy a very human characteristic?" I said, trying to be skeptical. "Isn't it a word to describe humans? Isn't this anthropomorphism?"

"I don't think so," Cynthia said, sitting up in her chair. "You watch a pair of elephant sisters that have been apart for a few days greet each other. All right, we can call this elephantine joy. But what word other than 'joy' or 'happiness' or 'elation' could we use? These elephants are not experiencing some scientific reaction. They are expressing joy."

"What about sadness?" I said. "Do elephants get sad? Do they get lonely?"

"They certainly get sad. I've seen elephants mourn when they lose a relative. Loneliness is more difficult. Some animals are naturally solitary. But elephants, apart from some old bulls, are social animals. They like to be with other elephants. So they probably can get lonely. Elephants are very emotional animals, you know. I've seen them happy, sad, frustrated, angry."

"They sound like people."

"Well, in some ways they are a lot like people."

Cynthia paused and frowned at her own words.

"Look," she said, "I have to be careful here. I'm not interested in turning elephants into little humans—or even big humans. I'm not really interested in the comparisons between people and animals. I'm interested in elephants in their own right. But one of the reasons that we seem to share so many emotional characteristics with elephants is that the pattern of our lives is so similar to theirs."

"What, in terms of longevity and social ties?" I said.

"Partly. They have the same life span as us and the same long childhoods. They also live in close families. And like us, they are born with only a small amount of their brain weight."

"What does that mean?"

"Well, most animals are born with almost their full adult brain weight. A wildebeest calf already has almost all the knowledge it needs for life. But humans have only twenty-six percent of their adult brain weight at birth. And elephants have thirty-five percent. They both have a lot of learning to do, a lot of intellectual and emotional growing."

"Like what? Learning what?"

"Some are simple things, like what food to eat. Or how to drink through the trunk. For the first few months, calves can't suck up water with their trunks. They have to put their mouths into the water when they want to drink. But they also learn more sophisticated things like how to communicate, how to react to each other, how to be themselves. Each elephant is very different. Elephants are very flexible animals. They are not beetles. You watch a thousand beetles and the chances are that each one would react to an event in exactly the same way. With elephants it's different. You never know what they are going to do. They do not lead programmed lives."

"So elephants have feelings," I said. "They are flexible. They are intelligent. But do they think? Are they aware? Do they know that they feel?"

"It's a hard question," Cynthia said. "But perhaps the best way to answer it is by looking at the way elephants communicate."

As I drove back into town, I considered the differences between men and animals. Some were vast. A chimpanzee could be taught to drive a car. It could even be taught to build parts of it. But it could not begin to design it. However, other differences were less clear-cut. Elephants and people share many emotions. Chimps use simple tools. Our intellect is incomparably more sophisticated than any animal's. But the idea that we are somehow made of a different substance than animals is really a piece of biblical homocentrism. Aristotle believed that the differences were only ones of degree. So did another wise old man, George Adamson, who along with his wife, Joy, had raised the lioness Elsa, made famous by Joy's book *Born Free*.

George was now dead, shot down by bandits. But one dry season, when I was living in Kenya, I had traveled up to see him at home in the remote Kora National Reserve, on the banks of the Tana River.

George was then already eighty-two and coming to the end of things. Elsa, Joy, and his brother Terence were all dead. George was no longer well. His limbs were stiff and slow. There was a fog in his soft blue eyes and a harsh rasp to his breathing. With his long yellow hair, brushed back from his head, and his yellow goatee tuft, he did still look —as he had always loved to look—like a lion. But he was a ragged and toothless lion now, no longer the rangy dominant male he had been.

In the thirty years since Elsa's death, George had raised and released dozens of other lion cubs. But the last of these cubs had been freed more than a decade earlier. Slowly, George's prides had been killed or had disappeared from Kora. For a while, George had come to think he would never see any of his lions again. But then, a few weeks before my visit, an old friend had unexpectedly turned up. This was Growe, the daughter of an orphaned lioness George had set free in Kora long ago. As a cub, Growe had been brought to see George by her mother. Now, many years later, she had returned to show George her own cubs.

Campi ya Simba, Camp of the Lions, George's home for seventeen years, was a simple dusty compound of a dozen open wooden huts. The lavatory was a fenced corner with a couple of elephant jaws balanced over a ditch for seats. George slept under the stars, and we ate at a wooden table where vervet monkeys would perch and pick grain delicately from George's hand. The only concession to changing times was the wire fence around the whole area that George had built to keep out both lions and the bandits who would eventually shoot him dead.

Kora lay in the furnace heart of Kenya. In the middle of

the day, the cracked earth and rocky outcrops were beaten into an arid silence by the force of the sun. But when the shadows began to lengthen one afternoon, George and I went for a walk. George was bare-chested, his loose brown skin dappled with freckles and long soft white hairs. We walked slowly over to the base of a rumpled rocky hill near the camp. The dry earth groaned beneath our feet. Even the rocks suffered in the sun: a boulder lay split in half by the heat, like a watermelon sliced with a machete.

It was up on these rocks that Arusha, one of Elsa's successors, had turned on George. She had thrown him onto the rocks and fractured his hip.

"Why did she do it?" I asked.

"Oh, she didn't mean anything by it," he said. "She was just playing. We had been having a game of hide and seek and she got a bit boisterous. You see they are very strong, lions. So much stronger than us. But she didn't attack me. She didn't use her claws or teeth."

"Had you raised her from a cub?"

"No, she was born in Rotterdam in a zoo. She was already big when she got here. But she adapted well. She survived in the wild for at least six years and had three litters."

"Then what happened?"

"She disappeared. I'd like to think she moved on, but she was probably poisoned by cattle herders."

"That must be hard."

"Of course," George said softly. "You become so fond of these animals. Then one day they go off and you may never see them again. But it's something you just have to learn to accept."

George had not always been so sentimental about animals. As a young man, newly arrived in Kenya, he had been a professional hunter. But the more animals he had killed, the less he had liked it. Eventually, he stopped hunting. He

handed in his license and for the next twenty-five years became one of Kenya's most respected game wardens.

Out in the bush, George had finally had time simply to
watch the wild animals. Elephants in particular had enthralled
him. He was continually amazed by their humor, their emotions and "the intelligent look" in their eyes. "The more I
saw of them," he wrote, "the more they seemed human. The
care they took to bring up their offspring, the way families
continuously kept in touch, and even the lengths of their
lives, were so like us."

One story George liked to tell was of an elephant his
brother Terence had found trapped in a well. Terence was
building a road at the time and he instructed his crew to bring
rocks, which he dropped, one by one, into the well. The
elephant "understood exactly what was happening," lifting
its feet when the rocks fell and then standing on them. Eventually, the floor of the well was raised enough for the elephant
to climb out. The elephant remained with Terence for several
minutes—"paying thanks," as George put it—before trudging off to rejoin its herd.

Another time, George had been called in to deal with a
bull that had been raiding maize cribs in a town. He waited
by the crib at night and when four bulls walked in, George
shot the leader: "He fell immediately. But then his comrades
gathered round him and, supporting him, made off with him
to the forest. It would have been futile, not to say suicidal,
to have pursued them that night, so I waited until dawn.
Lembirdan [a tracker] and I followed the spoor and splashes
of blood till we came on the elephant lying dead in the forest.
It must have taken enormous strength and determination to
get him so far."

From experiences like this, George had developed his own
credo of nature. In his own way, he had come to conclusions
similar to later animal researchers like Cynthia Moss and Jane

Goodall. Animals were individuals, he felt. They had characters and minds. They could experience joy and suffering. It was this approach to animals that George and Joy had used when they had taken on Elsa.

The sun was throwing a last soft rosy glow on the world as George led me back to Campi ya Simba. The local flock of vulturine guinea fowl had gathered impatiently for their regular feed, and George brought out a bucket of corn. He scooped up handfuls of grain and scattered it in circles in the dust, drawing the birds round and round with him, their cobalt-blue feathers flickering in the embers of dusk.

In the evening, after supper, we sat drinking whisky and talking about lions beneath the black ocean of the sky, splashed with the spray of stars. After a while, a growl floated through the night. George called out for a bucket of camel meat, opened the gate and walked out into the night.

"Come on, girl," he whispered. "Come on, Growe."

At first, I saw nothing. Then two red embers shone out. A dark shape padded forward and I could see the embers were the eyes of a lioness. She slunk low to the ground and bared her teeth. George took a piece of camel meat and held it forward.

"Here, Growe," he urged.

Growe came forward, growling softly. When she was just a few feet away, George slung the chunk of meat in front of her. She grabbed it in her teeth and backed away half a dozen steps. Then she settled down to eat, grunting to herself. Slowly, other shapes emerged. Growe's three young cubs sniffed nervously forward, followed by another adult lioness and two more cubs. This was Growe's pride. Whispering hoarsely, the lions padding all around him, George tossed slabs of meat into the shadows.

Though George had known Growe since she was a cub, he had never touched her. She was a wild lion: wild-born and wild-raised. She had never crossed the line into man's world. But somehow, on this dark night, George seemed to be crossing the line the other way. Standing amid the cats, with his yellow hair and yellow beard, he no longer seemed contained by his humanity. For a moment, in the ghostly light, my imagination fired, I was no longer sure what was man and what was lion.

There were four Amboseli elephant women: Cynthia, Norah, Soila, and another American named Joyce Poole. Joyce had recently joined the Kenya Wildlife Service as elephant officer. But before that she had spent more than a dozen years in Amboseli. One of her lines of study had been Amboseli's bulls. Another had been elephant communication.

I found Joyce one afternoon at the wildlife headquarters by the gate to Nairobi National Park. Her office was in a bare, prefabricated block, without electricity or telephone. Joyce was still in her thirties. She had a strong chin and nose, dark eyes, a page-boy haircut and a lopsided smile.

We started talking about why some animals were more intelligent than others. One of the reasons often given for man's intellectual development was his hands. With such manipulative tools, man was able to explore and manipulate the world around him. Chimpanzees and gorillas, two of the most intelligent animal species, had similar hands. But what about elephants?

Joyce raised her right shoulder and pressed it against her cheek. She held her arm out directly in front of her and waved it up and down, twisting her hand around.

"The trunk?" I said.

"The trunk," Joyce agreed. "It's such a fantastic thing. I don't know why no other species has developed one. You can do anything with it. You can pick up a tree or a crumb, touch a friend with it, throw dust on your back, splash mud, toss a person thirty meters, carry a dead baby. The trunk has allowed the elephant to investigate the world, to bring it closer, to look at things, play with them, use them."

"And smell them," I said.

"Yes, and smell is really important for an elephant. Far more important than sight. If an elephant hears something going on behind, it often won't turn around. It will just reach out behind with its trunk—feeling the air, smelling."

Joyce flickered her own hand over her shoulder like a trunk to show me.

"If you want to know what an elephant is thinking, just watch its trunk," she said. "It's always on the move. Swaying, lifting, curling, finding out about the world."

"OK," I said. "I do want to know what elephants are thinking. What are they thinking?"

Joyce smiled her lopsided grin. The trunk was an indicator of what elephants were thinking about. But as Cynthia had said, the best way to try and get inside elephant heads was by observing their ways of communicating.

Like all social creatures, elephants are seldom quiet. They are always making noises: rumbles, screams, squeaks, trumpets, bellows and roars. Many of these sounds are hard for the human ear to separate or identify. But they all signify something. Over the years, Joyce and Cynthia had uncoded nearly thirty different elephant "words" or "phrases."

Trumpets might mean "I want to play," "I'm feeling silly" or "I am indignant at what you have done." Rumbles express ideas such as "Let's go," "I'm lost" or "I'm pleased to see you."

"Does this amount to language?" I asked.

Joyce narrowed her eyes.

"It depends on what you call language. But elephants are

doing more than merely making meaningful noises. Quite often, when something happens, there is a lot of rumbling. I don't usually know what to make of it, but it sounds like everyone is making comments."

"Saying what?"

"Well, you might have a situation where one elephant gives a 'Let's go' rumble. It faces in the direction it wants to go, points with its leg, starts moving in that direction. The others hesitate. Then another one, perhaps the matriarch, makes another 'Let's go' rumble and starts moving in another direction. Then the others seem to comment with different sounds."

"How many different sounds?"

"It's difficult to tell because so many of them are on the edge of our hearing—or even outside our hearing."

This was a new discovery. Back in 1984, an American biologist named Katherine Payne was visiting the Washington Park Zoo in Portland, Oregon. Payne had previously worked a lot with whales. Standing by the elephant compound at the zoo, Payne felt what she described as a "palpable throbbing in the air." This reminded her of the throbbing she had felt when finback whales used infrasound—sound below the level of human hearing.

Payne returned to the zoo with electronic recording equipment and left it by the elephant compound. The results revealed a previously unguessed-at world of elephant sounds. Between two-thirds and three-quarters of elephant rumbles were below the level of human hearing. Much of what elephants were saying had previously been missed by researchers.

In 1985, Payne contacted Joyce Poole and came out to Amboseli to investigate this new discovery. Recordings made in the park gave similar results. The Amboseli elephants contacted and talked to each other with infrasound all the time.

The infrasound, which could carry for miles across the bush, was particularly useful for communicating over long distances.

"It explained a lot," Joyce said. "Elephants seemed to be telepathic. They always seemed to know where other elephants were, even if they were out of sight a mile away. Now we understand how they had kept in touch."

"So elephants are always talking, discussing things, letting each other know what's going on," I said.

Joyce nodded.

"But is it just instinctive language, like a bird giving a warning call?" I asked. "Or are they thinking about what they are saying?"

"Look at it this way," Joyce said. "Elephants almost seem to have names for each other."

"What do you mean?"

"Well, I've seen a herd standing around. One elephant will make a contact call and her sister will look up while all the others ignore it. Then the same elephant will call again and only her daughter will look up."

"And if you saw a group of humans doing this, you'd assume that the calls were names?"

"Mmmm." Joyce nodded.

The telephone rang in my hotel room. It was a Kenya Wildlife Service vet named Dr. John Jonjo. He was flying down to Amboseli the next morning to treat a wounded elephant in the park. He understood I was interested in the Amboseli elephants. Perhaps I would like to come along.

I woke early and drove out to Wilson Airport. Dr. Jonjo had not yet arrived, but someone else was waiting in the hangar: a stocky man in a Hawaiian shirt and a tight-fitting suit. He had a gold watch, a belt buckle that said EXCELLENT, and a pair of smart suede shoes.

"Yah, yah," he said. "Eliud Miringuh, *Kenya Times.*"

He shook my hand. His fingers were manicured, but the hand was sweating. Eliud's face was eager and innocent. He had a drooping lip, ornamented with a neat mustache, and wide, feminine eyes.

"So you are from England," he said. "Yah, yah."

I agreed.

"Mrs. Thatcher," he said. "The Iron Lady. Very good, very strong. She is very good. I am pleased she has left. Yah, yah. Mr. John Major, he is very good. He pleases me. I am the chief parliamentary reporter for the *Kenya Times.* We are very happy the Iron Lady is gone. We liked her very much."

Eliud's eyes darted around as he talked. There was something naive and predatory about him. He seemed to be on the lookout for something. He was scouting for an opportunity, searching for the main chance.

"Are you coming down to Amboseli?" I asked.

"Yah, yah," Eliud said.

I nodded and looked down at his tight-fitting trousers and expensive new suede shoes.

Dr. Jonjo arrived a few moments later. He was a slim, neat man with surprised eyes and a soft, humorous way of speaking. He busied himself around the plane, loading his dart gun and various wooden boxes. When he was ready, we all climbed in and the plane rolled slowly out onto the runway.

From the air, it was easier to appreciate the vast sweep of the land beneath. Once we had left Nairobi and climbed past the Ngong Hills, there was little civilization on the way to the park. A few roads cut across the pale expanse of the Rift Valley. The odd town or village drifted by beneath, but the land was mostly uninhabited.

Eliud was amazed by the emptiness. He had been born and

raised in Nairobi. He had never been up in an aircraft before. He had seldom been out of the city.

"Look down there," he kept saying. "Not a single body in sight. Nobody. Not a single body." He looked up at me, his eyes gleaming with delight. "Nobody," he repeated.

The dull cloud dissipated as we neared Amboseli. The park burned beneath the blue sky and white sun. We came in slowly and landed easily on the Tarmac strip. The warden, a thickset middle-aged man named Anderson Koyo, was waiting for us with half a dozen men and a couple of Land Rovers. We loaded up and drove off.

I sat beside Dr. Jonjo. As we bumped over the beaten earth, he explained the situation. The elephant he was going to treat was a young bull known only by number, M235. It had been reported three weeks earlier limping around the swamp with a badly swollen leg. Dr. Jonjo had flown down then and darted the animal.

"But it fell on its bad side," he said. "We had no ropes to pull it over onto the other side, so there was not much I could do. We slid some spare tires under the leg and I had a feel and a look. I think it must have been speared. It was quite serious. The bone was infected. I injected some antibiotics. This time I want to get a better look."

"Is it still in the swamp?"

"Yes, but not in the deep water, so we should be able to get to it. It stays in the swamp because it has water and food all around and it doesn't have to move. But the water is bad for the wound because it stays wet. It is more difficult to heal."

"So you're going to dart it again."

"Yes. We are going to see what state it's in. Maybe it will be worth treating. Maybe we'll just have to put a bullet in its head. We shall see."

We were approaching the swamp now. The deep water

where I had seen the AAs lay a couple of miles to the south. Here the water was not permanent but seeped out onto the earth for part of the year. Thick yellow grass marked the edge of the wetland. We stopped and peered into the swamp. Dr. Jonjo stood on the roof with his binoculars.

"There he is," he said. "Just ahead. Half a mile."

We drove slowly into the swamp. The wheels sank into the water and mud beneath, but the grip held. Bit by bit, searching out the driest route, we approached the elephant. When we were about a hundred yards away, the driver stopped. The elephant was hunched up miserably in the grass. It flapped its ears feebly and reached out its trunk to try to smell us. Dr. Jonjo was already loading the dart with M99 tranquilizer.

"We can walk from here," he said. "The elephant is not going to move. He is too weak."

Eliud edged closer to look at the dart.

"Be careful," the warden warned him. "This *dawa* is worse than the famous virus. It's worse than this AIDS. One drop will kill you instantly."

Eliud pulled away sharply. A moment later, Dr. Jonjo was ready and we all climbed down into the swamp. Eliud's suede shoes were immediately soaked. Dr. Jonjo led the way and we fell in behind. We needed to get within fifteen or twenty yards of the elephant. The dart gun was not very accurate.

As we drew closer, the elephant reared up. A month ago, it had been speared by men. Since then, it had been suffering terribly. Now more men were advancing menacingly toward it. The creature shook its head, whipped its trunk, and with an agonizing dipping and tugging motion began to drag itself away. At every jerked step, it screamed in agony.

We walked quickly after it: there was no point letting the pain continue. Eliud was now splashing happily through the mud, content that his shoes were ruined.

"This beast is unhappy," he giggled. "Yah, yah."

Dr. Jonjo whispered for him to keep quiet and raised his gun. There was a plop and the dart looped toward the elephant and fell into the mud. The doctor cursed under his breath and we retreated. After a few minutes, another dart was ready. The doctor fired again and this time we could see from the red tag on the end of the dart that it had stuck in the elephant's haunches. The beast pulled itself a few more paces and then stopped in the long grass. We held back and waited, but the elephant still wouldn't go down. It stood trembling in the water, a single white egret perched carelessly on its back.

"This elephant is very strong," Eliud whispered in my ear. "It is so strong. I like it very much."

"He's very dizzy," the warden said.

"I think he's just come from a drink in Loitokitok," Jonjo joked nervously.

After ten more minutes, Jonjo prepared and fired a third dart. This time, the elephant eventually dropped onto its stomach and fell asleep, sitting upright like a dog.

"Quickly," Dr. Jonjo said. "It cannot sit like that. The pressure is too great on the respiratory system. We must pull it over."

This time, we had ropes. We splashed up to the elephant. It was utterly asleep, sitting in the water and snoring loudly. The ropes were produced and tied to the tusks. There were ten of us. Half pulled at the ropes and the other half pushed against the creature's flanks. With one massive effort, we succeeded in rolling the elephant onto its left side.

Dr. Jonjo made sure that the trunk was not under water. He flapped the ears forward over the elephant's eyes, to protect them from the sun. I came forward for a better look. The beast was huge. Its head was the size of a big soft armchair. Its trunk seemed as thick as a man's torso. I touched the rough, warm, dusty skin and smelled its mustiness.

Eliud crept up nervously beside me.

"I've never seen an elephant before," he said.

"What? This close up?"

"No. At all. This is my first-ever elephant."

Dr. Jonjo was now kneeling beside the wounded leg. The whole lower joint was swollen to twice its normal size. The gash was six inches long and covered in mud. Jonjo slipped on a pair of plastic gloves and washed the wound. Now I could see the blood and muscle and tissue. Jonjo slowly pushed his hand into the wound. It went in all the way. Blood and pus oozed out onto the elephant's leg and Jonjo's arm.

Jonjo used his fingers and a pair of tweezers to pull dirt and grass and stones from the wound. Then, with a pair of scissors, he began to snip away the dead skin and flesh.

"Stop that!" someone shouted.

We all looked around. One of the men was languidly shoving his foot up the end of the elephant's trunk.

"What are you doing?" the warden shouted. "What do you think you are doing? I will throw you out of the park."

The man pulled his foot out, a bemused expression on his face, uncomprehending of his crime.

"The wound is better now," Dr. Jonjo said. "It's not as bad as I thought. Maybe the antibiotics from last time did the job. I am going to clean it and then it should be OK."

He swabbed the wound with disinfectant and squirted antibiotics into the open flesh. Then he dusted the entire area with powder to keep away birds and insects.

"Sometimes birds peck away at the wounds," he said. "And insects can lay their eggs here if I don't protect it."

Finally, the doctoring was finished. The men all went back to the safety of the car and Jonjo stuck a needle into the elephant's flank, injecting the antidote to the tranquilizer. We waited. Nothing happened. Dr. Jonjo walked forward and picked up handfuls of water and splashed them over the animal's face. It twitched and then started snoring again.

The doctor prepared another syringe of antidote. This time, the elephant stirred almost immediately and we all ran backward through the grass, laughing nervously at each other. The animal was now awake, but it made no effort to stand up. It lay on the ground, flicking its tail and pulling bits of grass into its mouth. We stood around anxiously. These injections were a risky business. The elephants did not always survive.

"Is he all right?" I asked.

"I think so. He's just being lazy."

We moved in closer, shouting and throwing sticks at the creature. One of the rangers crept forward and pulled the elephant's tail. The beast's reaction, a sleepy flick of its tail, sent the ranger hurtling back toward the vehicles.

Finally, the elephant shook its head and painfully pulled itself to its feet. It stood with its weight on three legs, looking fuzzily over toward us. Jonjo was happy that it was now all right, so we drove away.

"Amazing, really amazing," Eliud said. "I've seen conservation in action. I'm very impressed."

The elephant women of Amboseli were not the only animal watchers in Amboseli. For twelve years, two Americans, Dorothy Cheyney and Robert Seyfarth, had been studying vervet monkeys in the park. That evening, I lay on my bed in the lodge at Amboseli and read through their new book, *How Monkeys See the World.*

Over the years, animal studies had forced science and philosophy to reassess the divisions between men and animals.

It was now known that animals had capabilities that were previously believed to be uniquely human. They used tools. Some even made tools. Others had simple languages. They felt emotions. They could even solve problems.

But one puzzle remained. Were animals self-conscious? Were they self-aware? Did they know who they were and what they were doing? Did they make choices based on this knowledge? Did they have conscious aims and motives? Did they understand the world around them? These were the questions I had begun to raise in my own head when I saw the picture of Dicksie all those years ago. They were also the central questions that Cheyney and Seyfarth had set out to answer in their book.

There was no doubt that even the simplest animals could behave intelligently. When an ant dies in a community, the other ants remove its body from the nest. This is very sensible. A dead ant would decay and contaminate the nest. But if a live ant is dabbed with oleic acid—the dead-ant smell— it is also removed. The ants are behaving intelligently. But the intelligence does not belong to the individual. It comes from nature. The ants' actions are simply instinctive. They have no self-knowledge. They are not self-aware.

Was it the same with higher mammals? Did they know what was going on or were they, as Cheyney and Seyfarth wondered, "just sleepwalking through life, acting out complex strategies without being in any sense aware of what they were doing?"

Cheyney and Seyfarth set out to resolve these questions by watching how vervet monkeys in Amboseli reacted to the world around them. One clear reaction was the alarm call. If a monkey saw a predator such as a snake or a leopard, it would let out an alarm call. Over time, Cheyney and Seyfarth realized that the monkeys had several different alarm calls. One denoted a snake, another an eagle, a third a leopard. The calls also elicited different reactions from the other monkeys. An eagle alarm would make all the monkeys look into the sky. A snake alarm prompted them to stand up and look into the grass.

This was relatively complex behavior. But it was not necessarily anything more than instinct. But then Cheyney and Seyfarth began to notice that the monkeys did not always make alarm calls when they saw predators. Sometimes a monkey would look up, see an eagle far away in the sky, and appear to decide an alarm call was not immediately necessary. It would wait until the eagle came closer. This behavior suggested the possibility of some kind of conscious decision making.

Moreover, when monkeys were on their own, they very seldom gave out alarm calls. Cheyney and Seyfarth watched a solitary male crossing a patch of open country on its own. It was surprised by a leopard and, scampering across the field, just managed to reach a tree and climb to the safety of the highest branches. The entire chase took place in silence. The monkey seemed to understand that there was no need to waste energy by giving an alarm call when there were no other monkeys to warn.

Even more intriguingly, vervets sometimes made warning calls when there was no danger at all. They used the calls to fool other monkeys. One male named Kitui was particularly fond of this trick. Whenever he got into a scrape with other males, he would suddenly give a leopard warning call. The other monkeys would flee and Kitui would emerge as the dominant male. The reaction of Kitui's rivals was entirely instinctive. But Kitui seemed to have risen partly above instinct.

When Cheyney and Seyfarth turned to chimpanzees, they found even stronger evidence of mental awareness. Captive chimps in the United States had learned to use human sign language designed for the deaf. They even put words together to make new ideas. Older chimps had also taught younger ones signs.

Chimpanzees also seemed to have a sense of their own identity as individuals. In one test, researchers daubed sleeping chimps' heads with odorless paint. When the chimps awoke and were given mirrors to look at, they immediately reached for the paint spots on their own heads. Each chimp clearly understood that the animal in the mirror was itself.

Jane Goodall's wild chimpanzees had also given telling displays of apparent reasoning and conscious thought. Goodall had taken to leaving out bananas every day to keep the chimps in her area of the forest. The older, dominant chimps usually ate the main share of these bananas and the younger chimps were always coming up with ways to try to get a larger proportion of the food. The smartest of all the adolescent chimpanzees was a male named Figan.

At first, whenever Figan got hold of a bunch of bananas, he would hoot with pleasure. The older chimps would immediately descend on him and take most of the bananas away. After a few days, Goodall saw Figan find some bananas. He had worked out that hooting was a bad idea. But his instinct to hoot was still strong. Goodall heard faint choking sounds in his throat, but Figan managed to control his instinct and stay quiet. As a result, he kept all the bananas for himself.

On another occasion, when most of the bananas had been appropriated by the older chimps, Goodall saw Figan stand up and make loud departure noises. He then strolled ostentatiously out of the clearing. In chimp society, a group usually follows an obvious movement like this. The troop left the clearing and went off into the forest. Five minutes later, Figan doubled back and finished off the bananas in peace.

I closed the book and walked out into the Amboseli night. The sky was clear and the moon full. The park was bathed in a ghostly white light. *How Monkeys See the World* raised as many questions as it answered. It was easy to distinguish the far ends of the animal spectrum. Ants were unconscious sleepwalkers. Humans were self-aware. But the minds of vervet monkeys were less definable. At some point up the mental ladder, animals became aware. Were only humans above this point? Or did vervet monkeys have an active mental life? Did chimpanzees? Did elephants?

In the morning, I borrowed a car and drove out onto the pans in the east of the park. The wisps of early cloud had burned away and the air seemed to quiver with the heat. In the distance, I saw a line of shadows floating on the watery horizon. I stopped my car and waited.

At first, the shapes were as insubstantial as a mirage. Their hazy outlines trembled in a wavering pool of heat vapor. But as they advanced across the pan, their bulk rose above the shimmer and solidified into a herd of elephants.

There were eight of them: four adult females and four calves, the youngest a tiny rubbery creature no more than a few weeks old. The adults strode one behind the other with the calves scuffing along between. Their color was almost white. They had come out of a dry land and their skin was powdered with a ghostly coating of pale dust.

They seemed to be heading for a small swamp behind me. They would not have drunk since the previous day and they had the look of thirsty beasts. They walked deliberately, their heads held low, their trunks swishing rhythmically from side to side. At every low thudding step, a puff of white dust drifted up from the earth.

They were about thirty yards away when they changed direction and stopped. Until now I had not noticed the pale splinters lying in the dust. The lead elephant was standing over them. The other elephants waited behind in absolute silence. There was no swishing or thudding or rumbling. The matriarch swung her trunk slowly back and forth over the bleached bones of what had once been an elephant like herself.

Even from a distance, I could sense the somberness of the scene. These were old bones, but they seemed new to these elephants. Perhaps they had recently been unearthed by the wind. The matriarch ran her trunk gently along the rim of a large piece of bone, flaring her nostrils and extending the soft tip of the trunk. Then she picked it up and lifted it up to the eye on the side of her head. She looked at it for a moment and then let it fall.

The rest of the herd came slowly forward, nosing at the bones in silence. The tiny calf crept up and nudged a bone with its foot before its mother steered it back under her belly with her trunk. Each of the elephants had to have a sniff and a feel. The examination lasted for several minutes before the matriarch lifted her trunk and caught the scent of water in the air. Then the herd began to lumber on again toward the water in the swamp.

Elephant interest in their own dead was well documented. Over the years, Cynthia Moss and Joyce Poole had collected scores of elephant jawbones and taken them back to their camp in Amboseli as a record of elephant deaths. The jaw-bones lay in a wide circle around the eating hut and proved a regular attraction for elephants. One night, a herd passed through the camp. As usual, the elephants stopped to look at the bones. But one seven-year-old male paid particular attention to the newest of the jawbones, stroking it with his trunk and foot. When the other elephants moved on, this youngster remained for a few moments.

Cynthia watched the whole scene. She knew the identity of the calf. The new jawbone had recently been collected from the park. It belonged to the calf's dead mother.

On another occasion, in *Elephant Memories*, Cynthia described the death of a young female named Tina who had been speared by a Masai warrior. Tina fled with her herd until she fell down and died from her injuries. Teresia, her mother and the herd matriarch, tried lifting Tina to her feet. She slid her tusks under Tina's body and heaved until the effort painfully snapped off one of her own tusks at the root.

The herd "gave up then but they did not leave. They stood around Tina's carcass, touching it gently with their trunks and feet. Because it was rocky and the ground was wet, there was no loose earth; but they tried to dig into it with their feet and trunks, and when they managed to get a little earth up, they sprinkled it over the body. Trista, Tia and some of the others went off and broke branches from the surrounding low bushes and brought them back and placed them on the carcass."

Eventually, Tina's body was completely covered. Her family stayed with her through the night. "Teresia was the last to leave. The others had crossed to the ridge and stopped and rumbled gently. Teresia stood facing them with her back to her daughter. She reached behind her and gently felt the carcass with her hind foot repeatedly. The others rumbled again and very slowly, touching the tip of her trunk to her broken tusk, Teresia moved off to join them."

What did all this mean? Elephants seemed to understand the connection between elephant bones and elephants. They had some comprehension of death. They were emotionally affected by the death of a relative or even the discovery of elephant bones. The scene I had watched in Amboseli was not uncommon. Elephants seldom passed the bones of their own species without stopping to sniff and touch. These scenes were always silent and somber.

An animal that understands death must also have some concept of life. It must have some awareness that it is alive and that it may die. It might even have some understanding of the process of growing up and growing old. Perhaps I had been right about Dicksie. Perhaps she knew that she was dying. Perhaps somewhere in her great head she had worked out that for creatures, as much as man, there is nothing that ever runs unmingled.

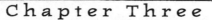
WHAT THE
GOMPHOTHERES ATE

South of the Ol Tukai
Orok forest lay a region of Amboseli that looked like a bat-
tlefield. The hollow grey trunks of a few dead trees stood in
the dust like weary scarecrows. The rest of the woodland had
been reduced to stumps and flakes of chalky wood that still
lay scattered over the earth. It was as if a great arm had swept
across the plain, shattering every tree into a thousand pieces.

"What's happened here?" I had asked Soila.

"You are not blaming our elephants, are you?" she replied
guardedly.

"Oh, I see," I said. "Too many elephants."

"You can't say that. What about the water table?"

The destruction of Amboseli's acacia woodland was a matter of controversy. Over the previous twenty years, many
of the park's acacia trees had died. Some people claimed that
salts in a rising water table were responsible. But others
blamed the 600 elephants crammed into Amboseli's 150
square miles.

Traditionally, Amboseli had been home to far fewer elephants. But in the early 1970s, poaching had increased and herds from all over the Amboseli region had sought out the safety of the park. Acacias were a favorite elephant food. And the destruction of the acacia woodland in the park had directly coincided with the increase in elephant numbers.

One of Africa's best-known ecologists, David Western, had been studying Amboseli's habitat for more than twenty years. He had made the role of the elephant in its environment his speciality. He had an office on Harambee Avenue in Nairobi and one afternoon I went around to talk to him.

Western was born in Tanzania of British parents. He had started studying the ecology of Amboseli for a doctorate in 1967. He was a short, dapper man with thinning hair and the intense blue eyes of a fanatic or a dictator.

"Is it fair to blame the elephants?" I asked.

"Oh, completely," he said. "The loss of trees in Amboseli is fifteen percent due to the water table and eighty-five percent due to elephants. It's quite simple. There are a lot of elephants in Amboseli and they have very large appetites."

The 600 elephants consumed around 60 tons of vegetation a day, or 220,000 tons every year. They stripped the acacia bark, tore off the leaves and branches, and often simply pushed down the trees. They also uprooted saplings and so prevented new growth.

"I have a house in the park," Western explained. "There used to be no trees around it at all. Then in 1984 I put up a fence to keep out the elephants. Now the house is completely hidden by new acacias. They've grown up because the elephants can't get to them."

Western spoke quickly and impatiently. His voice had a sharp, almost metallic tinge.

"And it's not simply a question of trees," he continued. "By reducing the woodland, the elephants have altered the entire ecology of the park. All sorts of animals that rely on trees for food or homes are disappearing. Giraffe numbers have fallen from two hundred to thirty. Lesser kudu and bushbuck are extinct. Baboons are down from twenty-five hundred to three hundred. Vervets only live around the lodges. And numerous birds, small mammals, and insects have been similarly affected."

It was not much of an advertisement for elephants. They seemed to be natural bulldozers who turned woodland into dust bowls and pushed out other animals. But this was not the whole story. In the core area of the park, an excess of elephants had certainly reduced plant and animal diversity. But Western had also looked at the areas outside the park. These had been vacated by elephants because of the threat of poaching. Here Western also found diminishing plant and animal diversity. This was because of the *lack* of elephants.

In these regions, the loss of elephants had allowed the acacias to grow unhindered. The trees had rapidly formed dense wooded thickets, which blocked out most of the light and severely reduced plant growth at ground level. This in turn had driven out animals that relied on grass and low shrubs, such as zebra, wildebeest, buffalo, and Thomson's gazelle. Too few elephants was apparently as much of a problem as too many.

Then Western had examined the fringe areas of the park. Here there was a better balance of elephants. As a result, there was also a better balance of nature: a patchwork of forest and open grassland and a broad diversity of wildlife, both woodland and plains game.

Elephants were not destroyers. In fact, in natural numbers, elephants were the ensurers of diversity. They kept back the growth of woodland without destroying it. They also opened up paths and trampled down thick sedges beside swamps so that smaller animals could reach the water. Elephants were the creators and guardians of rich, mixed habitats. Western called them the "architects of the savanna."

"And it's not just the savanna," Western said. "Wherever you find elephants, it's the same."

"Even in the rain forests?" I asked.

"Especially in the rain forests."

It was a muggy Saturday afternoon when I landed in Bangui, capital of the Central African Republic, the geographical hub of the continent. This had been French Africa, and driving in from the airport, I caught a whiff of the enduring French influence. The air hung with an enticing mix of scents: wet earth, diesel fumes and warm baguettes.

I was hoping to meet an American named Phil Hunsicker, who ran a World Wide Fund for Nature project in the forests. He lived in the far southwest corner of the country, but he was expected in town this weekend. I had no contact address. But it was still early and Bangui was a small town. So I decided to go out for a walk and see if I could track him down.

Downtown Bangui was rich with Gallic style. The street hawkers in Hawaiian shirts, with their fluent French, seemed as much Parisian as African. Even their insouciance—a blend of French shrugs and African fatalism—seemed half-caste. Down one street, African pop music, all dizzy throb and outrageous scale-sliding, danced out from open-slatted shutters and trellised iron balconies.

Dusk settled as I wandered the streets. I tried the American embassy and the bar at the French cultural center. I peered into restaurants with names like Le Pili Pili and L'Oubangui Grill. On a side street, in the purple glow from the neon light of a bar, I came across a group of boys poking a stick at a chameleon. It was a grubby, frightened creature with hunched shoulders and big cone eyes that rotated nervously. It was trying not to be noticed. It had stopped dead on three legs. The fourth dangled stiffly. But its heart was working overtime and I could see the puffs of movement in its chest.

The boys gasped as I slid my hand under the chameleon. Like many Africans, they seemed to think lizards were poisonous. The creature advanced slowly onto my wrist and I carried it to a nearby tree and left it gulping on a branch.

Eventually, in front of the Hotel Minerva, I found what I was looking for: a Landcruiser with a telltale World Wide Fund for Nature sticker. I walked inside. There were only two white people, a man and a woman, at the bar.

"Phil Hunsicker?" I said, walking up.

"That's me."

I introduced myself. The woman was Phil's girlfriend and WWF colleague, Denise Stromme.

"Pull up a chair," Phil said. "Have a beer."

A waiter clunked a bottle down on the sticky table and I took a gulp of warm, sour, gassy beer.

Phil and Denise lived in Bayanga, on the edge of the Dzanga-Sangha rain forest reserve, in the southwest of the country. This was where I wanted to go. I was hoping to catch a ride with them. But they were behind schedule. They had only driven the twelve hours up from Bayanga the day before. They would be in Bangui for at least a week.

"No problem," Phil said. "We'll find you your own vehicle. When you get to Bayanga, you can stay in our house. Now, to more important matters. Have you eaten?"

We left the hotel and drove through the unlit town. Pairs of headlights wove back and forth across the road like Dodgem cars in the dark. The restaurant lay in a courtyard under a thatched shelter. The patron was a sleazy Frenchman who had the look of a child pornographer. He gave us a horrible smile and explained that the written menu was supplemented by various specials. These were animals that were still alive. We could pick them out to be killed and cooked to order.

He waved casually toward the wall. I went and had a look. There was a baboon, a pair of mangabey monkeys, a couple of tortoises, and a tank containing a half-grown crocodile. I ordered a cheese omelette and another round of beers. Then I sat back and had a look at my two new companions.

They were an odd couple. Phil had a boyish smile, a thick dun beard and a hankering for wild places. In his early twenties he had joined the Peace Corps, America's overseas voluntary service. He had asked for the remotest post available and had been sent to Central Africa. He had stayed for three years and then gone back rather aimlessly to the States. He ended up getting a job at a fishery in Alaska. He spent his winters holed up in the snow and his summers sailing alone around stunning empty coves. Eventually, the isolation became too much and Phil returned to university to take a graduate degree. There he met Denise.

"Another beer?" Phil said.

"Sure."

Phil and Denise had little in common. He was a loner, a wanderer, a skeptic. She was bouncy, cheerful, blond and cute—from a big friendly Bible Belt family. But they had fallen in love writing their thesis together—a children's educational book about a giant butterfly that takes a little African girl on a dream journey to teach her about conservation. And when Phil was hired to take over the WWF project at Bayanga, Denise was also taken on to supervise conservation education.

"How long have you been here?"

"Nearly a year."

"And what exactly is your project?" I asked.

"I am codirector of the Dzanga-Sangha forest reserve," Phil said. "I am funded by WWF to work with the African director. The reserve is 2,500 square miles of primary rain forest. We've inherited it from a logging company and our job is to protect and develop the reserve. You know, stop poaching, involve the local people, bring in tourists."

"Are there many tourists?"

"A few. Mostly overlanders and backpackers. But the forest is wonderful. There are rivers, trails, gorillas, chimps, bongos and thousands of elephants."

Phil gazed at the pile of empty beer bottles on the table.

"Talking of elephants," he said. "How can you tell that an elephant has its sexual organs in its feet."

"I don't know. How can you tell?"

"When it steps on you, you're fucked."

"Oh."

After that, we swapped elephant jokes until I began to feel woozy and swollen from the gassy beer. It was time to go back to the hotel. I stood in the open back of the Landcruiser, holding on to the roll bar. The cool wind in my face kept the nausea at bay. When we reached the hotel, I clambered down.

Phil smiled from inside the vehicle.

"One or two things to remember in Bayanga," he said.

"Yes."

"Avoid the mayor."

"The mayor," I repeated solemnly.

"He's the main elephant poacher in the region."

"I see."

"And don't give any money to the police."

"The police."

"Whatever official documents they show you," Phil stressed.

"No money," I assured him.

"Oh," Denise said. "Hopefully, the kittens will have won

the battle with the rats. If not, keep some books by your bed."

"Books, yes, of course," I said. "Why?"

"To throw at the rats."

"Absolutely," I agreed. "Any particular author?"

Denise smiled and they drove off. I stumbled up to my room and woke later, sprawled out on the bed, still dressed, with a taste like rats in my mouth.

Many African leaders have behaved like emperors, but in modern times only two have actually gone so far as to have themselves crowned.

The first had history on his side. His name was Ras Tafari. He was a high nobleman of the ancient Christian civilization of Amhara. His royal family claimed descent from the union of King Solomon and the Queen of Sheba. And his coronation, as Emperor Haile Selassie of Ethiopia, on a hot day in Addis Ababa in 1930, was attended by two European royals, the colonial governors of Somaliland, Sudan and Eritrea, a French marshal, and a British newspaper correspondent named Evelyn Waugh.

The second emperor found justification for his elevation only in fantasy. He was a mission-school boy who joined the French army and rose to the rank of captain. Six years after his country was given independence from France, he took power in a military coup. His heroes were Charles de Gaulle (whom he called Papa) and Napoleon Bonaparte. After twelve years as president, he decided to proclaim himself Emperor Jean Bedel Bokassa of the Central African Empire.

Only one Western dignitary attended Bokassa's coronation, which cost the impoverished nation £12 million. This was Robert Galley, France's minister of cooperation. Galley answered foreign ridicule by saying: "I find it quite extraordinary to criticize what is taking place in Bangui while finding the Queen of England's Jubilee ceremony all right. It smacks of racism." Twenty months later, Galley's government sent in the paratroopers and overthrew the emperor. Bokassa was now rotting in a Bangui jail.

The morning I left Bangui, the world was washed in a pale mango-colored glow. The road westward led past lush grasslands and uncrowded villages. An hour out of town, between Yaka and Pissa, I came to a huge white wall stretching for half a mile along the side of the road. This was Bokassa's abandoned imperial country mansion.

A lone soldier stood guard beneath a huge rotting gate. I parked and went over to talk to him. He was wearing a tatty green uniform and had a hideously pockmarked face. I gave him a few francs. He pushed open a door in the gate and we entered a world of ruined fantasy. Broad overgrown boulevards led away in every direction. The crumbling white ruins of ostentatious neoclassical buildings stood among the weeds and vines. On either side of us was a line of high white pillars. All were cracked and several had fallen down.

We waded through the golden waist-high grass to Bokassa's private garden. There were two huge metal statues among the weeds. Both were of the emperor, in full imperial garb, his monkeyish face grimacing through a mockery of uniformed dignity. One statue was still standing, a little lopsidedly. The other had tumbled into the grass. Both were streaked with white bird droppings. Here was Bokassa: Look on my works, ye Mighty, and despair!

Bokassa's reign had combined generosity—he happily doled out French money—with terror. He murdered his opponents and was widely believed to indulge in cannibalism. His downfall came after he helped to beat more than a hundred schoolchildren to death. The children had refused

to buy a new official school uniform, emblazoned with Bokassa's portrait and manufactured by Bokassa's own company. "I'll show you what we do with children who
misbehave," Bokassa was reported to have said, poking out
one child's eyes.

Bokassa also stole much of his nation's meager wealth,
including vast amounts of ivory. In the 1970s, he set up a
company, La Couronne, to run all the ivory dealing in his
country. He sent out his soldiers to shoot tens of thousands
of Central African elephants. He also bought large numbers
of poached tusks from neighboring countries. The Central
African Republic was to the ivory trade during the 1970s
what Burundi became during the 1980s. In the last years of
Bokassa's reign, La Couronne was exporting more ivory—
nearly five hundred tons between 1977 and 1979—than any
nation in the world.

When Bokassa had come to power, there were more than
70,000 elephants in the Central African Republic. Now, the
4,000 elephants that remained in the forests of the Dzanga-
Sangha reserve, where I was heading, were the last large herd
in the country.

"*Venez*," the soldier said.

We climbed the stairs above a huge courtyard. These had
been the sleeping chambers of Bokassa and his wife and various mistresses. Everything had been looted. Weeds were
growing through the walls and floors. There were graffiti all
over the peeling paint. In one room, I found the crushed
remains of the empress's circular red satin bed. None of the
looters had wanted this. I walked out onto the empress's
balcony. Below was the swimming pool where she was said
to have fed those who displeased her to awaiting crocodiles.
It was still full of water—a dark stinking greeny brown.

Beckoning me forward, the soldier walked down more
stairs and marched across another courtyard to a long, low

building. This was the kitchen. A dozen ovens lay overturned amid piles of cement dust on the floor. The soldier pushed me around a corner toward a dark, cavernous chamber.

"Le Frigidaire," he said. *"Les hommes."*

He opened his mouth and made a grotesque eating gesture. This was the cold room where Bokassa was supposed to have kept his stocks of human flesh. I peered in, but all I could see was a dead cockroach, lying on its back, with its spindly legs in the air.

Outside, I gulped at the fresh air. We walked back through the ruins, and the soldier grinned happily from his pocked face as I drove away. A few miles beyond, the tarred road gave way to a dirt track. Bokassa, builder of roads, had not cared much for the uncivilized western regions of the country.

At Mbaikï, a market town with a petrol station, the main road veered north. I continued westward on a broad, well-maintained dirt track that was soon tunneling into the forest. This was the road to Bayanga. It had been built by the logging company that had worked the Dzanga–Sangha for hardwoods before the forest became a reserve. Once it had been full of trucks and logging vehicles. Now it was virtually empty, a great folly of a highway leading grandly into the emerald shadows.

There was little habitation along the road. Through the morning and into the afternoon, I passed only a couple of police posts and half a dozen ragged villages. The Central African Republic was nearly three times the size of the British Isles, but it contained only 3 million people. Few of them lived in these forests. Once, around noon, I came to a river. Three grizzled ferrymen squatted in the leaves. I warmed some food over their fire, and then they pulled the Jeep across on their ferry: a raft of tree trunks lashed together with vines.

Only once did I see signs of elephants: an uprooted sapling and a line of fresh, steamy droppings. If there were any more beasts, they remained hidden in the forest. I could see no farther than the first few feet away from the road. The vegetation was dark and thick, a tangled imbroglio of thrusting saplings, choking weeds, fattened stands of bamboo shoots and dense clumps of parapluie trees, their foliage like so many limp, splayed hands.

Most of the way, I had only insects for company. On one stretch, I saw thousands of large black caterpillars shuffling across the road. But the most common and colorful insects were the butterflies. These winged vagabonds were the scavengers and hitchhikers of the forest road. They moved in huge throngs, settling on any rotting branch or carcass on the track. Multicolored clouds of them—diamond harlequins, striped rainbows, spotted clowns—rose up as I passed. Sometimes they would smack against the windscreen, leaving bloody trails on the glass. I left many more squashed in my tracks.

It was dark by the time I reached Bayanga. The cook let me into Phil's house. It had been built by the logging company for one of the expatriate managers. It had facilities for electricity and running water, but there was no petrol for the generator. I looked around with my torch. The house was made all of wood. There were two stories, with a large porch and slatted shutters for windows. It would have been as much at home on the Mississippi River as on the Sangha.

The kittens soon tumbled in. They were delighted to see me and dug their claws into my leg. One settled down to suckle on my shoelace. Leaving them in the sitting room, I went to bed in the spare room and slept soundly. There was no sign of rats.

In the morning, I walked down to the Sangha River. It was a quarter of a mile wide, a shallow brown sheet drifting southward toward its appointment with the Zaire River. Lush green bushes and trees glinted picturesquely on the far bank.

Bayanga itself was a model rural African village. All the houses were made of neat wooden planks. There were schools, shops, bars and restaurants. There was even a floodlit volleyball court, though the lights no longer worked. But walking around, I sensed an angry listlessness.

This was a world bemused by changes. Less than twenty years earlier, Bayanga had been an isolated cluster of mud huts inhabited by only a few dozen simple fishing families. There had been no road. The nearest town was eighty miles away. The fishermen had had more contact with the forest Pygmies, with whom they traded for meat, than with any outsiders. But then, one day, a forest surveyor arrived. He saw all the valuable ebony and mahogany trees. Some time later, in the distant world of Bangui, a government official granted a concession to a Yugoslav logging company.

The logging road was cut and eventually the first trucks arrived in Bayanga. It was like a visitation from another planet. Huge trundling vehicles arrived by the hour. They carried with them massive metal machinery. Soon an entire sawmill was being constructed just above the village, along the river. Its buildings were a hundred feet high. The machinery was twice as long. The saw blades were ten feet wide and the length of a cricket pitch. The men who supervised it were white and spoke a strange language that was not even French.

Timber workers were also trucked in from all over the country: Muslims from the north, Bimu from Nola, Gbaya from the northwest, Mbanda from the drylands, Mbaka from farther east. Lights that glowed in the dark were erected. Soon beer became freely available. Prostitutes arrived. Every night there were parties. For a decade, Bayanga boomed.

Then, as suddenly as it had begun, the boom ended. The logging company's problems had become insurmountable. The corruption, the sudden taxes, the paperwork, the distances, the rains, the forest, the superstitions, the mosquitoes, the heat, the damp. It had all proven too much. The company could not make a profit. The managers were being driven to distraction. One night, the foreign workers pulled out. They left an empty plant and dozens of trucks and vehicles neatly lined up in the grass. They also left a host of unpaid salaries and broken promises.

Bayanga had been altered forever. The original villagers and the Pygmies in the surrounding forest had been introduced to an alien world. Two thousand outsiders had also settled in Bayanga. This was now their home. They had nowhere else to go. So they stayed on, waiting for the loggers to come back, for their salaries to be paid, for the promises to be fulfilled. They survived from a bit of farming, a bit of tourist business, a bit of smuggling diamonds, and a bit of poaching the animals in the forest. They set traps and acquired guns and went after buffalo, bongo, gorilla, kudu and elephants.

Visitors to Bayanga were supposed to register with the police, so I ambled over to the wooden police station. Two men were sitting on a bench outside. Neither was in uniform. They were like a pair of B-movie small-town cops. One was fat and sweaty and over-friendly. The other was slim and masked his eyes with dark shades.

They took me into the dark police hut.

The fat one peered at my passport.

"Nationality?" he asked.

"English."

"What are you doing here?"

"I've come to see the elephants."

"You are a resident?"

"No."

"So you paid airport tax on entry to the country?"

"No."

"Ah," he breathed in triumph. "Then you must pay here."

"Airport tax?" I said.

"Yes, look."

He showed me a tattered piece of paper on the wall. It was a closely and badly typed list of regulations. No. 7 was airport tax at Bayanga.

I remembered Phil's warning.

"Do you expect me to believe this?" I said.

The fat man smiled. The thin man said nothing.

"I'm sorry," I said. "I'm not paying."

"You have to pay," the fat man said.

I shrugged.

"Then you must stay here."

"No, I'm going."

"Then you must leave your passport."

"No."

The fat man looked at the thin man.

They only wanted a couple of pounds. But it was the principle. Phil and Denise had told me that the police chief was one of the main elephant poachers in the region. I felt I ought to make even this little stand on behalf of the elephants.

"I'll come back later," I said and walked out into the bright midday light.

Phil and Denise had told me about an American woman who was living in the forest studying gorillas. In the afternoon, I drove out along an old logging road to her camp. The last few miles of track wandered between the bases of towering trees, twisting and rocking the Jeep over an obstacle course of loose roots, trailing creepers and torn branches abandoned carelessly in the road by passing elephants.

The camp stood in a shaded clearing. There were two wooden cabins built on stilts with green mosquito mesh across the windows. Smoke was rising from a kitchen hut and a hammock hung between two trees. An old Suzuki Jeep stood on the bare ground.

When I pulled up, a woman strolled over to the car.

"*Bonjour,*" she nodded.

"Hi, are you Melissa?" I said.

"Oh, English," she said. "What a relief."

Melissa Rimus was a big, tough woman from California. She had broad shoulders and mousy hair pulled back into a ponytail. She had been living in these forests for a year, with only her cook and Pygmy trackers for company.

I explained that I was hoping to accompany her into the forest to look for gorillas. But Melissa had a problem. Her Pygmy trackers were on strike.

"On strike?" I said.

"Yeah," she said. "They don't want to track. They are frightened of the gorillas."

"Oh," I said. "Why?"

"Well, it's not really gorillas. It's the Pygmies disguised as gorillas. They think Pygmies disguised as gorillas are out to get them. You know the sort of thing."

"No," I said. "Not really. Perhaps you can explain."

Melissa rolled her eyes.

"We had some kind of heavy stuff with a silverback gorilla. You know? A dominant male. It charged us a few times when we were out in the forest and the Pygmies were not happy about it. They grumbled all the way back and that night they both claimed to have had the same dream. They were being attacked by gorillas. Only the gorillas weren't real gorillas.

They were Pygmies who had turned into gorillas. And these
Pygmies were trying to kill them."

"Why would other Pygmies want to kill them?"

"They say it's because the others are jealous of the money
they are making out here. I don't know if that's an excuse.
Maybe they just want to go back to their wives for a while.
Maybe they don't want to admit that they can be scared by
ordinary gorillas."

"Why would they be scared?" I asked. "Surely the Pygmies
know how to deal with the animals in the forest?"

"Look, I've read Dian Fossey. I know that a silverback
charge is usually only a mock attack. I know that if you sit
and look down nothing will happen. But the Pygmies haven't
read the book. They've never tried to sit out a charge. When
they meet a gorilla, they usually get out of the way. Or if
they are hunting gorillas, then the gorillas really do fight
back."

"What happens then?"

"Sometimes the Pygmies get hurt. There's one in the hospital up at Nola whose foot was mauled by a gorilla. He's
probably going to lose the foot."

"So what's the situation with your trackers now?"

"Well, this morning I tried to persuade them to track again.
They refused, so I lost my temper and said I was going into
the forest alone. I tramped off, knowing that they would
follow. They couldn't let me go alone. But they didn't even
try to track, so we gave up. Now we are in deadlock."

"Can you try talking to them again?" I said. "Perhaps you
can shame them by saying you have a guest."

"I can try."

The Pygmies were sitting in the shade behind one of the
huts. These were Baka Pygmies. They stood almost five feet
high. They had broad faces with bulbous, splayed noses. One
was young and good-looking. He refused to meet Melissa's

eyes. The other was older. He had a paunch and skinny legs, but Melissa said he was the best tracker in the entire area. He was happy to talk, but unhappy about tracking.

"They're not going to change their minds," Melissa said. "It's a pity too, because the silverback charges were the end of my best-ever few days of gorilla sightings."

"What can you do?"

"I'll just have to get new trackers."

"From where?"

"Their village is near Bayanga. There's no problem getting new trackers. It's just a case of letting them know and bringing them back up here."

I had to go back to Bayanga anyway, so I offered to drop the two striking Pygmies off at their village. Then I could collect new trackers the following morning and bring them out. Melissa readily agreed. The Pygmies collected their stuff and we drove back down the track. It was dusk by the time we reached the Pygmy village. Huts the shape of igloos were hunched in the gloom. Fires flickered against the damp khaki backdrop of the forest. I dropped off the two men and said that I would return at dawn to collect the new trackers.

Back at the house, the cook had made supper. I ate by lamplight and then sat out on the porch in the dark, watching the sandbanks glisten silver in the ink-black current of the Sangha River.

I woke before dawn and drove up to the Pygmy village. The forest was a silhouette against the purple of the sky. Two Pygmies strolled idly down to the car. One jumped into the back while the other climbed in beside me. His name was Huanga. He had a handsome dreamy face and shorts that came down to his knees, like an old-style soccer player.

We drove in silence out to Melissa's camp. The cook

provided a quick breakfast of sweet milky tea and lumps of doughy bread. Then we filled our water bottles and set off down a winding path to the clearing below the camp. We squished across a muddy stream and climbed up a grassy bank. Then the canopy closed in overhead and we entered the forest.

It was a couple of hours after dawn, and the uppermost stories of the trees were dappled with glistening spots of light. A few bright shards dropped farther down. But in most places the forest floor was without any direct sunlight. It was a muffled, colorless, watery world: as though the canopy was the surface of an ocean and we were far below on the grey sandy ocean bottom.

The vegetation was a mixture of massive, towering trees and thick hard brown tangles of vines, leafless bushes and creepers. Some of the trees were so tall they needed buttresses, broad supporting webs that spanned out from their trunks, to hold them upright. The tangles got everywhere. The two trackers slipped lithely along the paths, dipping and swerving without a thought. Melissa was surprisingly agile for her size. I stumbled after, caught by every thorn, root or loose branch. Before long, my arms were covered in raised welts and tiny trails of blood.

At first, I felt that my blundering passage was the only sound in the forest. But soon my senses became more tuned to the noises from the trees and the sights along the way. Birds cawked in the foliage. Small animals rustled in the undergrowth. Several times I walked blindly into huge glistening webs and had to brush giant spiders out of my hair. On other occasions, we crossed dense lines of soldier ants cruising the forest or running silently across the mottled bark of fallen trees.

The noisiest creatures, apart from Melissa and myself, were troops of mangabey monkeys that we came across two or three times high up in the canopy. When we approached too close to the base of their tree, they would shriek at each other and take off through the foliage. All we would see were dark sinewy shapes, all arms and tails, leaping through the air and landing on branches that sprung back like trampolines and were still wobbling long after the monkeys had leaped on ahead.

As the morning progressed, the forest grew hotter and more steamy. Eventually, we stopped beside a short, stubby tree with red berries. I picked one up from the floor. It smelled like a cherry.

"This is a mokangenje tree," Melissa said. "This was where I first found the gorillas a few days ago. I sat over there, down the track, and watched them for a couple of hours. They were eating these berries. Some of them were up in the tree."

"Was this where you got charged?"

"No. That was two days later. They didn't know I was watching them here. I came back the next day and tracked them to another feeding place. I watched them again. It was on the third day that we had our confrontation with the silverback. They were the three best days I've had since I arrived in the forest. At first, the gorillas would run at the sight of me. Charging is a good sign. It means they are no longer completely afraid."

We followed the trail on through the forest to the spot where the charging had taken place. It was a large patch of bare earth in the deep shade underneath a huge tree.

"What exactly happened?" I said.

"We saw a young gorilla in this tree and moved in for a closer look," Melissa said. "We didn't realize that the silverback was just on the other side of the trunk. He came round and charged us, tearing up branches, smashing them on the ground, opening his mouth threateningly."

She stood in the forest with her hands on her hips. She was twice the size of the Pygmies, but smaller than a gorilla.

"I crouched on the ground. The idea is to try and look like a submissive gorilla. You look down, don't move. But the Pygmies' natural instinct when a gorilla charges is to stand up and wave their machetes. So I was trying to look submissive and take notes and at the same time reaching behind me to grab the Pygmies and stop them jumping up."

"How long did the charging last?"

"About twenty minutes. He'd charge a little and then stop and sit down and start eating as if we weren't there. That was great. But every time we tried to move back, he'd jump up and start displaying again."

I looked at the beaten ground and the torn branches. I had seen wild gorillas once, in the Rwandan mountains. There had been no screaming or charging then. I had sat and watched a huge silverback for the best part of an hour. He had lain on his back, stuffing leaves into his mouth and picking at his fur. When he sat up, I had looked at his face. He had a high forehead, a broad flat nose and thin pouty lips. His eyes were dark and sunken and intensely human. I looked at him and he looked at me, and then he fell asleep.

The Pygmies called out.

"They've found the trail," Melissa said.

There were still a few half-fresh clues: broken branches, footprints, drying droppings. Huanga led off. The trail soon left the path and plunged into vine and thorn thickets. The branches were now like grasping claws. The scratches multiplied. My skin was becoming blotchy with the heat and sweat. Inchworms were tumbling inside my T-shirt. The trail wove through thickets, clearings and more thickets. Finally, we came out onto a path. Able to stand upright, Melissa and I stretched out our necks and shoulders and caught our breaths. A little farther down the path, Huanga stopped and pointed into the undergrowth.

"Gorillas?" I said.

"No," said Melissa. "Have a look."

I slid down a little slope between two bushes into a cavern of flattened leaves. Big yellow bones lay amid the leaves. I dug around with my foot and found more bones. An elephant had died here. These were its remains.

"We found this six months ago," Melissa said. "It had been speared by poachers."

"Who?

"Villagers. Pygmies. I don't know."

We pushed on down the path until it opened into a clearing. Huanga stopped and sniffed. I followed his lead and caught a faint musty odor. This time it was gorillas. Melissa bent down and picked up a broken stem. It was a slender yellow-brown plant with green leaves. She bit into it and told me to do the same. It tasted familiar.

"Wild ginger," she said. "Favorite gorilla food."

Huanga took the ginger and examined it.

"Two days ago," he said.

The gorillas had probably stayed here awhile. Melissa and I sat down on the grass while the Pygmies wandered off to look for more tracks. Sunlight poured down into the clearing. The air was fresh and sweet. Short shrubs and grasses were growing happily—different kinds of plants from the fibrous undergrowth and sinewy creepers we had been pushing through all day. Insects buzzed around. Butterflies fluttered in the light. The forest had been dark and intent. Here, in the clearing, the world seemed more playful.

"Clearings like this are very important for the gorillas," Melissa said. "They find a lot of their food here. In most places in the forest the sunlight doesn't get through. The only food at ground level is fallen berries. Gorillas do climb trees to get food, but they can't get up to the canopy where the really good food grows. So they rely on the clearings where the sun reaches the ground."

"What grows here?"

"Herbs like this ginger. Fresh saplings. Young fruit bushes. All sorts of things. The minute the sun gets through, there's a riot of new growth. Other animals do a lot of their feeding here too. Buffalo, bongo, duiker, sitatunga, forest hog. And look, you see all sorts of insects and birds here that you don't see in the forest cover. The clearings are like separate little ecosystems within the forest."

"How do these clearings form?"

"Here some of them were made initially by loggers. But it can also be a natural tree fall. Wind or lightning. Or sometimes an elephant will push down a rotten tree. And once a clearing is made, it's always the elephants that keep it open by eating back the new growth and trampling down the weeds."

It was a similar story to the savannas. In the dense parts of the forest, most animals lived up in the canopy. But clearings allowed all sorts of other animals to thrive. The elephants helped to make and maintain these clearings through the forest. They contributed to a patchwork of different environments and so encouraged a broad diversity of plants and animals.

"How would gorillas do without elephants?" I asked.

"It would be much more difficult. The clearings would close up. Food would be harder to come by. Their existence would be more fragile. The gorillas don't like elephants. They run away if they hear them. But they need them."

The trackers had finally returned. They had struck out all around the clearing, but the trails were cold. We decided to head back for camp. On the way, we nearly ran into a herd of elephants. We were walking through a particularly dense part of the forest, unable to see more than a few feet on either side of the path, when Melissa suddenly halted. Huanga crept back, his finger to his lips. I halted and listened. I could hear rustling and chewing nearby. I shuffled slightly and a twig cracked. The forest around us erupted. There was a crashing of vegetation and a great pounding of feet. We froze, and though we could still see nothing, the elephants seemed to come by us in every direction. Then the noise faded and all was silent and peaceful again.

Huanga chopped off a vine with his machete and held it above his mouth. A milky liquid trickled out of the end. He drank happily and then handed the vine to me. The sap was slightly sour but refreshing. I watched the white drops fall to the ground and saw that Huanga had no toenails. The ends of his toes had been eaten away by parasites.

I suddenly remembered years back seeing a documentary film about Pygmies whose toes were similarly stubby. The film had also shown the Pygmies hunting elephants. It was an old black and white film, speeded up like a Keystone Kops movie, with an American commentary that talked about the "little people." The Pygmies had smeared themselves with elephant dung and dashed through the forest. But all it showed of the hunt was a close-up of a spear piercing the hide of what was clearly a dead elephant.

"Has Huanga ever hunted elephant?" I asked Melissa.

"I don't know," Melissa said. "I'll ask him."

Huanga smiled slowly. He hadn't, he said. But he knew other Pygmies who had. They used spears. They hunted alone, creeping up on an elephant and lunging the spear into the stomach. The meat was good. The ivory was good, too. But hunting elephants was a risky business, he said. Not all

elephants were really elephants. Some were Pygmies transformed into elephants—like the Pygmy gorillas that had
haunted the other trackers' dreams.

"Superstitions are strong here," I said.

Melissa nodded.

"Most of it's to do with people turning into animals," she
said. "I've had the camp raided twice by elephants. It was
built on an old elephant path and they are always coming
past. In the raids, they tear off the mosquito netting and
grab anything. They've eaten my books and bras even. The
Pygmies say these aren't real elephants, they are Pygmy
elephants."

"Your cook's not a Pygmy. What does he think?"

"Oh, he believes too. Everyone believes in magic around
here. Even Bolobo, the African director of the reserve. And
he was educated in France. Hey, sometimes I start to believe
in the magic. And there's an American who's studying the
Pygmies who says he saw a Pygmy turn into a duiker one
night."

"An American said that?"

"He had smoked a lot of dope."

It was time to get moving. We walked on in silence. A
little later, Melissa stopped to speak again.

"It's so hard to tell with this magic," she said. "You never
know how much people believe and how much they just use
magic to scare other people and get what they want. A few
years back, a man drowned in the Sangha River. Rumors
started that he had been killed by crocodile men: men who
change into crocodiles. The mayor and the police chief arrested about seventy people. Quite a lot of them were thrown
in jail."

"The mayor and the police chief," I said. "I've heard about
them."

"That's the thing. Quite a lot of these crocodile men turned out to be enemies of the mayor and the police chief. The whole crocodile event was very politically convenient. But then again, if you talk to the local people, they are all convinced that the crocodile men really exist."

Eventually, we trudged wearily up the hill into camp. "You should try the shower," Melissa said.

"Shower? Where?"

She pointed down a hill.

I clambered down a rocky path to a grotto in the shadows below the camp. A waterfall tumbled over a mossy cliff into a shallow pool. I stood knee deep in the water and the icy stream slipped deliciously over me, washing away the sweat and burrs and scratches of the day.

It may not have been Noah's Flood, but something did happen not so very long ago that washed from the face of the earth many a "beast and creeping thing and bird of the air."

This last of the great extinctions took place at the end of the Pleistocene period, between 30,000 and 10,000 B.C. It wiped out almost half the earth's species of mammals, including oddities like kangaroo rats, pocket gophers and giant skunks. The elephant, an oddity itself, was fortunate to survive, to make it onto Noah's Ark. Most of the other great land mammals, the "megaherbivores," disappeared.

These megaherbivores came in all shapes, if only one size—big. Some, like the woolly mammoth, the mastodon and the gomphothere, were cousins of the elephant. Others were related to different contemporary animals, like the toxodont, a huge guinea pig, or an eighteen-foot-long giant ground sloth called the megatherium. In Australia, there were even giant marsupials like the palorchestes, a pouched, hopping beast twice the size of a kangaroo, and the diprodont, a giant wombat, six feet high and ten feet long, with teeth like chisels.

When fossils of these creatures were first properly examined in the early part of the nineteenth century, scientists were bemused. Thomas Jefferson, the American president, proclaimed the fossilized jaw of a long-extinct ground sloth to belong to an unknown living species of North American lion. But as the century progressed and more fossils were uncovered, including the massive remains of dinosaurs, it became impossible to deny that all sorts of strange animals had once roamed the earth.

This raised the question of what had killed off all these extinct species. Even today, scientists are still divided on the answer. The dinosaurs all died out together, some 70 million years ago, and they were probably affected by some massive change in the earth's atmosphere: like a meteor hit which sent up huge dust clouds and blocked the sun. But the Pleistocene extinction was different. It was selective. It wiped out only half the mammals on earth. Some species survived while similar species living virtually side by side with them disappeared. What killed the smilodon, the North American saber-toothed cat, but spared the North American cougar?

The timing of the extinction pointed to the involvement of man. Between 30,000 and 10,000 years ago, bands of human hunters were spreading across the earth. In Africa, animals like the elephant had evolved for millions of years alongside humans and had learned to avoid these two-legged hunters as much as possible. But in other parts of the world, animals had never experienced organized intelligent hunters like men. The megaherbivores would have been particularly vulnerable. Their size made them easy to spot and worthwhile to hunt. They were generally slow and unaggressive. And they were comparatively few in number. Over several thousand years, animals like the giant sloth could easily have been hunted to extinction by men.

But the megaherbivores were not the only animals to disappear. Thousands of smaller species also died out. Humans could not possibly have hunted down every one of a species of mouse or rat or squirrel. So what could have nudged these creatures to extinction?

This remains a controversial question. But in 1987, a South African scientist named Norman Owen Smith came up with an intriguing answer. He suggested that the smaller mammals died out as a result of the disappearance of the larger mammals. As an example, Owen Smith used contemporary elephants. He suggested that the Pleistocene megaherbivores had dominated their habitats in the way elephants do today. By eating trees, grasses and hedges, they had maintained an ecological balance. When the megaherbivores were hunted down, this balance changed. Some species were able to survive the changes. Others were not.

This is precisely what had happened in the areas outside Amboseli which had been vacated by the elephants. Zebras and wildebeests had disappeared. This had been just a local extinction. But Owen Smith's ideas posed the possibility that if elephants disappeared from Africa, then other species might follow. The forests and savannas would grow quieter.

I w a s b a c k i n Bayanga, sleeping in Phil and Denise's house, when the rains began. I shivered beneath my mosquito net while a cascade of water drummed a violent tattoo on the iron roof. Later, the rhythm lulled me to sleep, and when I woke, just before dawn, the quiet was startling. The pounding had stopped and there was only a gentle drip-drip from the lemon tree outside the window.

I dressed and walked outside. In the blue shadows, I could see that the river had risen. The sandbanks I had gazed at in the moonlight a few evenings back had all disappeared. The ground was sodden beneath my feet. I breathed in the fresh earthy air. Then I climbed into my Jeep. I had an early morning appointment with a Central African ecologist named Joel. I headed out into the forest, the wheels of my Jeep sliding in the mud.

Joel was making tea when I arrived. He had an impacted, expressive face, with dark, deep-set eyes and purple-black skin. A red baseball cap was pulled tight over his head, the bill facing backward. Three Pygmies were also standing around. They were Joel's forest experts. One of them had filed his teeth down to points, but when he smiled, his expression was gummy and comic rather than fierce.

We left camp and slipped down a muddy bank onto a sunken, waterlogged path. The forest was even darker and cooler after the rains. The bark on the trees was black from moisture. The rain had stopped hours earlier, but the water was still working its way groundward, the drops plunking from leaf to leaf before spilling finally to the earth. The insistent sound was like the dull tinkling of a thousand untuned pianos.

The path meandered to the edge of a broad stream, deepened and widened by the rains. In the middle, the water came up to my thighs and the waists of the Pygmies. It was cold and clear and I could feel the spongy, streaky sand beneath my feet. We splashed through and squelched out onto higher, dryer land.

By the side of the path, a tree trunk was daubed with a splash of mud, as though a giant paintbrush had been wiped across the bark. Something similar had in fact happened: an elephant, still wet from a mud bath, had brushed past.

"Just one hour ago," Joel said. "Look here also."

A few yards beyond the tree, half a dozen boluses of fresh elephant dung sat on the wet earth. Each was the size of a sweet melon: slightly squarish, still wet and warm, the color of dark honey, the consistency of horse droppings.

"Lots of seeds in here," Joel said. He eased a bolus open with his finger and hooked out a seed that looked like a flattened chestnut. He showed it to the Pygmies and they nodded. Then he handed it to me. The dung was slimy on the nut. It smelled high and sweet, but not unpleasant: a stronger version of the composty odor of the forest itself.

"Nguruma tree," he said. "There are lots around."

Happy at his rich find, Joel instructed the Pygmies to gather the droppings, and they carefully picked up the boluses and dropped them into a canvas sack. Over the past few months, Joel and the Pygmies had done this hundreds of times. When they returned to camp, the Pygmies would sort through the dung and pick out all the seeds. Joel had found scores of different kinds of seeds in the elephant dung, and he was still trying to match some of them to different trees in the forest.

His aim was not just to see what elephants ate. It was to find out how this eating actually helped the forest.

"The elephant is the bee of the forest," he explained. "Bees collect pollen and distribute it so that the flowers can reproduce. The elephant does the same thing. It pollenates, it fertilizes the forest."

It was a good parallel. Flowers make nectar to attract bees, which then become unwitting carriers of their pollen. The forest trees did the same with the animals of the forest, and especially the elephant. They wrapped their reproductive seeds in sweet fleshy fruit. Elephants then came along and ate the fruit. The flesh was digested but the seeds passed through the elephants' digestive systems and were eventually deposited in new parts of the forest in large piles of hot, wet, rich manure.

"Just look here," Joel said.

In a patch of subdued, dappled light trickling through the canopy, he had found an old pile of elephant dung. It was dark and shapeless, without smell, but clearly recognizable. Sprouting from the surface were several small green plants. Each one was just a few inches high: a stem and four leaves. Glistening from the rains, they looked like weeds or flowers.

Joel grinned delightedly.

"Nguruma," he said. "These are nguruma seedlings."

Some months back, an elephant had eaten some nguruma fruit. Later, it had deposited the seeds here. Now they had germinated into healthy seedlings. I peered up into the upper story of the forest. One day, perhaps, these seedlings would reach the distant sunlight above.

Joel saw me looking and waved his arms at the canopy.

"So much of this is due to the elephant," he said. "The elephant is the gardener of the forest."

Joel smiled happily and walked on down the path. As I followed, I thought about another ecological story from the Pleistocene that related specifically to Joel's work in the forest.

Daniel H. Janzen and Paul S. Martin were American scientists studying trees in the Santa Rosa National Park in Costa Rica. Their attention was drawn to one tree, a type of forest palm. This palm had two puzzling characteristics.

The first was that it appeared to be in decline. It seemed to be diminishing in both number and range—and to have been doing so for several thousand years. The second was that the tree produced far too much fruit. At the end of every dry season, each palm dropped thousands of oval yellow fruits. A few were eaten by agoutis, tapirs and peccaries. But most simply rotted beneath the parent trees. And most of the seeds, the trees' reproductive tools, were eaten by a voracious species of burrowing beetle.

What was going on? The tree was wasting nutrition and energy and diminishing in number. It almost looked as though the palm was expecting a big animal like the elephant to come along and eat all its fruit. With such help perhaps it would then start to spread through the forest again.

There were no elephants, nor any other large animal, in the Santa Rosa forest. But in the past, there had been. More specifically, until the Pleistocene extinction, there had been a relation of the elephant, the gomphothere. Over the millions of years, there had been various kinds of gomphotheres. Some had long trunks, others short ones. One type, the platybelodon, had tusks like shovels. Another had four tusks. But the type that had lived in these forests was a short-trunked, fruit-eating beast, somewhat like a huge pig.

The palm fruits looked to be specially well suited to gomphothere appetites. They were dull-colored but strong-smelling. Like elephants, gomphotheres had a better sense of smell than sight. The fruits were also fleshy and good to eat. And they were deposited in the large numbers necessary to attract a beast like a gomphothere. This suitability had probably evolved over millions of years. Palm and beast would have developed together: helping each other like the elephant and the nguruma.

Then the gomphothere suddenly died. In ten thousand years, the palm had not had nearly enough time to adapt to this loss. It still produced thousands of useless fruits. And without the gomphothere's help, its range continued to diminish. Perhaps eventually the palm would die out.

I caught up to Joel at the next stop.

"What would happen to the nguruma if there were no more elephants?" I asked.

"*C'est mal,*" he replied. "There would be many fewer seed-lings. And it would not just be the nguruma tree."

There were dozens of trees in the forest whose seeds the elephants ate and helped to distribute. Other animals, like the gorilla, also performed the same task. But the elephant was the main carrier. And the gorillas anyway depended partially on the elephants for their own existence.

Research in the Dzanga-Sangha and elsewhere in Africa had also shown that some fruits actually needed the specific juices and nutrients in elephant dung to germinate. And a few seeds could not germinate unless they had actually passed through the digestive system of an elephant, undergoing some kind of chemical change in the process.

"Shhh," Joel said.

He held up his hand and put his finger to his lips. The path had grown wetter. We were now up to our ankles in brown water. I slushed gently forward and Joel pulled me in behind him. He held aside a dripping bush and I looked into a flooded clearing ahead of us.

Just a few yards away was a herd of elephants. I peered closer. There were four adult females and three calves: forest elephants, smaller than the savanna species, with rounded heads and straighter, slimmer tusks. We watched them suck-ing up the water with their trunks and squirting it into their mouths. The calves played between their mothers' legs, tum-bling and splashing each other. The forest seemed to vibrate with the creatures' rumbles of contentment.

Then Joel shifted his weight. The mud plopped and the elephants started at the sound. They looked up and began to taste the air with their trunks. The calves drew back beneath the adult bellies. Suddenly, the largest of the females tensed: she had caught our scent.

She came quickly forward, waving her trunk. I could al-most feel her bulk. Her head and ears eclipsed the light from the sky. I was sure she would hear the frantic thumping of my heart. Then, without warning, like a truck skidding on oil, she wheeled around and there was an explosion of splashing. The water turned white and the ground shook. I looked up to see the last elephant haunches vanish into the trees on the far side of the clearing.

Joel and I breathed out and turned around. The Pygmies were nowhere to be seen.

"Where . . . ?" I began to ask.

Joel pointed.

The Pygmies were clambering down out of a tree, shamefaced and muttering to themselves in their own language of forest sounds.

About a week after I had arrived in Bayanga, Phil and Denise returned home. They brought with them a boy named Josh. He was twelve years old and Phil's son. When Phil had been a Peace Corps worker in Central Africa, he had lived with a local woman and Josh was the child of the relationship. Phil had kept in touch with the family and he had now brought Josh to stay in Bayanga for his school holidays.

Josh was short and quiet. He had light brown skin, pale curly hair, and Phil's blue eyes. He had grown up in a remote rural African village. He had never before had any real contact with his father's culture. When we sat down to supper, he ate with his hands and threw the bones from his food on the floor.

Phil and Denise were in a dilemma. Josh was a poor rural African, but his mother had suggested that Phil take him back to America when he left. The idea raised all sorts of questions. Could Josh cope with the change? Where would he be happiest? Was a richer society better than a poorer one?

How could Josh choose when he had no real conception of America?

We talked it over into the night, and I could see that it would take all of the two more years Phil and Denise expected to stay in Africa to reach a decision.

In the morning, I rose early and tiptoed out of the house. The Pygmies from Huanga's village were going hunting and I had arranged to join them. About twenty of us set out into the forest. The men led the way, carrying spears and machetes. The women carried woven baskets on their backs. As we walked, they collected fruits and nuts along the way.

Eventually, we came to the spot where the Pygmies had left their hunting nets on a tree branch. There were about a dozen of them. They were made out of rough brown twine. They were long and narrow, like tennis nets. The men slung them over their shoulders and walked deeper into the forest until we came to a likely area of thicket. The men hung the nets on the vegetation in a long semicircle. Then they walked around to the other side. The nets now formed a trap. Anything that ran away from the men was likely to end up in the nets. At a signal, the men began to walk forward, shouting and clapping their hands. I waited, listening for the sounds of an animal, but the Pygmies eventually reached the nets without having flushed anything.

This was hit-and-miss hunting. The first four times the nets were set, we missed. The fifth time, I was sitting on a fallen tree just outside the sweep of the nets. By now, I was expecting nothing. Suddenly, there was a crashing through the undergrowth, and by the time I had scrambled over to the noise, a dark shape was writhing in the nets.

The Pygmies held the animal down for me to see. It was a duiker, a small, ugly antelope with high haunches, stubby legs and a curved, snub-shaped head. It lay on its side, its heart beating so fast and heavily in its barrel-shaped chest that I thought it might expire from shock. Every few seconds it wriggled, in a sudden attempt to escape.

I stood there, gripped with mixed emotions. One of the Pygmies spoke to me and made a gesture. It seemed to me that he was asking if I wanted to let the animal go. Perhaps this was a courtesy extended to squeamish visitors.

I nodded my head.

"Yes, yes. Let it go."

In response, with a flick of his wrist, he snapped the duiker's back leg. I had got the general idea right, but the question wrong. He must have asked if he should kill it. The duiker's tongue now slobbered out of the side of its mouth and it shrieked: a horrible scream like a child caught in a trap.

It was too late to save the animal's life. It could not survive with a broken leg. So I gestured for the Pygmies to kill it and end its pain. A teenage boy grabbed hold of the animal's neck and twisted until its head faced back toward its flickering tail. The duiker still failed to die. Its soft wet eyes bulged out and blood started to pour out of its mouth from its bitten tongue. The boy then picked up the duiker and smacked its head against a tree until it was dead.

The Pygmies laughed and I felt sick.

The women quickly cut up the corpse with their knives. They wrapped the pieces in leaves, each Pygmy receiving a small slab. Then, happy with their catch, they strolled back through the forest.

As we walked, I thought about these Pygmies. In a way, they shared Josh's dilemma. They were cultural half-castes. They were strung out between two worlds: the forest where they had been born and the village on whose outskirts they now lived. Now that they had experienced the bright lights of the village—the beer, prostitutes, clothes, money, new foods and radios—they could never return completely to the forest. Yet they were living only at the scrappy edge of the modern world. The villagers treated them with disdain. They got them drunk and stole their possessions. They raped their women. They ordered the Pygmies about.

In the forest, the Pygmies were the kings of men. In the village, they were the dregs. But the Pygmies knew what they were doing. They had made their choice. All around me they were laughing and chattering, wearing their torn Beck's beer and Coca-Cola T-shirts and carrying their little parcels of duiker meat, wrapped up in forest leaves.

I drove back to Bayanga and found Phil, Denise and Josh heading out to play volleyball in the village square. I grabbed a drink and ran to join them. At first, the village boys watched us, giggling, from the sidelines. But eventually they joined in, and we bashed the ball back and forth over the net until the sun began to sink in the sky.

We walked back to the house and drank cold Cokes from the gas fridge. Then we clambered down the riverbank for a wash and a swim in the muddy waters of the Sangha River. The current was strong from the recent rains, so we lazed in the shallows by a little sandy beach and watched the sun set orange and purple on the far side of the river.

Later, dry and dressed, I went out for a walk. The moon was rising and I could see my way by its pale light. I walked past the last few houses and up toward the abandoned mill. I had been here before during the day. It was an enormous plant. Hangars and vast machines covered several acres. The whole place was like an alien station in the forest. In the dark, the place was even more threatening. The machines loomed like monsters in the shadows. There were even eyes flickering in the darkness—gangs of fireflies.

But as I walked around, it sunk in that these monsters were dead. The loggers had come and changed this world. But now they had gone. The mill was a massive graveyard. Without electricity and workers, the machines were merely carcasses, skeletons. The scene suddenly felt more peaceful, and I sat on a low wall and watched the fireflies turning their lights on and off.

As I got up to leave, a shadow drifted out from behind a machine. I started, but it was only an old man, a lone night guard, who must have been woken by the echoes of my footfalls. He came forward and spoke to me in Sango. I replied in French and we had a brief conversation. I said I had come to look for elephants and his eyes lit up.

"Elephants, they come here every night," he said.

"Here?"

"Yes, they come right to the edge of the factory. I see them myself. They eat the grass around the factory."

I waited for a while with the guard, but no elephants came. This night, they were staying in the forest. But I was still gladdened by the old man's words. For the time being, the elephants, not the trucks and great saws and logging machines, were the masters, and the architects, of the rain forest.

Chapter Four

WHITE MAN'S GRAVE

One morning in Nairobi, I drove out toward the hazy knuckled ridge of the Ngong Hills to the suburb of Karen, named after Karen Blixen, to visit an old friend named Terry Mathews.

The Mathews dog pack, half a dozen squat, piebald mutts, were the first to greet me. They bowled across the grass and leaped up, barking and licking and wagging their stubby tails.

"Go on, Champ. Get out of it, Topi."

Terry hobbled out of his studio and waved his crutch in the air. When the dogs had quietened, we went over to the porch to have tea. Terry swung muscularly along beside me on his good leg and the crutch. His bad leg, the left one, hung stiff and scarred from the surgeon's knife.

"I see you're up and about," I said.

"Not exactly running," Terry snorted.

He screwed up his good eye. The other one was sightless, hidden by a black patch. Even with all his wounds, and after nearly sixty adventurous African years, Terry was still boyishly handsome. His blond hair, hawkish nose, glinting blue eye and raffish expression gave him the look of a middle-aged Hollywood film star. With the patch and crutch, he could have passed for Stewart Granger playing Long John Silver.

The lost eye was an old injury, from 1968. As a young man, Terry had been a professional hunter, one of the most popular and respected in Kenya. He was a charming guide, a first-rate naturalist, and a fast and accurate shot. Working in a risky business, he was also always careful and well prepared. But there was one animal even Terry could not prepare against: his human client. A careless shot took out Terry's lead eye and put an end to his hunting career.

Terry had then taken up his second love, sculpting. His bronzes were mostly of the animals he had hunted. It was not easy being a one-eyed sculptor. I had seen him working: he weaved his head from side to side all the time, trying to give his one eye the perspective of two. But Terry was a good artist. His bronzes sold well and he established himself as one of Africa's leading wildlife sculptors.

But by the time I first met Terry, when I was living in Nairobi, nearly five years earlier, he was injured again—with these leg wounds and a hole in his belly. He was laid up in a bed on this porch, as frustrated as a caged leopard. He spent his days spotting birds in the garden and flicking at flies with a length of rubber. He had grown good at the flicking. Nine times out of ten, squinting with his one good eye, he zapped his fly.

These latest injuries, his first serious wounds from a wild animal, had come long after he had given up hunting. He had made a life-size sculpture of a rhino for the Kenya Wildlife Service, and an American television crew had interviewed him about the sculpture and then asked if he would accompany them to Nairobi National Park to film a live rhino. In the park, they found a mother rhino and calf. The idea was to film Terry talking in the foreground with the rhinos in the background. But the plan went badly wrong, and through no fault of his own Terry found himself facing a charging rhino. The film was still rolling, and I had seen the whole sequence. Terry knew there was a film crew behind him and his hunter's instincts told him to stand his ground, to protect the people at his back. He picked up a stone and threw it at the rhino. He was stooping to gather another stone when the rhino hit him.

Its first contact was a sideways sweep of the horn that shattered Terry's left shin and knocked him from his feet. As he fell, the rhino thrust upward. Its horn sliced through Terry's groin and penetrated sixteen inches into his belly. Only Terry's thick leather belt prevented him from being ripped open as the rhino jerked back its head. Instead, Terry was thrown a dozen feet into the air. It was touch and go whether he would survive the physical trauma and the infection from the wound in his belly. When he was finally released from hospital, he picked up a lump of clay and began to model. Typically, the piece was a rhino, in the act of striking. Terry called it *Left Hook*.

Since then, Terry had recovered from the internal wounds, but his leg had healed badly and it was only after a series of operations that he was even hobbling. It had not been easy sculpting. Terry liked to work standing up. But now, five years after the rhino incident, he was finally preparing a new exhibition of his bronzes.

"Are there any rhinos in the exhibition?" I asked.

"Yes, one or two," he said. "But more elephants. I seem to have done a lot of elephants. While I was laid up, I went through my output over the years. Almost a third of all my sculptures have been elephants."

As we were talking, Terry's wife Jeanne came out onto

the porch. She was a tall, striking blond woman, renowned among Africans in Nairobi for having produced five sons.

"I was just saying that almost a third of my bronzes are elephants," Terry said to Jeanne.

"Of course," Jeanne said. "They always were your favorite."

Terry pressed two fingers thoughtfully to his forehead.

"Were they?" he said.

"Oh, yes," Jeanne said. "I've always thought of you as an elephant man. You even think like an elephant."

"When I was hunting, there was something about elephants," Terry mused. "They were the biggest creatures in the bush. And the cleverest. When you hunted elephants, you had to think."

"That's what I mean," Jeanne said. "You always knew what they were up to. You thought like an elephant."

Terry's favorite hunting country was up along the course of the Tana River, which ran from George Adamson's camp at Kora across the barren outlands of northeast Kenya to the Indian Ocean between Malindi and Lamu.

"There were certainly some big bulls up there," Terry said, chewing on his finger. "But they were also smart. They knew they were being hunted. We'd set up camp by the river and suddenly there'd be no elephants around. They'd come down to the river at night to drink, but by morning they'd be long gone, thirty miles out into the bush."

His hands moved all the time while he talked, following the elephants, becoming the elephants, scratching his neck and running through his thinning blond hair.

"Then you had to try and work out the tusk size from the tracks," he continued. "You see, there was no point going after just any bull. You wanted one with big tusks. So you'd look at the size of the tracks and the texture. Elephant feet are like tires. They have grooves or treads. Cows and calves have fine treads. Young bulls' tracks look like a guy with new tires on. The old bulls have smooth tracks like old, worn tires."

"So the bigger and smoother the better?"

"Right, though sometimes you had more tantalizing clues. One elephant got me very excited. Elephants tend to get their sleep between two and four at night. They lie down, and big elephants often rest their heads on slopes or anthills. This bull had leaned against a wet bank and left an impression of one of its tusks in the mud. It was huge, as big as anything I'd ever seen."

"Did you find the elephant?"

"No." He shook his head. "Never caught up with him."

His eye went a little dreamy.

"You know, when you do catch up with a bull, it's something else," he said. "You're in thick cover, you're bloody close, your heart's in the back of your throat. The tusks are glinting white. The thing looks monumental."

Terry lifted his arm and lined it up like a rifle on an imaginary bull.

"Pufff," he whispered.

Then he lowered his arm and sighed, boyish and bashful.

I h a d n e v e r s e e n an elephant shot, but I had been on a hunting safari a few years back. One of Terry's old colleagues, a professional hunter named Robin Hurt, had invited me along: not to do any shooting myself, but simply to observe. Hunting was banned in Kenya. But it was still allowed in Tanzania, and Robin had a concession in the remote Moyowosi swamps, 120 miles inland from Lake Tanganyika.

I flew down from Nairobi in a small Cessna. The swamps

were a vast waterlogged region, infested with tsetse flies and
mosquitoes and inhabited only by wildlife and a few poachers. For the last few miles, the pilot skimmed the plane low
over herds of buffalo and elephant, wading through the deep
waters and high green grass. The camp was sited on a dry
headland in the swamps. This was an old-style, thousand-
pound-a-day safari. Robin Hurt had hacked a road more than
a hundred miles through the bush and trucked in a luxury
camp. We had tents with beds, thatched hot-water showers
and chilled champagne.

Sitting around the fire on the first night, it felt as if the
Cessna had brought me into a different world. The Africa I
was covering as a reporter at the time was the modern continent of wars, coups, famines, social misery and economic
collapse. But this was more like the Boy's Own Africa I had
read and dreamed about as a boy, the Africa of Stanley,
Livingstone, Tarzan and Allan Quatermaine, the elephant
hunter in *King Solomon's Mines*. I drank my whisky and shivered with anticipation.

The next morning, we went for a ride into the swamps.
Robin had brought in two amphibian buggies designed for
use by deer stalkers in the Scottish marshes. They were made
of hard green molded plastic and looked like a pair of Jacuzzis
on wheels. As we rolled across the land and then churned
noisily through the water, I studied my companions. Robin
could hardly have looked less like a hunter. He was short
and bandy-legged, with a plain square face and square spec-
tacles. Jim and Harry were more likely hunting clients.
Both were grizzled and white-haired and delighted to be out
here, away from their businesses, their worries and their
families.

We chugged through the water and reeds. A buffalo eyed
us from the shade of a palm tree on a sprout of an island.

Later we stopped on a larger patch of dry land and had a picnic lunch. When we explored the island on foot, a huge reedbuck leaped out of a patch of reeds just ahead of us and bounded away. It sidestepped and swerved to put us off, but we were not carrying the rifles.

I had only come for a few days, and in the evening I asked Robin what our chances were of making a kill.

"You never know," he said. "Jim and Harry only want good trophies. They're not going to shoot smaller versions of animals they've already got. It depends what we find. Last time Jim came on safari with me, he stayed for three weeks and took home only two trophies."

I went to bed wishing for good luck. The morning was fine and cold. We ate breakfast and climbed into Robin's open Landcruiser. This time, we were going to drive along the tracks around the edge of the swamps. There were some leopard baits to check, maybe some buffalo to have a look at. We cruised slowly out of camp. Birds took off from the trees. The clouds drifted overhead. The bush buzzed with insects. Then, around a corner, scarcely a mile from camp, we saw beneath an acacia tree the forms of three big lions.

The next minute was a blur. Robin braked and bustled Jim out of the car. The gun bearer handed down Jim's gun. Robin positioned a tripod made of bamboo on the ground and Jim rested the gun in the center.

"The one on the left," Robin whispered.

The lions had stood up by now. They were big, broad-shouldered, black-maned beasts, in the prime of life.

Jim took aim and fired. A terrible transformation came over the lion on the left. It seemed suddenly immensely tired, as though it had aged ten years in a moment. I felt I could sense a puzzlement on its face as its legs were no longer able to hold it upright. It crumpled slowly—almost in slow motion—to the ground. Jim fired again. A spasm shot through the beast's body like an electric shock, and then it was still.

Harry was already placing his gun on the tripod. These lions had never been hunted. They had no instinctive fear of men or guns. The remaining two simply stood and stared in confusion at us. An awful guilty sorrow gripped my body. I wanted to stand up and shout at them to run. Then Harry fired. The second lion dropped immediately and lay writhing on the ground. Another shot and this beast was dead too.

The third lion now came forward, low to the ground, snarling, flicking its tail. Two corpses lay behind: almost certainly its brothers. I waited for another shot. But we only had two lion licenses. Robin shouted and waved. Everyone now joined in. Robin raised his gun in case the lion charged. But it didn't. It simply turned, its tail drooping behind, and walked away into the dry crackling scrub.

Jim and Harry and Robin were all grinning. The gun bearers were whooping. I felt like a black man in a white hood at a Ku Klux Klan meeting. My noble, romantic vision of hunting had vanished at the moment of the first shot. Trembling, I followed the others up to the carcasses. The lions lay with their eyes open in the dust. Blood seeped out onto the golden hides. I reached down and touched a lion flank. It was still warm. "I had never shot an elephant and never wanted to," George Orwell wrote in "Shooting an Elephant." "It seemed to me that it would be murder." This too, I felt, had been murder.

The carcasses were loaded onto the car and we drove back triumphantly into camp. Jim and Harry had cut off tufts of black hair from the lions' tails and stuck them in the rims of their hats. The gun bearers were singing a song in Swahili about the big bwanas who had killed the big lions. In the

afternoon, the animals were skinned and I saw the pink hide-
less bodies, grotesque remnants of what the lions had been.

I was a guest on this safari. I tried to hide my feelings. But
my misery was transparent. And Robin was an evangelical
hunter: a proselytizer. He seemed to need my approval. At
dinner, he advanced the case for hunting.

"Hunting is the best thing for conservation," he said.
"There are thousands of lions in these swamps and we take
out only a handful every year. But the money we bring in
means that the Tanzanian government is prepared to keep
this area as a wilderness. Do you know what would happen
to the Moyowosi swamps if there were no hunters?"

"Tell me," I said.

"It would be turned into rice paddies, man. They'd clear
out the tsetse and bring in the farmers."

I had no argument with this. I knew enough about the
issues to accept that hunting, when properly controlled, was
beneficial. It did provide justification for the continued existence of wilderness areas like this. It did persuade African
officials that wildlife was worth keeping and using.

This was not my problem. My distress was personal.
Whenever I had seen lions before, I had always watched them
in awe and wonder. They were magnificent creatures. It had
seemed a privilege simply to see them in the wild. Now we
had just shot two lions. I hadn't even had a chance to have
a proper look. I was still peering through the grass when the
first one was shot. I was mourning not just the killing of the
lions but, in a way, the loss of my own innocence.

"You are not going to write anything bad about hunting,
are you?" Robin said.

"Well, um, I don't . . ." I stuttered.

"Perhaps I shouldn't let you go back," Robin said. "Perhaps I should just shoot you here."

I giggled nervously and looked up. Everyone's eyes were

turned away. No one was laughing. There was a faraway expression on Robin's face.

It was dark by the time Terry had finished telling me about elephant hunts. I asked if I could have a look at his new work. We walked over to the studio. Terry flicked on the light and dozens of sculptures glinted on white exhibition stands. It was as though a Midas with a bronze touch had strolled across a miniature savanna.

Right in front of me was a charging rhino, a reworking of *Left Hook*. On the next stand were a pair of courting ostriches, wings aspread. Behind was a yawning hippo and a startled kudu, its neck thick and sinewy. A family of warthogs caught my eye. These creatures were the clowns of the bush and Terry had captured them perfectly. They were running in a line, their ugly snouts low to the ground, their tails sticking up into the air as though held up by helium balloons. The piece beside the warthogs was more serious, more arty. It was a stunningly fluid sculpture of three giraffes, loping along, their muscular necks curling and flexing like nervous snakes.

But Terry was right. Almost half the pieces were elephants. Here stood a big taut bull. Over there were two mothers and calves. Beyond was another bull, its trunk resting on its tusks like a leopard lounging in a tree. Behind that a tusker scratched its back on a rock, a cow and calf drank from a stream, a baby rolled in the mud.

The bronzes were technically perfect. Terry could roll a piece of plasticine between his fingers until it became a miniature animal. But in the best of them, there was something more than simply a good likeness. These pieces had a certain tension, a sense of expectancy, as though some dramatic act were about to occur. Then I realized where this tension came from. The act would be the pulling of a trigger. These animals were seen through a hunter's eye. Somewhere, out of the picture, Terry was raising his rifle.

I looked again at the sculptures, pleased at this piece of insight. But then I had another thought. My memories of the hunt in Tanzania were not merely of this moment of beautiful tension. They were of the blood and horror that came afterward. These sculptures had nothing of this. There was no bronze of the bullet thudding home, the tearing of flesh and bone. None of the animals in Terry's art had been shot. None was wounded or dead.

I looked across at Terry. This omission seemed like some kind of unconscious admission.

"When you're hunting, Terry," I said, "you've got an animal in your sights, a beautiful wild living creature, like one of these sculptures. Why do you then pull the trigger? What makes you want to kill it?"

Terry stuck out his chin as though I had challenged him to a fight. Then the chin dropped and his expression softened.

"The killing is rather an anticlimax," he said. "Many of the best days you wouldn't even fire a gun."

"But some days you would."

Terry lifted his eye patch and rubbed his dead pearly eyeball with his knuckles.

"Yeah," he said. "Some days you would."

"So why?" I said.

Terry twisted his face in thought.

Why did people hunt? It was the question I had been trying to answer ever since I had been on my hunting safari. Back then, I had asked Jim and Harry. They said hunting was good for conservation. They said they liked being in the wild. They said the killing was just the excuse for the rest. These weren't really answers to my question. But I did understand one thing. Men like Jim and Harry hunted because they enjoyed it. They liked the hunt and they liked the kill. It was as exciting as anything they did in life: as exciting as a business killing. They had no need to shoot the lions. They did it for fun.

"Look," Terry finally said, interrupting my reverie. "You grew up in London, right? I grew up in the bush, catching snakes, shooting small animals. This is Africa. Hunting is a part of life in Africa. It's normal here, it's natural."

I could see his point. It was not a question of absolutes. It was a matter of degree. There was something obscene about rich foreigners like Jim and Harry coming to Africa specially to shoot beautiful, intelligent wild animals so that they could hang the horns on their walls and spread the skins on their floors. But hunting for the pot, even hunting to make a living, this changed things a little.

And I had to accept the confusion in my own attitude. My horror at the killing of the lions was not merely moral indignation. It was also, quite simply, that I hated having to witness the bloodletting. It was squeamishness. As Terry said, I had grown up in London, in a plastic-coated world where coq au vin looked nothing like chickens and steak nothing like cows. I was happy to eat meat as long as I didn't have to visit a slaughterhouse or kill the animals myself.

On safari once, I had seen a pack of wild dogs chase down a young wildebeest. The calf had been hamstrung and then eaten alive. It had stood on the savanna, the dogs ripping at its belly, and turned its eyes toward me and my companions. As it was eaten alive, it bleated at us. I had not liked this either, but I could not argue that the dogs were immoral. Similarly, I had been upset by the incident in Central Africa with the Pygmies and the duiker. Yet I had no right to criticize the Pygmies. If I objected to such natural hunting, then I had to accept that the problem was mine, not theirs.

"Come and have a look at this," Terry said.

We walked across the studio to one of the sculptures. This was a unique piece. It depicted a simple scene. In the middle stood a baobab, Africa's broadest and most ancient tree. To one side was a huge old bull elephant. On the other, peeking around the base of the tree, just able to see the tips of the elephant's great tusks, was a tiny African hunter, a bow and arrow in his hands. The piece was titled *Giants of the Bush*.

"The giants?" I said. "The elephant and the baobab."

"And the Waliangulu," said Terry.

"The Waliangulu?"

"The best elephant hunters Africa has ever seen."

I looked down at the sculpture. I felt Terry was trying to tell me something, trying to help me cross the gulf between my urban English sensibility and that of a man like this Waliangulu hunter.

"Tell me more about the Waliangulu," I said.

"They live beyond Tsavo," Terry said. "There aren't many of them around any more. But if you really want to find out about them, you should go and talk to Bill Woodley."

It was a lovely early morning. The air was cool and fresh. Clouds fluttered like white flags in the baby-blue sky. I threw my bag in the back of the Jeep and headed down the main highway eastward out of Nairobi.

Life in Kenya is slow. People walk and work slowly. Service in shops and banks is given in slow motion. But once a Kenyan gets behind the wheel of a car, all this changes. Driving is a test of manhood, an expression of sexual prowess, an outlet for all the frustrations and slowness of the rest of life. As I drove, vehicles of all shapes and sizes roared and careered past. There were cars, slung low to the ground with ancient suspension, trucks heaving up and then hurtling down the hills, and *matatus*, Kenya's myriad brightly painted private buses, death on wheels, hooting, slewing violently and vomiting black diesel fumes.

Just beyond the Tarmac, at the side of the road, Kenya's normal sleepy self resumed. Old Wakamba women sat beneath yellow acacia trees, waving pots of sweet wild honey. Herdboys lounged dozily among their cattle. Muslims in cloth caps stood beside the wooden shacks where they sold cigarettes and warm Cokes. As the road fell gently away from the Nairobi plateau, the land became hotter and browner. The rolling hills flattened. Toward the end of the morning, I turned off the main road. At a gate, I paid a few shillings and drove through onto a dirt track. I was now in Tsavo East National Park.

It was not until 1848, three and a half centuries after Vasco da Gama landed at Mombasa, that the first white man ventured the sixty miles inland to the Tsavo area. This was Johann Ludwig Krapf, the German missionary. But Krapf was not walking on untrodden paths. African traders had been bringing ivory from Tsavo to the coast for centuries. And more recently, Swahili Arabs from the coast had been plying the same routes for the same commodity. By the time Krapf arrived, Tsavo was empty of elephants.

"How quickly these animals diminish and recede farther into the interior," Krapf wrote. Without elephants, Krapf found that Tsavo had become a "dreadful jungle," a dense tangle of acacia forest and thorn scrub. Krapf spent days crawling under bushes and vicious thorns while crossing the region.

Within fifty years, the British were building a railway line across Tsavo. Animals caused constant problems, as Colonel J. H. Patterson, a chief engineer on the line, described in his book *The Man-eaters of Tsavo*. Rhinos charged the men and ran off with tents on their noses. And two rogue lions carried off at least twenty-seven Indian coolies and an unrecorded number of Africans before the colonel finally shot them both. But in all his time in Tsavo, Patterson did not record the presence of a single elephant.

It was only when the First World War interrupted the ivory trade and the British colonial authorities introduced strict game laws that elephant numbers began to recover. Herds from more remote regions moved back into Tsavo and began to breed. By the 1930s, Tsavo was again good elephant country, patronized by professional hunters like Bror Blixen (Karen Blixen's husband) and Philip Percival. And on April Fool's Day, 1948, 8,000 square miles of the Tsavo scrub— an area the size of Wales—was turned into Kenya's biggest national park.

Three men, a warden and two assistants, were sent down to Tsavo to supervise the new park. One of the assistant wardens was a raw, good-looking eighteen-year-old who had been born and brought up in Kenya. This was Bill Woodley. Four decades later, Woodley was still working in the park.

I drove southeast through Tsavo for most of the afternoon. The rains were just beginning and the land was no longer bone-dry. But the colors were still the sunburned browns and yellows of the acacia trees and *commiphora* thorn bushes —and the shimmering ocher of the bare earth. As I drove, small groups of zebras, reddened from the dust, wandered across the track. Once I saw a gerenuk, up on its hind legs, reaching into the thorns with its long neck and prehensile tongue.

It was already late by the time I reached the park head-quarters at Voi. Several men were just walking into a meeting in the warden's office. One was an elderly, leathery-faced white man.

"Bill Woodley?" I asked.

"Yes?" He stopped short.

I explained my interest.

"Come up to my house in the morning," he said. Then he followed his colleagues and shut the door.

Bill Woodley lived on the side of a red hill at Mtito Ndei. He and his wife were still eating breakfast when I arrived, so I walked up the hill and sat on the ground to wait.

The sun was beginning to warm up the world. I watched a line of black ants hurrying across the loose earth. They were following a scent trail. Idly, I brushed my finger across their path and broke the line of scent. The ants were suddenly confused. They scuttled furiously back and forth on either side of the tampered soil, waving their antennae and snapping their pincers. Eventually, one ant dashed across the gap and found the trail. The others followed, and the procession continued.

By now, breakfast was over. An African servant came out to call me and I followed him down. The house was a typical simple cement bush dwelling. The servant led me into the sitting room. It was full of assorted family heirlooms, animal art and uncomfortable furniture. I sat on the protruding spring of a dying couch and was given a cup of tea.

Bill Woodley was sixty now, though he looked older. A lifetime of guns, dust and whisky was etched deeply in his face. One eye behind the slitted skin no longer worked. His voice, ravaged by throat cancer, was quiet and hoarse. He had an old man's hair: silver and lifeless. Time had moved on. Life in the bush was no longer so simple.

Back in 1948, Tsavo had been divided into two sections and Woodley was put in charge of Tsavo East. This was a huge dry land. There were no roads and only two main rivers, the Tiva and the Galana. With little water, the park could not support the profusion of animals found around the swamps in Amboseli, but there was still a good number of lions, leopards, rhinos, zebras, giraffes, buffaloes and elephants. For a young man in love with the wilderness, it was a grand place and a grand existence. But as Woodley explored the park, he found that all was not well in Tsavo. There was still a lot of hunting going on. And elephants seemed to be the main target.

Week after week, Woodley stumbled onto elephant carcasses. These had invariably been killed with poisoned arrows. Sometimes, he even found wounded elephants. "Today we found a terror trail of diarrhea from a herd of about forty elephants," Woodley wrote in his diary on September 23, 1948. "One had been shot with a poisoned arrow, and we came across it after two hours. It was still alive and in terrible agony, but I ended its suffering with a bullet in its head."

The people living in the Tsavo region were mostly Wakamba. But the Wakamba were not great elephant killers. They preferred to hunt smaller game and their short, accurate bows were designed for bringing down antelopes and warthogs on the run. So who was killing the elephants? As Woodley asked around, he began to hear of another, less numerous tribe. These people lived to the east of the park. They were said to use long, powerful bows. And their favorite prey was the elephant. Their name was the Waliangulu.

Before Woodley could find out much more about the Waliangulu, events took a turn in Kenya. The Kikuyu tribe's Mau Mau uprising—Africa's first serious rebellion against colonial rule—broke out. All efforts were put into containing Mau Mau, and Woodley was drafted into the security forces. For the first half of the 1950s, he was away from Tsavo.

Eventually, Mau Mau was defeated and Woodley returned
to Tsavo. The new warden of Tsavo East was a man named
David Sheldrick. He and Woodley soon established that the
elephant killing was continuing and that the main culprits
were still the Waliangulu. The Mau Mau uprising had been
a brutal guerrilla war. Woodley and Sheldrick had learned
sophisticated anti-insurgency tactics. Over the next few
months, they set about using these same methods against the
Waliangulu hunters.

The wardens set up a well-paid informer network and
found out that the entire Waliangulu tribe numbered only
some four thousand. They started to keep file cards on every
Waliangulu man. They also learned to recognize the signature
marks on Waliangulu arrows. And they continually hounded
the Waliangulu, tracking them through the park and raiding
their villages, time and again, day and night.

The campaign was so intense that one Waliangulu was
broken under interrogation when the wardens told him what
he had dreamed the previous week. (He had unwittingly told
his dream to a park informer.) Over this period, more than
four hundred Waliangulu men, almost half the adult men in
the tribe, ended up in jail. The Waliangulu were supreme
bushmen and intelligent people. But they had never experienced anything like this. They had neither the physical nor
psychological resources to withstand the onslaught. By the
end of eighteen months, their elephant hunting had virtually
ceased.

The final act took place at the end of 1957. The most wanted
Waliangulu was a middle-aged hunter named Galogalo Kafonde. He had been too smart for Woodley and Sheldrick
and had slipped their grasp on a number of occasions. But
he had grown weary of the chase. One morning, he walked
into Malindi police station and gave himself up.

At his trial, Galogalo was asked whether he had ever hunted

elephants. "Of course," he replied. "I am the greatest elephant hunter of them all." Then he was sent to jail.

As far as the authorities were concerned, that was that.

Old black and white photographs of the Kenya Game Department, as it was then called, in the late 1950s show a dozen young men, handsome, thickset, confident. One figure stands out as slightly different from the rest: a scrawny boy with an ironic smile, a snub nose and jug ears.

His name was Ian Parker and he was as much a maverick in character as looks. He loved to question the conventional wisdom. As a warden, he had helped to put the Waliangulu behind bars. But after the Waliangulu had been forced to abandon their elephant hunting, Parker had continued to visit their villages and talk to their elders.

One morning, back in Nairobi, I called him on the telephone and said I was interested in the Waliangulu.

"Are you free today?" he asked.

"Yes."

"Come round at three."

By white Kenyan standards, Parker's was a modest house. He kept cattle in the backyard and visitors had to open and close the drive gate themselves: for ten pounds a week, most whites employed Africans to do this.

It was more than thirty years since the photographs I had seen were taken, but Parker had hardly changed. The skin was a little rougher and there was a touch more suspicion in his eyes, but the jug ears, turned-up nose and close-cropped hair were just the same. He was wearing a sweater and shorts. His legs were skinny and knobbled, like a chicken's.

Parker remained a maverick. He lived by dabbling in a variety of different wildlife matters: ivory dealing, elephant management consultancy, culling (he had personally shot several thousand elephants), publishing and writing. He had theories on everything: elephants, history, English journalists, and of course the Waliangulu.

After the Waliangulu had been defeated in Tsavo, Parker had slowly begun to see things from the Waliangulu point of view. Before 1948, Tsavo had been simply a wilderness. The Wakamba and Waliangulu had hunted freely there. But after 1948, when Tsavo became a national park, hunting became poaching. To the Waliangulu, this was absurd. They had lived on this land for hundreds of generations. Parker had delved into the history books and reckoned the Waliangulu had been around in East Africa for at least two thousand years. And they had always hunted elephants.

Moreover, the Waliangulu were not casual elephant hunters. Their whole existence had evolved around the hunting of elephants. Waliangulu life began with the killing of an elephant. The men would go out into the bush and make a kill. Their families would then follow, camp beside the carcass and eat the meat and fat—they particularly loved the fat—until it was all gone. Then the men would head out again and the whole cycle would restart.

"Elephants and elephant hunting were their religion," Parker said. "Killing an elephant was a boy's rite of passage into adulthood. A man could not become a man without killing an elephant. You aspired to hunt elephants, you were praised for doing so, you got the girls for doing so. You had to hunt elephants. These people loved elephants. They even spoke about elephants in human terms."

"What about the ivory?" I asked. "Did that have any special significance?"

"It was important socially. They used it for bride price. And it was their only form of money. They bartered tusks for anything they needed, especially palm wine. Ivory was very special to them. It was in their souls. They had lots of words to describe it and taboos surrounding it. I once saw a man hit with a tusk and pull a knife on his attacker on the spot. He tried to kill him. Hitting a man with a tusk—you just didn't do that."

Parker was now in full swing. He lectured and I sat and nodded.

"You know, they had an uncanny nose for ivory," he said. "A lot of the ivory came from natural deaths. If you have tens of thousands of elephants wandering around a national park, several hundred are going to die naturally each year. The Waliangulu always seemed to be finding ivory."

"What? Just lying on the ground?"

"Sometimes. But they knew where to look. You'd be walking along with a group of them and suddenly they'd all run off in a certain direction. When you caught up with them, they'd be stripping the tusks out of a three-year-old skeleton. They knew it was there because they'd seen a tree with branches broken in a certain way. This meant that vultures had sat there after gorging so much that it had to be an elephant."

"It sounds a bit like prospecting," I said. "You just have to recognize the signs."

"That's right. One time, we were walking through a swamp, knee-deep in mud, and one of them suddenly stopped. He didn't move his foot but rolled up his sleeves and put his hand down into the mud. Immediately, the rest knew what had happened—that he must have trodden on an old elephant tusk with his foot. Before he had pulled the first tusk free from the mud, the others were searching round for the other half of the pair. Within minutes, they'd found it. They just thought ivory all the time, like gold panners think gold."

The Waliangulu were similarly obsessed with their hunt-ing. Much of a man's time was spent lovingly creating his bows and arrows. The bows were made from a combination of woods from five different trees.

"The bows were taller than most Waliangulu men and among the most powerful ever used," Parker said. "Their draw weights were up to a hundred and seventy pounds—higher even than the old English longbows. You had to be trained to use them. It was as much technique as muscle. And they were designed specifically for elephants—for power, not distance."

The arrows had to be strong and sharp enough to penetrate an elephant's hide. They were up to three feet long and veined with vulture feathers. The tips were forged from iron and coated with poison.

"The poison was made from the *Acocanthera* tree," Parker said. "That was the main ingredient, though they added a variety of different things, like sap from the euphorbia tree, which gave the poison a tackiness and made it more irritating. If the muscles are irritated, the blood flow increases and the poison works faster."

The poison caused massive heart failure. The hunters would test it when they made it by dipping a thorn into their mix and then pricking a toad or a frog. Before hunting, they would check that it was still potent by cutting themselves and mixing some blood with the poison. The stronger the poison, the more quickly the blood coagulated.

The hunters' favorite shot was a hand's breadth in front of the hind leg into the abdomen on the left side. Here the poison was introduced most quickly into the bloodstream. In order to make an accurate shot, a hunter would need to stand within twenty paces of an elephant. The Waliangulu's shooting and bravado while hunting were unequaled.

"They were men in the mold we would like to have been ourselves," Parker said. "One of the hunting aces, Abekuna Gamunde, became a very good friend. He was a unique human being. I feel privileged to have known him. He had a major intellect. He had no desire to cross over into Western culture, but he was as interested in my culture as I was in his."

Like Parker, Bill Woodley and David Sheldrick had also come to admire the Waliangulu. They felt bad about what had happened. So on Parker's suggestion, a plan was launched to set aside an area outside the park for the Waliangulu to continue elephant hunting. But the scheme was fraught with problems. The government in Nairobi decided that hunting with bows and arrows was too cruel. Guns should be used: but because of memories of Mau Mau, the Waliangulu had to collect these guns in the morning and return them in the evening. After a couple of seasons, it was not surprising that the Waliangulu gave up this mockery of their previous life.

"A few of them became trackers for white hunters," Parker said. "Abekuna worked for Tony Archer. Oh, he enjoyed safaris. He even went to Nepal to hunt tiger with an American client. He stayed at a big hotel in Delhi. Tony found him one evening, sitting in his hotel room with a big Sikh in gloves serving him and calling him Sahib, and Abekuna was laughing and laughing. He couldn't get over it."

Parker smiled wistfully himself.

"Then when Abekuna retired, Tony fixed him up with a pineapple shamba and he lived there. But he didn't think much of it. He would always shake his head and say, 'Pineapples! Pineapples for an elephant hunter!' "

Abekuna was luckier than many others. The Waliangulu who did not take up tracking quickly slid into poverty and turned to drink, crime and petty poaching. They even began to marry their children into farming tribes.

"Their society was blown apart," Parker said. "This was a people who had been hunting elephants in this part of Africa for more than two thousand years. They were living the same

life while the English were being invaded by the Romans.
Then in the 1950s, we came along and in the space of two
years simply blew them apart. They didn't stand a chance.
They've gone the way of the American Indians. It's finished.
They'll never get back on their feet again."

Whatever had been done to the Waliangulu,
the Tsavo authorities could still take heart that they had carried out their primary job: they had saved the park's
elephants.

Through the 1960s, Tsavo's elephant numbers soared. Elephants already in the park bred rapidly. And herds in less
secure regions outside the park soon found their way into
Tsavo. By the end of the decade, there were an estimated
42,000 elephants in Tsavo—one of the largest populations on
the continent.

These huge numbers of elephants were good for tourism.
But they were less good for Tsavo's vegetation. The same
process that I had seen in Amboseli soon began to occur in
Tsavo. The elephants pulled down and killed the trees. The
vegetation thinned out. There was even talk of culling some
of the excess elephants. But having expended so much blood
and effort to stop the poaching of elephants, the park authorities were unwilling to turn around and shoot thousands
of the beasts themselves.

Then, in 1970, the rains failed in Tsavo. The water holes
dried up. The rivers shrank. The vegetation shriveled. The
pressure on the land increased enormously. It was a terrible
dry season, but somehow most of the park's animals made
it through to the following year. The rains were eagerly
awaited. Then they failed again. And the next year they failed
once more.

The combination of too little vegetation and too many

elephants began to turn Krapf's "jungle" into a desert. The most dramatic regions were the stretches near the rivers. The wildlife had to drink every night, so they would walk down to the rivers in the cool of the darkness. By morning, they would still be walking back toward an ever more distant line of bushes. Eventually, Tsavo's wildlife began to die. The hyenas and lions did well from all the carcasses—but the grazing and browsing animals perished in their tens of thousands.

By the time the rains finally fell in 1973, at least 10,000 elephants had died. In the mid-1950s, David Sheldrick reckoned that the Waliangulu were killing a little less than 1,000 elephants a year. Between 1957, when the Waliangulu hunting stopped, and 1970, when the drought began, the Waliangulu would probably have hunted down some 10,000 elephants.

Toward the end of his hunting career, Terry Mathews had sometimes employed a Waliangulu tracker named Badeeva Kiribai. When last heard of, Badeeva had been living in a remote village between Tsavo and the Indian Ocean. The village was called Kisiki cha Mzungu: the white man's grave.

As it happened, Terry and Jeanne were heading down to the coast for a few days.

"Why don't you join us there," Terry said. "We could drive up to Kisiki cha Mzungu and see if Badeeva is around."

I met up with Terry and Jeanne in Malindi. The town was founded by Arab seafarers around the tenth century. Even back then, Waliangulu hunters were probably already trading ivory with the Arabs. In the sixteenth century, Malindi was taken over by the Portuguese. Now most of the money in

Malindi was Italian: invested in hotels, casinos and, it was said, drugs.

We set off just after dawn. The sandy beachfront was empty and the palm trees creaked like old houses in the wind. We drove north out of the town and crossed the bridge over the Galana River. The early morning light rippled on the water like white flecks on brown cloth.

"This place used to be thick with crocodile," Terry said. "I actually shot one from this bridge. The locals used to spear the crocs. They think the meat makes good eating."

"Have you tried it? Does it?"

"Yes, it's quite nice. Tastes like fishy chicken."

"Of course," Jeanne said, "Terry's got little love for crocodiles."

"Why not?"

"Not after what happened when he was a little boy."

Half a century earlier, Terry had watched a woman carried off by a crocodile in the shallows of Lake Victoria. He was seven or eight years old at the time, living near Entebbe in Uganda, spending his holidays like Huck Finn, lazing, drifting, trapping animals and fishing. One afternoon, he had gone fishing on an old wooden pier on the lake. He was sitting on the pier, waiting for a bite, when a woman came down to wash her clothes in the water.

"I was half watching her," Terry said. "She washed the clothes and then waded in deeper to draw clean water in her bucket. The croc must have been waiting because as she dipped the bucket in, it came up and grabbed her hands. I saw her pulled out into the deep water and disappear. I ran up the hill to tell the police and eventually they came down and shot the croc. The next time I saw the woman, she was in pieces inside the croc's sliced-open belly."

Past the bridge, we turned west, away from the coastal

strip. The palm trees and bougainvillea bushes gave way to dense, crackling amber scrub. It was hot and dry: the sun had sucked the moisture from the air.

For an hour, there was little to see. Occasionally, the track carried us past a primitive Giriama village. Once, an old woman stood up from her digging and stared hollowly at us. She had bare breasts that hung down like empty triangular water bladders. Another time, we passed an old man singing as he freewheeled down a hill on his bicycle.

Then the land suddenly opened out. We came over a rise, and the view stretched away across a vast rolled world to a distant dry haze. Forty years earlier, fresh out of school, Terry had worked here for the Survey Department. He had cut tracks and made simple maps of the region.

"You have to watch yourself out here," Terry said as the road slid down the rise into the plains. "These lands go on for a hundred miles. In some parts there isn't even a single small hillock. There's nothing to give you direction. At some times of year, it can be overcast for days. No rain, just cloud covering up the sun. If you get lost, you are in big trouble."

"Have you ever been lost out here?"

"Fortunately not. But I remember four Waliangulu who were lost while escaping from the antipoaching squads. They were never seen again. They must have walked in the wrong direction. You can always find something to eat—roots, bark, honey. But there's no water. Water is the thing. Without water, they wouldn't have lasted very long."

Terry narrowed his eye and stared into the distance.

The track eventually brought us to Baricho, the last village marked on Terry's old map. Beyond, only footprints and a single bicycle track led down a narrow sandy path. We eased the vehicle between the thorny bushes and followed the bicycle marks until they veered off into the bush and disappeared. There were no more signs of people. I was driving and Terry was directing.

"When were you last here?" I asked eventually.

"Oh, more than twenty years ago."

"Don't you think the tracks would have changed since then," I said. "You are sure we're going the right way?"

Terry grinned in amazement at the cheek of the question and rubbed his eye patch. Then he started another story.

"Years back, a family got stuck out here. Trying to cross the dry Tiva River. Stuck in the sand. I think it was an American, a banker with his wife and *totos* and houseboy. Anyway, it was an American sedan, a Chevy or something. This fellow, the American, sent the houseboy to get help, but the houseboy got treed by a lion."

Terry paused, jutting his chin out across the scrub.

"After two days, they'd drunk all the water in the radiator. They didn't know how to dig for water. Everything was gone and they were starting to go mad from thirst. The hyenas had been around during the night. The man got out his gun. He was going to shoot his wife and kids and then himself. He was loading the gun when there was a shout in the distance and the local chief turned up out of the blue, riding his bicycle. The houseboy had got through."

It was now midday, and we had been driving since dawn. The outside of the Jeep was too hot to touch. The sky had turned pale white. The only animals we had seen were a small herd of oryx that had turned away as we approached, side-stepping through the scrub, their black tails swishing against their pastel grey haunches and dusty white legs.

Then, ahead, we saw a black dot beneath a tree. It shimmered in the heat and almost disappeared. As we closed in, it took shape. It was a man, sitting against the trunk of an acacia tree. We pulled up and the man looked slowly over to us.

"*Jambo mzee,*" Terry said.
"Eh."
"*Habari yako.*"
"Eh, *zuri.*"
"We are looking for Kisiki cha Mzungu," Terry said.

The man nodded. The dust in the creases of his skin had given him red whiskers around his eyes and red lines across his forehead. There was a stem of grass between his lips. That was all. He had no bag, no water, no food. There was nothing to suggest how long he had been waiting beneath this tree.

"Eh, I know this village," he said. "I am going that way. I will show you."

He climbed inside, leaving a patch of scuffed earth beneath the tree. As we drove, he grunted directions: "Leftie, rightie, eh." Eventually, at a crossroads of sorts, he told us to stop and climbed out. Kisiki cha Mzungu was just ahead, he said, flicking his hand. As we pulled away, I saw him settle down in the shade of another tree, still chewing on his grass.

The track led us down toward the Galana River. The sand became moist and the air cooler. The brown vegetation grew greener, less brittle and more luxurious. Then the river itself appeared: less wide here than near the ocean, but faster and more alive. It slipped swiftly past the lush banks, a lithe brown eel with somewhere to go.

A few minutes later, the path wandered into the village. A dozen huts lazed in the shade of heavy-boughed trees. A chicken stood in the dust, jerking its head idiotically. A cooking pot rattled untended on a crackling fire. A movement caught my eye and I saw the gleam of a body slipping through the bushes: a bare chest, an angled arm, a wooden bow. The Waliangulu were hiding: the rare arrival of a vehicle usually meant the antipoaching squads.

We parked the car under a tree and Terry climbed out. Swinging on his crutch, he loped toward the riverbank.

Standing by the car, Jeanne and I heard grunts and then an outburst of greeting.

"Eh, Mathews. Bwana Terry!"

"How are you? How are you?

"Eh, eh!"

"Mathews, I thought you were dead!"

"You have come."

Immediately, bodies began to drift in from the bush. Children's faces peered around the edges of the huts. By the time Terry reappeared, there was a crowd of smiling brown faces around the car.

Swaggering alongside Terry was Badeeva. He was short, sinewy and compact. He made Terry look huge and ungainly, like a lean black hunting cat beside an oversized pink mongrel. He came over and greeted Jeanne. Then he shook my hand and sized me up, grinning happily.

He was drunk. It was a Sunday and he had been sipping warm palm wine all morning. But he had a face to trust: calm, amused, able, knowing. His skin glimmered with sweat. His beard made a black knitted circle around his puckered mouth. One front tooth was a dead yellow. He was wearing only a *kikoi*, rolled around his waist.

He was delighted to see Terry. The last time he had been in Nairobi, another white man had shown him the film of Terry being thrown by the rhino. He was told that Terry had survived, but words were words: now he could see with his own eyes.

"Eh, this Mathews he is strong," Badeeva said.

Of course, Badeeva went on, only a fool would have given the rhino such a chance. He too had been charged by rhino and elephant. It was an occupational hazard. But to be caught?

Badeeva was happy with palm wine. He had an unexpected audience. It was not an opportunity to let pass. He planted his bare feet in the dust and began to tell his story.

He too had been working with a film crew. The producer wanted a shot of a charging elephant, and Badeeva had been hired as a tracker to provide this. The crew set up their camera on a rise, and Badeeva was sent in to provoke a large bull.

Badeeva began to act out the part. He crouched, holding his head forward, opening his eyes wide, swaying as though he were creeping toward the elephant. Then he swiveled round. Now he was playing the elephant. He raised himself up, reached out with his arm and stuffed imaginary leaves into his mouth.

"When I was close enough," he said, "I stood up."

He showed us how the elephant reacted. It backed up and then came forward. Badeeva swelled out his chest, flailed his arm and stretched out the fingers like an elephant tasting the air. Then he charged.

"I was ready. I took off my shirt and held it in my hand. When the elephant charged, I threw the shirt. The elephant smelled the shirt and ran after it. It stamped on it and gored it. I jumped behind a tree and watched. When the elephant was finished, the producer was happy. The elephant went away."

The show was now over and the novelty of our arrival began to fade. Most of the village went back to their Sunday tasks: drinking, eating and sleeping. Even the Waliangulu, way out here, had picked up British Sunday habits.

Badeeva's antics had exhausted him—and sobered him a little. He sat down on a chair and talked more calmly. His English was rapid and incomprehensible. Terry translated.

Badeeva was now in his fifties. He had come of age as a hunter in the years before Sheldrick's and Woodley's anti-poaching operations. By his early twenties, he had killed more than fifty elephants. In 1957, he was arrested and jailed for eight months.

"Were you bitter?"

He shrugged. When he was released, he picked up work as a tracker and driver.

"Did you ever hunt again?"

He laughed. "Of course. I am a Waliangulu."

"And now?"

"Now I am too old," he said, hunching his head into his shoulders like an old man. "I shoot only small game. And even when I hunt rabbit, I take my wife with me to carry my bow."

I asked about the famous bow. Badeeva gesticulated and his bow was brought. It was a long, narrow, knobbly piece of wood, like an ostrich's leg—a weapon to be used rather than admired. It had been shaped with a knife, but not finished. The string was woven and rough. Badeeva gestured for me to try it.

I planted my feet on the ground and held out the bow. I wrapped my fingers around the gut and pulled. The string cut into the flesh at the base of my fingers, but the bow hardly moved. I gritted my teeth and pulled with all my might. I managed to draw back the string twelve inches.

The watching children collapsed with laughter.

I handed the bow to Badeeva. He was, by Waliangulu standards, an old man, and his belly had begun to sag. But the rest of his body was still like a bantamweight boxer's. He lazily drew back the string. The tendons knifed on his neck, his chest and his arms. Waliangulu stories told of hunters dying mid-pull from the effort. But Badeeva eased the string back the length of his arm before gently releasing it.

"When did you last use the bow?"

"The other day. You could have come with us. We were hunting warthog. This boy here, he hit one on the run."

He gestured toward a tall, muscular young Waliangulu. There was something familiar about his features: the yellowish face, the piercing eyes, the high handsome forehead.

"Who is he?" I asked.

"Galogalo Kafonde."

Waliangulu eldest sons take their father's name in reverse. Badeeva Kiribai's first son was Kiribai Badeeva. Grandsons therefore have their grandfather's name. This was the grandson of the greatest of all the Waliangulu hunters. I had seen pictures of the old Galogalo Kafonde. The grandson resembled the grandfather.

Even in these times, the young Galogalo had managed to take a few elephants in Tsavo. He too had been arrested, a couple of years back, and had spent a few months in prison.

"But hunting is not like the old days?"

"No." Badeeva scowled. "Then we lived from the game. Now, now—look around. We have a few chickens and goats. We grow some maize. We survive mostly on my savings from my years as a tracker. Is this the life for a hunter? What life is left for our children? Life is not good. There is no road to follow."

With his toe, Badeeva slowly drew a circle in the pale dust. It was an impression of an elephant's print. His thoughts lay on the surface of his face like oil on water.

"Today," he said, "I would be happy just to see one elephant footprint."

"What would you do if you saw one?" I asked.

"Do?" Badeeva said. "I'd look for the next footprint. And the next. Then I'd follow them to the elephant. Then I'd take out my bow and shoot it. Then I'd feast on elephant fat."

He rubbed his stomach and laughed at the joke.

Chapter Five

WHEN CONSERVATIONISTS FIGHT

P atrick Hamilton stood
beside his aircraft on the flat dusty plain of Tsavo National
Park. In his Kenya Wildlife Service flying uniform, he looked
like a Boy Scout leader. His maroon beret was pulled down
to his eyebrows. His khaki trousers came to a sudden halt
above the rims of his boots. He was a slight man and he
stood awkwardly. Only his eyes suggested something more
cowboy than Boy Scout: taut, drawn, impassive slits, habit-
uated to squinting across the glare of the African bush.

"How are you at flying?" he said. His voice was clipped
and military. "It might be bumpy."

"I'm OK," I said. "I can fly a bit myself."

"Good."

I took another look at the plane. It had the fragile, primitive
elegance of an origami dart. Its walls were paper-thin. The
wings looked as though they were about to fall off. There
were two seats, one behind the other.

"I've never seen one quite like this before," I said.

"Christen Husky," Hamilton said. "It's new."

"What happened to your old one?"

"Super Cub? Lovely old plane. Just kept putting me down in the middle of nowhere."

We took off with ease, like a gull stepping off a cliff perch into a rising current. Our shadow, thrown ahead by the sun, skated across the ground and startled a zebra. The beast jerked its head up and shied away, its fat striped haunches bulging like the buttocks of an overly optimistic plump lady squeezed into a pair of striped lycra trousers.

As we climbed, the land shrank, wobbled and then settled below. The trees compressed into squat, flat bushes. We crossed the silver river of the main road and skimmed into the air above Tsavo East. Hamilton leveled the plane at a few hundred feet. His hands and feet instinctively kept the Husky on course as he cast his eyes across the endless terrain, searching for signs of disturbance.

I sat hunched between the paper walls in silence. The back of Hamilton's neck, a few inches in front of my eyes, was red and deeply etched. When I looked down, I saw similar patterns: the crisscross of animal tracks and the veins of newborn streams, agleam with daggers of early morning light. The rains had arrived in Tsavo a few days earlier, and the park was already awash with water and new green growth.

It was more than a decade and a half since the terrible drought of the 1970s. Tsavo seemed to have recovered well. The scenery was a patchwork of scrub, open grasslands and acacia woods. Against the bright green of the new grass, the black and white zebras, silver wildebeests, fawn gazelles, and red and yellow giraffes looked like colored candies emptied onto the baize of a pool table.

As the sun rose, the inside of the Husky heated up like a sauna. Down below, the shadows shortened and grew more severe. The animals drifted in toward the shade of the trees. The colors became washed-out. Pale lands stretched toward pale horizons.

"Down there," Hamilton said. "Three o'clock."

He swung the plane around and lowered the flaps. We circled and gently sank. Trees and bushes rose upward. A vulture's nest came into focus in the flattened foliage of an acacia tree.

"There," Hamilton said, pointing down.

White splinters lay like a spilled box of matches on the bare earth beside a water hole. At first, I thought they were the shattered remains of a dead tree. But as we dropped farther, I realized that they were bones: hollow-eyed skulls, cowlike jawbones, toothpick ribs, ashtray-shaped hips and leg bones picked clean like the bones cartoon dogs always fight over. The size of the bones made them unmistakable. These were the remains of a host of elephants.

"May twenty-eighth," Hamilton said over the crackle of the radio intercom. "I found them freshly killed."

Unexpected emotion softened the clip of his words. The date seemed burned into his memory.

"It happened during the night," he continued. "The manager of a nearby lodge reported hearing the automatic gunfire. I went for a look in the morning. There were twenty-four fresh carcasses. All ages."

He had landed at the lodge and taken a vehicle. When he arrived at the water hole, dozens of vultures flapped up from the carcasses and landed grumpily on the branches of nearby trees. The elephants lay in a huge huddle, like a pile of soft rocks, their grey skins streaked with the white and yellow of vulture feces.

"The poachers must have been waiting for the elephants down by the water hole," Hamilton said. "They came out firing. The elephants fell down on top of each other. The shooting would have been over in minutes. A couple of hours later and all the tusks were gone."

When morning came, the vultures arrived. They had not been able to tear away the elephants' thick skins, so they had begun at the exposed areas, the faces hacked away by the poachers, and the eyes, a particular vulture delicacy.

Times had changed in Tsavo in the thirty-three years since the Waliangulu had been driven out of the park. Those days now almost seemed like an age of innocence. The park staff had been armed with bolt-action rifles. The poachers had used bows and arrows and killed one elephant at a time. When the wardens defeated the Waliangulu poachers, they felt guilty and provided an area for the tribesmen to hunt elephants. Modern Tsavo was vastly different. It was a far more brutal place.

For the past two decades, the park had become an elephant killing field. The killers were both poaching gangs and corrupt park officials. The weapons were often AK-47 and G-3 automatic rifles. Gunfire had become a sound of the Tsavo night, elephants without faces a sight of the Tsavo day. Before the drought, there had been 42,000 elephants in Tsavo. A recent aerial count had found just 4,327. In the northern regions of Tsavo East, the counters had sighted more dead elephants than live ones.

Similar stories were true all across Africa. For most of the century, the African elephant population had grown steadily. As late as the 1960s, talk of an elephant problem meant too many elephants, spilling over into farms and villages. In countries like Zaire, Uganda, Kenya, Tanzania and Zambia, tens of thousands of elephants had to be shot for control every year. But in the 1970s and 1980s all this had changed.

What had happened?

The leading chronicler of the elephant crisis was Iain Douglas-Hamilton, the biologist who had introduced Cynthia Moss to elephants in Lake Manyara National Park in Tanzania. He blamed two main factors.

The first was a sharp rise in the price of ivory. Between 1950 and 1970, ivory remained at a level $5 a kilo. By 1978, the price had soared to $75 a kilo, a sixfold rise in real terms. The causes were difficult to pinpoint—something to do with the world recession and increased demand for ivory in Japan, where it was used for *hankos*, or signature seals. But the effect was clear. An ordinary bull elephant with a pair of fifteen-kilo tusks was now suddenly worth more than $2,000. The poacher on the ground could expect to collect a quarter of this: $500, an average annual salary in Kenya.

Douglas-Hamilton's second factor was the spread of guns across Africa. During the 1970s, Africa armed faster than any other region on earth. Arms imports increased from $500 million in 1970 to $4.5 billion by 1980. The number of men in the armed forces in just six East African countries tripled during the same decade, from 141,000 in 1971 to 441,000 in 1980. And all these men had rifles or semiautomatic weapons.

These indicators were both crucial. But they were not the whole story. Between the days of the bow and arrow and the AK-47 in Tsavo, Africa had undergone a cataclysmic transformation. During the 1960s, thirty-three new African nations had stumbled to independence. But the continent was still only three or four generations from the Iron Age, and it was utterly unprepared for self-government in the computer age. The result was Alice-in-Wonderland anarchy: the chaos of wars, coups, corruption, famine and social confusion that I had written about as a newspaper correspondent.

I had caught my first glimpse of this Africa on my very first morning on the continent. It was a Sunday and I had just flown into Nairobi. I bought the *Standard* newspaper and flicked through to the classified advertisements. The entire "To Let" column was filled with the name of one real-estate agent. I called the number and within half an hour Wakambo Kambo was knocking on the door of my hotel room.

Wakambo was tall and lean, with a glossy face and a studied mystical expression. His clothes were mix and match. He wore a tight pinstripe jacket and loose black linen trousers. His shirt was red and his tie bright yellow. Wakambo's profession was also mix and match. His business card was so big it had to be folded over like a Christmas card. Its listed skills included accounting, computer systems design, advertising, manpower recruitment, urban planning, translation and language teaching as well as estate management and house finding.

"I have many good houses for you," Wakambo said. "I am the best estate agent in Nairobi. In fact, I have a house for you that is perfect. It is five bedrooms with a swimming pool and a very good grass tennis court."

"How much?" I said.

"Ten thousand shillings a month."

This was about £400. Dreams of colonial splendor filled my head.

"All right," I said. "Let me see it."

"As it is a Sunday," Wakambo said, "and I am ready to spend my day of rest with you, I will have to charge you five hundred shillings service charge."

Wakambo's car harked back to the dawn of motor transport. Driving out of town, we were overtaken by pedestrians. There was a large hole in the floor beneath my feet. I looked down. If things got even slower, at least I could slip my feet through and help the car along. Eventually, we pulled up on a bare-earth shoulder by a busy traffic circle. Wakambo led me down a wet alley and through a broken gate. The house was older and more dilapidated than the car. The roof appeared to have moved on to better quarters. The swimming pool was a cesspit and the tennis court a patch of bare earth and rock. When Wakambo saw my expression, he turned to the house and gave it a fierce, accusing look.

"Don't worry," Wakambo said. "I am putting you in my action book. I will find you the very best house."

I never heard from him again.

Wakambo relieved me of twenty pounds, but he helped me to understand Africa. He was a poor man with a rich man's dreams. He had been exposed to the material Western world and was no longer happy with a less cluttered African life. He wanted Mercedes-Benz cars, Levi's jeans and Rolex watches. But the reality of the poor African world was unlikely to give him these things. So he resorted to fantasy. He built castles in his head and sold them to unwitting new arrivals like myself.

Wakambo was ludicrous—but not unsuccessful. The twenty pounds he had earned in a couple of hours was as much as a young civil servant with a university degree would make in a week. The way I came to see it, Africa itself was like Wakambo: a wild blend of greed, fantasy and low cunning.

It had not always been like this. Before the coming of the white man, Africa had possessed its own coherence. It had not been an innocent idyll, but it had been its own land. Its faiths and culture were drawn from its own experience and traditions. Its laws and taboos had evolved naturally. But with colonization, the Europeans brought new religions, new languages and new laws. They built churches and jails. They drew lines on maps and created nations. They set up governments, parliaments, civil services and judiciaries. All these systems worked while the Europeans remained to preside over them. But then, almost overnight, the Europeans left. There were few trained civil servants or professionals. The new African leaders had had far too little time to grasp the new ways. And Africa's own traditions were no longer enough. The continent was stranded in a no-man's-land between the old and the new.

In Liberia once, I had met a highly educated political journalist. He was a thoughtful, deep-eyed man who shamed me with his moderate, considered opinions about Africa and the rest of the world. We went out to lunch and our discussion ranged from the soccer World Cup to Gorbachev, Reagan and Thatcher. But when I asked him about Liberia's mysterious bush schools, where rural children were sent to learn magic, he turned his face away. "If I were to tell you," he whispered, "I would not live. I would be split in half."

This Liberian was not unique. All over the continent, the old and the new were intertwined. Underneath suits from Savile Row lurked skin etched with tribal scarring. Inside Christian churches were African idols. Behind English words were African thoughts. The two personalities were like tectonic plates on the surface of the world: as they rubbed against each other they threw up jagged mountains and exploding volcanoes. The way I saw it, this confusion, this rubbing together of the old and new, lay at the heart of many of the continent's troubles.

War grew out of this conflict. Most of the new African nations were unnatural European creations that embraced several tribes. These tribes were often traditional enemies. As each country came to independence, similar patterns of events occurred. One tribe attempted to seize most of the power. Other tribes objected. In many countries—Chad, Uganda, Sudan, and Biafra in Nigeria, the objections flared into civil war.

Even Africa's most severe problem, its population explosion, was a direct result of the mix of old and new. Africans had always had as many babies as possible, so that a few would survive to adulthood and look after their parents. Then the Europeans brought modern medicines: antibiotics, malaria pills, rehydration salts and the like. Suddenly, most children no longer died. But Africans still drew pride and comfort from the size of their families. They continued to have as many babies as possible. In Kenya, in the late 1980s, the *average* woman was still giving birth to eight babies. The consequence was the fastest-growing population of any place on earth at any time in history.

And it was this same confused blend of old and new that bubbled over to produce the widespread poaching of elephants. Africans had always hunted for food. From the sixteenth century onward, Europeans taught Africans that elephants could be hunted for money. Then, in the twentieth century, the same Europeans declared elephant hunting illegal. But they continued to pay lots of money for tusks. At the same time, the white man provided Africans with increasingly efficient guns to kill elephants. And when colonialism ended, the Europeans left in place park systems that were extremely vulnerable to corruption. When the price of ivory rose in the 1970s, the result was inevitable.

"S h o t s   h e a r d .   I n   t h e   night. *Shifta*. Have a look."

The words crackled through the radio static. Patrick Hamilton pushed the aircraft into a rapid climb and swung around toward the east. I watched him reach into the bag by his side and pull out a revolver, which he fastened to his belt.

"Did you get the message?" he said eventually.

"Some of it."

"The shots were on Galana Ranch. Maybe poachers. We're going over to have a look."

Galana Ranch lay along the eastern border of Tsavo. We flew for an hour until we crossed the fence between the park and the million acres of ranchland. Apart from the better roads and the occasional herd of cattle, there was little to distinguish between park and ranch. The land and vegetation were the same. And while lion and leopard were shot on Galana to protect the cattle, other wild animals were left alone. Flying over, I saw zebra, wildebeest and eland.

The report of the shooting had come from herdsmen at a cattle *boma* in the northeast section of the ranch. We headed that way and Hamilton brought the plane down on a bumpy strip of grass. The *boma*, a circle of thorns and fencing, was empty. The cattle were out in the bush for the day. A lone cattlehand, a willowy man in a T-shirt and torn shorts, stood and watched us impassively. Hamilton climbed out, adjusted his gun, and went over to talk.

"They've heard nothing here," he said when he returned.

He climbed back into the plane and we took off again. There were *bomas* all over the ranch and we tried two more. On the second occasion, I watched a group of men nod at Hamilton's query and point out into the bush. We rose once more into the hot air and followed the meandering of a sandy riverbed. The river was still mostly dry, but the trees were thick and green along its banks. Hamilton put full flaps on and we cruised as slowly as possible, peering out on either side.

"What are we looking for?" I said.

"A camp, a dead animal maybe. We won't see the poachers themselves. The vegetation is too thick. They would hear us long before we saw them and just slip under a tree."

"Who would they be? Somalis?"

"Yes. *Shifta.*"

Somali *shifta* were responsible for much of the elephant poaching in Kenya. The government liked to claim that they were Somali nationals sneaking across the border. But the majority of them were actually Kenyan Somalis.

At independence, the southern end of what had been Greater Somaliland was given to Kenya, along with several hundred thousand Somalis. These people were tough nomadic herdsmen, fond of fighting and feuding. Karen Blixen, who adored them, compared them to the feuding clans of the Icelandic sagas. Early travelers through Somaliland found that the Somalis could be unparalleled hosts when the mood took them. When the mood didn't, they were equally happy to slaughter any visitors.

Most of the Kenyan Somalis concentrated on their cattle herding, punctuated by the occasional cattle raid. But a few took up raiding full-time. They formed bandit gangs, or *shifta*. They stole cattle, robbed buses and held up villages. In the 1960s, these gangs acquired automatic weapons. Somalia was the Soviet Union's first foothold in Africa, and Moscow poured shiploads of guns into the country. Some of these weapons inevitably trickled across the border to Somali cousins in Kenya. When the price of ivory began to rise in the early 1970s, the *shifta* turned their AK-47s onto elephants.

I scanned the ground as we flew. Every clearing seemed like a poachers' camp. Every bush looked like a carcass covered with branches. Once, I started at a movement, but it was only an eland breaking cover at the sound of the plane.

"We're not going to find anything," Hamilton eventually said. "We've given it a go. At least we've spooked anyone down there. Let's go and have something to drink."

The Galana River glistened in the afternoon sun. We landed on the northern bank and trundled up to a house at the end of the strip. A burly, white-haired man was there to greet us. This was Terence Hopkins, the manager of the ranch.

We walked through the house and sat on the porch overlooking the river. A servant brought lime juice and biscuits, and I ate and drank greedily. In the excitement, I had not realized I was so thirsty and hungry. It was already mid-afternoon and we had been in the air since early morning.

"You saw nothing," Hopkins eventually said. It was a statement rather than a question. Hamilton shook his head.

"What would they have been shooting?" I asked.

"Probably meat," Hopkins said. "Kudu or eland."

"Not elephants?"

"There are no elephants left here. We used to have around five thousand. But the *shifta* killed them all. There were a couple of bulls living just near the house until recently, but they've gone too now. I haven't seen a fresh print for three months. These days, the *shifta* just come through Galana on their way to and from Tsavo."

The *shifta* had first arrived in Tsavo in the early 1970s. David Sheldrick was still warden of Tsavo East and he stood up to the *shifta* with armed antipoaching patrols. Later, Bill Woodley was recalled from the Aberdare National Park to take on the Somalis in Tsavo. Several waves of *shifta* were rebuffed and the gangs eventually gave up on Tsavo. These were still the days of elephant abundance and there were tens of thousands of elephants roaming across large unprotected parts of northeast Kenya.

But Tsavo's troubles were not over. By the mid-1970s, bigger scavengers than the *shifta* had become interested in Kenya's increasingly valuable ivory. In 1975, it was revealed that a Nairobi company, the United African Corporation, was illegally exporting huge amounts of poached tusks. Documents recorded that one shipment alone was worth over £1 million. The head of the United African Corporation was a woman named Margaret Kenyatta. She was also the mayor of Nairobi and the daughter of Jomo Kenyatta, the country's first president.

The revelation was an embarrassment. The government announced a crackdown on ivory dealing and banned the hunting of elephants, but this did not stop government officials from making money privately from ivory. Some continued to buy tusks on the sly from Somali middlemen and arrange their lucrative export. Others greedily eyed Tsavo's rich stocks. In 1976, senior officials in the Ministry of Tourism and Wildlife made their move. David Sheldrick, who was uncorruptible, was removed from Tsavo East. Most of the wardens who followed him were more easily seduced—and their crooked superiors gave them orders not to protect Tsavo's elephants but to shoot them.

Throughout the 1980s, the killing escalated. Inside Tsavo, the wardens and rangers were the main poachers. Outside the park, the *shifta* were finishing off the elephants region by region, through Garissa, Kilifi, the Tana River and Galana. By 1987, the elephants outside Tsavo in eastern Kenya were finished. So the *shifta* turned their attention back to the park. They found little opposition. The park warden and rangers wanted the same thing as the *shifta*: ivory money. With their automatic weapons, the *shifta* could shoot more elephants faster. So the warden gave the Somalis the freedom of the park in return for a share of the booty. It was a *shifta* gang that had shot down the herd whose bones I had seen earlier in the day.

It was growing late. I drank a last lime juice and Terence Hopkins walked us back to the plane. We waved goodbye and climbed up into the late afternoon sky. The color of the world had begun to change. It was deeper and warmer now, like the amber glow from a glass of whisky.

We were just a few miles from home when we saw our first elephants. From the air, they looked curiously small and vulnerable. They had none of the thumping power and bulk so impressive on the ground. It was as if I was looking through the wrong end of a telescope—or a rifle's telescopic sight. I could have picked them off easily.

Hamilton slowed the plane with the flaps, and we cruised back and forth above the herd. There were twenty or thirty beasts, dirt-red, the color of the mud and dust. As we circled, they lifted their heads and made a token protest, waving their trunks and halfheartedly flapping their ears.

In early 1988, at the height of the killing in Tsavo, I had gone to see Iain Douglas-Hamilton in Nairobi. He was a tall, vain man in his mid-forties. We sat and talked in his airy, untidy living room, surrounded by images of elephants. Bulls loomed out of photos, cows rested in sculptures, calves played in paintings.

Douglas-Hamilton's main concern these days was elephant numbers. He had finished his studies in Lake Manyara National Park some fifteen years earlier. For most of the intervening period, he had been gathering information about elephant populations across the continent: traveling to parks and reserves, sending out questionnaires and organizing aerial counts. In 1979, he had produced the first estimate of Africa's total elephant population. It was a mix of fact, estimate and wild guess. The final figure was 1.3 million elephants.

There seemed little cause for worry. The Save the Tiger project had been started in India when the number of Royal Bengal tigers slipped below 2,000. Other flagship endangered species numbered even less. There were around 1,000 giant pandas and some 400 mountain gorillas left on the planet. Nonetheless, Douglas-Hamilton was worried. A stable population of 1.3 million elephants was fine. But the reports he had received from all over Africa suggested that the population was far from stable. Poaching was rife. Elephant numbers were tumbling.

There were exceptions. In South Africa, Zimbabwe and Botswana, elephant numbers were actually on the increase.

In these countries, most of the parks were secure, well managed and well funded. In Kruger National Park in South Africa, elephant numbers had grown from a few dozen at the turn of the century to some 8,000 by the 1980s. There were so many elephants that some had to be culled each year. The story was the same with Zimbabwe's 50,000 elephants.

But this was the end of the good news. In more than thirty other countries, elephants were under fire. In Uganda, Idi Amin's rule had reduced the country's 20,000 elephants to around 2,000. In Central Africa, Bokassa had presided over even greater slaughter. In Angola and Mozambique, rebel movements were buying South African guns with thousands of poached tusks every month. In southern Sudan, northern Arab horsemen and southern Dinka rebels, all armed with automatic weapons, had killed as many as 100,000 elephants in a decade. Deep in the forests of Zaire and the Congo, whole villages had given up farming and other traditional ways of life to concentrate entirely on the ivory economy.

And the elephant deaths did not stop with the killing. Almost every time an adult female was poached, one or more calves were endangered. Calves under two years old had no chance of surviving without a mother. From two to five, they had a 30 percent chance. From six to ten, the chance was 50 percent. On average, every poached mother meant the death of one calf.

"There are only a few areas left in Africa where the elephant is holding its own," Douglas-Hamilton said. "We are short of firm information about the forests, but we know what is going on in many of the savanna regions. We've got proof from counts. Ten years ago, I organized a count in the Selous Game Reserve in Tanzania and we found 110,000 elephants. Just recently, we went back and found only 55,000."

He pushed his glasses back on his nose.

"In the savannas of East Africa, the elephant population is

declining by nine percent a year," he said. "A similar decline across the continent would mean we are losing well over 50,000 elephants a year. That is completely unsustainable."

Part of this process was inexorable. Many of Africa's elephants still lived outside parks and protected areas. As the human population expanded, these elephants would inevitably continue to lose their habitat. But the poaching was not limited to these marginal and unprotected areas. Through the 1980s, elephants were being killed even in the most famous national parks. Tsavo and the Selous were not isolated examples. There were similar losses in parks like Garamba in northeast Zaire, Shambe in southern Sudan and Gorongosa in Mozambique.

Shortly before I talked to him, Douglas-Hamilton had published his second major elephant estimate. There was still a lot of guesswork, especially from the dense rain forest in the center of the continent. But the numbers were now far more accurate. The new figure was 750,000.

Elephants were still not in danger of extinction. But that danger was not so far away. In East Africa, the elephant had virtually disappeared outside the parks. The herds inside the parks were now under enormous pressure. When these elephants were wiped out, the poachers would inevitably turn to the safer havens in southern Africa. This was exactly what had happened with the black rhinoceros, whose horn was highly valued for dagger handles in Yemen and for medicines in the East. The black rhino population had fallen from 70,000 to 4,000. The last large population was in the Zambezi Valley in Zimbabwe. Here even the shooting of more than fifty poachers in five years had failed to stop the killing of rhinos.

"As long as there is a demand for ivory, it is virtually impossible to protect the elephant," Douglas-Hamilton said. "The ivory trade is a tragedy. Most of the consumers don't realize what they are doing. Even tourists that come to Kenya and see wild elephants happily buy ivory. They don't seem to make the connection between an ivory bracelet and a dead elephant."

Douglas-Hamilton had hoped that the publication of his new figures would help to stir the world into making that connection and accepting that Africa's elephants were in crisis. But the world had not been stirred. The conservation community had virtually snubbed Douglas-Hamilton. His figures had been questioned and his conclusions dismissed. By 1988, Africa was not losing elephants, it was hemorrhaging them. But almost nothing was being done.

Why?

The answer lay in a philosophy of wildlife management that had come to dominate conservation thinking both in Africa and within wildlife organizations such as the World Wide Fund for Nature. This philosophy was known as "sustainable utilization." Its most striking incarnation existed in Kruger National Park in South Africa. When my elephant travels eventually took me south, I drove down from Johannesburg to Kruger.

Kruger was a park on the same scale as Tsavo, comparable in size to Belgium or Wales or Vermont. It was also rich in wildlife. Driving around for a couple of days, I saw a pack of rare wild dogs, a pair of lions mating on the road, three white rhinos at sunset and scores of big-tusked elephants. But there were also noticeable differences between Kruger and Tsavo. The Kenyan park was an untended wilderness. Its roads were rough. There were no fences. Animals died when there was drought and grew fat when it rained.

By comparison, Kruger was a controlled, almost manicured environment. It was entirely surrounded by a high fence. The roads were all Tarmac or dirt tracks good enough for ordinary automobiles. Even the grass by the shoulders was regularly trimmed. On holiday weekends, parts of Kruger were like Disneyland. Thousands of trailers arrived. Traffic jams formed. Helicopters flew over the park and warned drivers to move on from viewing prides of lions by the sides of the road so others could have a look.

The park's animals were similarly monitored by the Kruger authorities. Every year, counts were made of all the large species in the park. The Kruger biologists had ruled that the populations of certain species with destructive feeding habits, like the elephant, buffalo and hippo, should not be allowed to rise above a certain set number. Every year, after the counts, the excess numbers of these animals were culled.

This culling was not merely a biological exercise. As soon as the animals were shot, they were loaded onto special trucks. They were then taken to the processing factory at Skukuza, a mile down the road from the main tourist center. Here the carcasses were cut up and processed. Their products were stored, canned and tanned. An elephant was particularly productive, yielding canned meat, dried biltong, leather for boots and belts, bones for cattle feed—and ivory.

The biltong and meat could even be bought in the Skukuza tourist shop. Various game meats were also available at the restaurants in the park. When I was in Kruger, the most expensive restaurant served dishes such as buffalo tongue in mustard sauce, medallion of crocodile with garlic butter, grilled kudu fillet and warthog stroganoff.

It was this, the warthog-stroganoff approach to conservation, the sustainable utilization of the warthog and other species, that lay at the heart of the dismissal of Iain Douglas-Hamilton's warnings.

Sustainable utilization is, in fact, the oldest form of conservation on earth. The first conservation areas were hunting reserves, set up by European kings, Indian maharajas and Chinese emperors. Wild animals were protected in these reserves so that a few of them could be hunted each year. The areas around the reserves could be taken over by villages, or grazing land, or arable fields. But the reserves had a value. The wildlife was treasured. So they remained natural wildernesses.

Modern sustainable utilization works the same way. During the 1970s and 1980s, world conservation became a serious business. It was no longer simply about saving a few species such as the panda. It was about conserving the world's resources, about protecting entire habitats. The World Wildlife Fund recognized this development by changing its name to the World Wide Fund for Nature (although the American and Canadian organizations stayed with the original name). The conservation community also accepted another home truth. Much of the world's wild resources survived in the Third World. And in these areas, nature could not be protected in isolation from man.

This was particularly relevant in Africa. This was the continent of Biafra, Ethiopia, Mozambique and southern Sudan. The people here were poor and hungry. Many were desperate for land and meat. It was not a world where wild lands and animals could be maintained simply for esthetic reasons. Esthetics was a Western luxury. The African reality was the struggle for survival. If animals had no commercial value, they would eventually be eaten and their land turned over to cattle or the plough. The best way to protect the animals was to use them, to draw benefit from them for the local people, to make them pay their way.

One highly profitable way of using national parks on a sustainable basis was tourism—people paying to look at the animals. More than 400,000 foreign tourists visited Kenya each year. Many were drawn by the parks and wild animals. This tourist business created tens of thousands of jobs and made more than £100 million a year in foreign exchange.

But sustainable utilization also involved killing animals. One method was sport hunting. I had seen this at work in the Moyowosi swamps in Tanzania. Wealthy men like Jim and Harry paid large amounts of money to shoot a few animals. This money helped secure the continued existence of the swamps. Hunting was even in some ways less destructive than tourism. It brought fewer people into the wildernesses. There were fewer car tracks, less rubbish, less general disturbance of the animals.

The other killing method was culling. Healthy wildlife populations were harvestable. This harvest could be profitable. Warthogs could be turned into stroganoff. Buffalo hide could be made into leather. The profits from these sales would help to run the park and justify its existence. The general populations of wild animals in the park would thus survive.

This argument was particularly relevant to the elephant. When well protected, elephant populations grew steadily. Eventually, for biological reasons, to stop the elephants from overrunning the park and eating all the trees, these populations would have to be culled. The carcasses were the wildlife equivalent of gold dust. In Kruger, a single dead elephant was worth £6,000. The 300 to 400 elephants killed each year in Kruger to maintain the population at below 8,000 were worth more than £1 million to the park.

To many conservationists, Kruger—along with a number of other parks in southern Africa, such as Hwange in Zimbabwe—was a model for the future. Kruger made money from tourism, hunting (in separate blocks) and culling. This money helped to buy guns, vehicles and helicopters, build fences, pay rangers proper wages, and so properly protect the park against poachers. Kruger's animals were therefore safe. They increased in number. They could then be culled further. It was a profitable cycle. It made sense. If all parks in Africa could use their wildlife, and in particular their valuable elephants, in this way, then they too could stop poaching.

Elephants were Africa's flagship wild species. The use of elephants—and particularly the sale of their ivory—had become the flagship of the sustainable utilization approach. So when Iain Douglas-Hamilton kept warning that sustainable utilization was not working with elephants, that the legal ivory trade merely encouraged a far bigger illegal ivory trade, that the elephant was being poached to extinction, the world conservation community chose to turn a blind eye. These arguments were a nuisance. The WWF and other organizations simply didn't want to know.

Before I set out from London for Burundi to begin my elephant journeys, I had gone to see a man named Dave Currey at the Environmental Investigation Agency in Islington. Currey was a blond, red-faced photographer-turned-wildlife-activist. The offices, at the top of a narrow terraced house, were a few ramshackle rooms, piled high with filing cabinets and boxes of leaflets about pilot whales, dolphins and parrots.

The EIA was five years old. Its founders were Currey and two former members of Greenpeace, Jennifer Lonsdale and Allan Thornton. The EIA's methods were energetic and unconventional. Their first success had been to film the annual killing of pilot whales in the Faroe Islands. Afterward, they had run a campaign against the trade in live parrots. It was while lobbying against this parrot trade that Thornton and Currey attended a meeting of the Convention on International Trade in Endangered Species (CITES) in Ottawa in

1987. There, by chance, they were introduced to Iain Douglas-Hamilton.

Douglas-Hamilton was a frustrated man. It was almost a decade since he had first warned of the elephant crisis and his words had still had little effect. For ten years, his numbers had been questioned and his interpretations ridiculed. Ian Parker, my Waliangulu expert, had even been prompted to write a book, *Ivory Crisis*, which argued that there was no ivory crisis. Now, in Ottawa, where Douglas-Hamilton had just announced his new elephant figures, he was being snubbed again.

But Thornton and Currey were outsiders themselves. They were ready to listen. They persuaded Douglas-Hamilton to explain the problem.

As Iain Douglas-Hamilton saw it, the system of culling was all very well in an ordered, wealthy country like South Africa. But most African countries were far more chaotic and corrupt. Most wardens and wildlife officials were too busy lining their own pockets with ivory money to worry about culling. In Kruger, elephants were culled to provide money to fight poachers. In most of the rest of Africa, elephants were poached to provide money to buy bigger and better guns to poach more elephants. The elephants were being used, but not for conservation purposes and—most important—not on a sustainable basis.

"What do you think is to blame?" Thornton asked.

"It's the bloody ivory trade that's doing it," Douglas-Hamilton said. "No question of it. But no one here wants to be told that, do they?"

CITES was the United Nations body that monitored trade in wild animal products. It also decided which species should be put on the endangered list. There was a small CITES secretariat. But the decisions were made by the ninety-one member states of CITES. The representatives of these states usually reflected the view of the world conservation community. This view, in 1987, was that the ivory trade was a good thing.

CITES accepted that too much poaching was bad. But legal elephant killing was good. The solution was simply to control the ivory trade so that only legal ivory could be sold. This would block the illegal ivory trade and so stop poaching. To this end, CITES had introduced a system of controls and licenses on the international trade in ivory.

This was fine in theory. But in practice it was a joke. The illegal ivory trade was like a smaller version of the cocaine trade. It was a highly lucrative criminal business. It involved armed gangs, crooked cops, corrupt government officials, and front companies both in Africa and in the Far East. It was run by leading Hong Kong Chinese businessmen and African cabinet ministers. It was not something that a few controls could stop.

For a start, the licensing system could easily be abused. In Africa, illegal ivory could be turned into legal ivory simply by bribing a government official for a license. This was exactly what had happened in Burundi for most of the 1980s.

Secondly, the controls covered only raw ivory. CITES could obviously not expect every century-old set of billiard balls or piano keys or paper knife or hair comb to carry a license every time it crossed an international border. So all the traders had to do was have their tusks cut up or lightly carved. They could then be legally traded without any licenses. For this purpose, a couple of factories were set up in Africa. But larger factories were also believed to exist in the free trade zones of the United Arab Emirates. There was no trouble shipping ivory out of Africa and into these zones. The ivory could then be lightly carved. It would then be shipped quite legally to the real carving factories in Hong Kong and China.

Iain Douglas-Hamilton had estimated that less than one-fifth of the ivory leaving Africa came from legally culled elephants. The rest was all poached. He was still collecting information to prove the level of elephant killing on the ground in Africa. But someone else needed to uncover the extent of the illegal ivory trade and to demonstrate that the CITES controls were not even beginning to work.

"The traders were laughing," Currey recalled, his eyes wide with bravado. "We had to get involved. There was nobody else we could see who was fighting for the elephant."

In April 1988, Thornton, Currey and a cameraman, Clive Lonsdale, Jennifer Lonsdale's husband, set off for Dubai. Posing as journalists putting together a feature on trade, the three men toured the Jebel Ali free trade zone in Dubai, searching through papers, interviewing businessmen and watching for signs of ivory. In one Dubai customs file, they found references to 150 tons of "unworked or simply prepared" ivory that had left Dubai. All of it was heading for Hong Kong. The trail then led them to a factory in Dubai belonging to a company named MK Jewellery. This company was in turn owned by the Poons, a Hong Kong Chinese family known to be at the heart of the ivory trade.

Thornton and Currey soon established that ivory was being carved in the MK Jewellery factory in Dubai. But there was no way they could simply walk in and film the carving. However, the factories here were all sited in huge warehouses divided by concrete walls that stopped a few feet from the roof. Thornton and Currey realized that the ivory carving could be filmed through one of these gaps. So they applied for permission to shoot in a Black & Decker workshop adjacent to MK Jewellery. If they could get the camera near to the ceiling of the Black & Decker unit, they would be able to film down into the ivory factory.

The plan worked perfectly. Filming the Black & Decker

workshop from various angles, Currey and Lonsdale arranged to be lifted high into the air inside a packing crate. From there, they shot film of huge stacks of ivory. And they took footage of the ivory carvers at work. The raw tusks were all whole. None was marked with CITES registration numbers. There could be no doubt that this ivory was poached and illegal.

Two months later, Dave Currey followed the trail on to Hong Kong. Here he met and filmed Poon Tat Hong, a leading member of the Poon family. The EIA now had documents and films showing how unlicensed raw ivory progressed from Africa to the factories in Hong Kong and on to the markets in Europe, the United States and Japan.

The film and the story were turned over to the press and shown on news programs in Europe and America in December 1988. The world was beginning to wake up to the fact that something was rotten in the world of elephants.

The EIA's investigations had helped to prove that illegal ivory could easily circumnavigate the CITES controls. But there was still fierce debate about the level of elephant killing and the numbers of elephants remaining in Africa. How accurate were Douglas-Hamilton's figures? Wasn't he a doomsayer? What about the rain forest? This covered an area the size of the United States. It was virtually impenetrable. No one knew how many of the beasts there were hidden in the trees. There could be 5 million. Even 10 million.

It was not a secret the forest seemed likely to yield. It was impossible to count elephants in the forest from the air. And ground counts were difficult, lengthy and usually inaccurate. But while the debate raged, an English biologist named Richard Barnes was quietly trying to find an answer. Barnes had an eccentric idea, the beginnings of a new computer program, and some figures about the length of time it took for a pile of fresh, smelly elephant dung to decay. In 1985, funded by the New York Zoological Society, he set out for the Ogooué-Ivindo forest of northeastern Gabon to see if he could count elephants by their droppings.

Barnes and his team, which included his wife Carol, spent two years in Gabon on their bizarre but important project, and earned themselves the title of the "dung runners." Although elephant dung was easier to find than elephants, it was not feasible to count every dropping in an area of forest. So Barnes settled for cutting straight lines, or transects, for a dozen miles through the forest and counting all the dung along the way. The transects had to be absolutely straight. They crossed rivers, marshes, and ravines. If a snake was in the way, the snake had to be removed. Even elephants had to be avoided. It was their dung the dung runners were concerned about. The twelve-mile transects usually took a week.

The finding of a pile of dung was always greeted with a bustle of scientific activity. The number of boluses was counted. The distance from the center of the transect was measured. Then the age of the dung was calculated. There were four general classifications: from "A" for "intact, very fresh, moist, with odour," to "D" for boluses that were "completely disintegrated . . . an amorphous flat mass." Testing often involved the technical procedure of dipping the forefinger into the dropping. The dung runners soon became as familiar with elephant droppings as the average dung beetle.

The collecting of the information was just the beginning. After two years, Barnes returned to Cambridge University. He then fed his facts—amounts, placing, decay rates and so on—into the computer. The methodology was as complex as the idea was simple.

When a dropping is seen by the observer walking down the transect centre-line, its distance x from the centre line is measured. The x values for all the droppings are used to estimate the probability density function f(x). From the probability density function one obtains an estimate for f(0), which is an estimate of frequency with which droppings occur on the centre line. The process of dung running has produced entirely new mathematical equations:

$$Y = \frac{nf(0)}{2L}$$

The methodology also took into account variance and confidence limits, steady state assumption, survival curves and exponential decay.

All this mathematics was a long way from elephants wandering through the rain forest and casually defecating balls of steaming droppings. But when Barnes completed all his computer work, he came out with numbers that closely matched more laborious counts of elephants in this one area of the forest.

Barnes now sent new dung-running teams into the forests of the Congo, Central Africa, Cameroon, and most importantly Zaire. The results of these counts trickled slowly back to Cambridge. They were then processed and passed on to Nairobi. Here the United Nations Environment Program mainframe was used to combine Barnes's data with other counts, estimates and variables such as human population, number of roads and rivers, logging operations, vegetation type, rainfall, political stability and the availability of guns in the forest areas.

The numbers that came out of the computer toward the end of 1988 were still extrapolations. But they were the most credible estimates yet. And the figures were certainly dramatic. In 1987, Iain Douglas-Hamilton had come up with a figure of half a million elephants for Central Africa. Some 330,000—not far short of half Africa's elephants—were estimated to be in Zaire.

The new figure for Zaire, using Barnes's information, was only 86,900 elephants.

The year from mid-1988 to mid-1989 was to prove the turning point for the elephant. The EIA's films were released. Richard Barnes's early figures were circulated. And studies of the sizes of tusks confiscated by Hong Kong customs confirmed that smaller and smaller elephants were being poached.

Greed was also beginning to catch up with the poachers. They had killed most of the elephants in unprotected areas and were now homing in on the parks. Poaching in Tsavo was at its height. Elephants were being attacked on all sides. Trying to find safe havens, they took up residence near the tourist lodges. But the poachers followed them even there. Tourists were woken by gunfire at night. And during the day, they stumbled over elephant carcasses. Stories began to filter back to Nairobi. Letters were sent to the Kenyan press. The Kenyan papers and the foreign press corps began to write articles about the elephant slaughter in Tsavo.

One photograph of a dead elephant in Tsavo was worth more than all Douglas-Hamilton's figures. Film crews began to turn up in Kenya. Journalists headed down to Tsavo. In September 1988, prompted by the international interest, Richard Leakey, the renowned paleontologist, who was chairman of the Kenya Wildlife Society and a Kenyan citizen, launched a damning attack against Kenya's government. "Last week people were cutting off elephants' heads with mechanical saws in our parks," he said. The poaching of a precious resource was a "national crisis."

The conservation community's support for the idea of sustainable utilization meant that the details of the elephant crisis had been partially suppressed. Now the WWF and other groups were being bypassed. Reporters, magazine writers and television crews were reporting directly from Africa's parks back to the general public. Elephants had always been a popular animal in the West. But the campaign was helped enormously by the growing concern in the West for all environmental matters. People were already talking about global warming and the Brazilian rain forests, and elephants could get on the bandwagon. Moreover, the elephant question was more tangible and more emotional than global warming. Dead elephants made dramatic film footage. Elephants quickly became a symbol of the world's endangered environment.

January 1989 began with the launch of the Year of the Elephant by the African Wildlife Foundation in Washington. Sensing the mood of the public, the AWF's campaign was emotional and aggressive. "Today in America," ran one ironic advertisement in a campaign designed by Saatchi & Saatchi, "someone will slaughter an elephant for a bracelet." Bumper stickers were soon produced telling people that ONLY ELEPHANTS SHOULD WEAR IVORY or SAVE AN ELEPHANT, SHOOT A POACHER.

Similar campaigns were launched in Europe. Brigitte Bardot became the figurehead for the elephant in France. In Britain, the *Daily Mail* started a Save the Elephant campaign. New organizations with names like Elefriends and Tusk Force sprung up. The connection between wearing ivory and killing elephants had been made, and almost overnight ivory had become taboo. "When I go to parties now, I just say I'm in import-export," a British ivory buyer told a newspaper.

"Otherwise I get thumped. If I said I was peddling drugs for a living, I wouldn't get a worse reception."

Back in Africa, changes were also taking place. Partly as a response to Western pressure, two new appointments were made. In Tanzania, Costa Mlay, an honest and highly respected biologist, was made the new director of wildlife. And then Richard Leakey was unexpectedly given the equivalent post in Kenya. Both men began purges of their departments. They invited the world's press to visit their parks and film and write about what was happening to their elephants. And most significantly, in May 1989, Costa Mlay and Richard Leakey made the first public call to scrap the CITES controls and ban the entire international trade in ivory.

This call was immediately supported by the African Wildlife Foundation in the United States. At the beginning of June, after considerable soul-searching, and the exile of its fiercely "antiban" head of African operations to a post in Cape Town, the World Wide Fund for Nature also came out in favor.

Within days, London's three most famous department stores, Harrods, Selfridges and Liberty, had all announced that they were removing ivory products from their shelves. A few weeks later, Steinway declared it would no longer use ivory for its piano keys. Japan's two main piano makers, Yamaha and Kawai, followed suit almost immediately.

Support for a ban was gathering pace. On June 4, the United States declared a unilateral moratorium on ivory imports. Britain did the same five days later. Australia, Canada, Taiwan and the European Community followed. Even Japan, the world's largest market and the least environmentally conscious of the economically developed nations, announced a ban on the import of raw ivory.

Back in Africa, on July 18, Kenya made the most dramatic gesture yet. Two thousand tusks—twelve tons of ivory, worth more than £2 million—were trucked into Nairobi National Park and piled into a huge pyre. In the late afternoon, at a moment carefully timed to allow live coverage on American breakfast television, President Daniel arap Moi set the pile on fire. The flames shot high into the afternoon sky and filled the television screens of viewers across the United States.

The next CITES meeting was set for Lausanne in October 1989. Support for a worldwide ban was almost universal in the West, but there was considerable opposition from producers in Africa and consumers in Asia. As the time for the meeting grew closer, lobbying became fierce and passionate.

"If an angry bull elephant with a poacher's bullet in its hide was looking for someone to gore, it could make no better choice than a self-assured French-Canadian bureaucrat called Eugene Lapointe," began one article in the *Financial Times*.

Lapointe was the head of the CITES secretariat, the body appointed by the United Nations. He was supposed to be neutral. But he had made himself a mouthpiece for the ivory traders. He had even taken money for the secretariat from many of the big ivory traders, including the Poons. This was technically legal, but highly dubious ethically.

Insults flew back and forth. "The ivory crisis was engineered," wrote Chris Huxley, a former CITES employee, in a veiled attack on Iain Douglas-Hamilton. "The strategy was to avoid serious scientific or technical debate and to appeal to the emotions. . . . The case for elephant conservation is dishonoured by the catalogue of lies, damned lies and statistics."

"I was surprised to read the vitriolic attack mounted by

Mr. Huxley," replied Douglas-Hamilton. "It would be difficult to exceed in fallaciousness."

"I don't respect hysterical screaming like Huxley," agreed Perez Olindo, a former director of wildlife in Kenya. "He's still writing, plotting, planning to control the trade in a diminishing commodity. Will he still be trading when there is just one elephant left in Africa?"

"That crook Perez Olindo," exclaimed a Zimbabwean who had never met Olindo and could produce no evidence for his accusation. "He's the biggest ivory poacher in Africa."

Months later, when I spoke to Cynthia Moss, she shook her head over the whole business. "Sometimes I felt that nobody was interested in the elephant," she said. "It was just their own egos and their own philosophies they worried about. You know there's an old African proverb that says when elephants fight, the grass suffers. Well, back then it should have said, 'When conservationists fight, the elephant suffers.' "

In October 1989, the spitting and snarling moved to Lausanne. The CITES secretariat kicked off the meeting with a characteristic lack of subtlety. Delegates signing in were presented by the CITES secretariat with personal vinyl briefcases donated by the International Fur Trade Federation.

The elephant was the only subject on the agenda and the argument was pretty clear. A few southern African states argued the sustainable-utilization line. They culled and sold elephant products. They were doing well. Therefore, ivory trading should continue. But East Africa and the Western delegates responded that the rest of Africa was in crisis and as long as a legal market for ivory remained, the whole elephant population would be threatened.

The argument went on for several days. None of the main players showed signs of budging. But the outcome was no longer up to only the key countries like America, Britain,

Zimbabwe, South Africa, Kenya and Tanzania. There were ninety-one members of CITES and each one had a vote. Most were countries uninvolved with elephants or ivory, such as Argentina, Afghanistan, Bangladesh, Chile, Costa Rica, Ecuador and so on. No one was sure which way these countries would vote.

In the end, there was little disagreement. Seventy-six nations voted to ban the international ivory trade. Four abstained. Only eleven voted against. Even Japan voted in favor. The elephant was now officially an endangered species, like the blue whale, the giant panda and the tiger.

In May 1990, six months after the vote in Lausanne, I ran into Richard Leakey on one of his flying visits to Tsavo National Park. It was a year since his appointment as Kenya's director of wildlife. He was thickset, handsome and charming. He was also extremely pleased with himself.

"A year ago," he said, "Kenya was losing hundreds of elephants every month. In the past twelve months, we have lost less than two hundred."

The killing had begun to diminish in Kenya even before the ivory ban. Leakey's appointment had shaken up the wildlife department. Scores of corrupt officials had been sacked. Warnings had been given to many others. Leakey had also appointed a military man, Abdi Omar Bashir, to set up new antipoaching squads with military training and brand-new automatic weapons to match the AK-47s of the poachers. In the early months, Bashir had even used army helicopter gunships to root out and kill poachers in Tsavo.

But Bashir's job had been made much easier by the ban. Many economists, including Professor David Pearce, an advisor to Chris Patten, Britain's environment secretary at the time, had argued that a ban would simply force the ivory trade underground and push up the price. This was what had happened with rhino horn. But this did not take into account the differences in the markets for the two products. Rhino horn was used for dagger handles by wealthy young Yemenis and as medicine in China. Neither Yemenis nor Chinese cared about rhinos. But ivory was sold primarily to the West and Japan. Westerners did care about wildlife conservation. And partly to please the West, Japan was beginning to care too.

These attitudes were perfectly reflected in the marketplace. The CITES vote had banned only the international ivory trade. Ivory already within a country could still be sold domestically. But in the months after the ban, despite heavy discounts, shops in Europe and America sold virtually no ivory. Even in Japan, the Mitsukoshi department store removed ivory from its shelves. And Sunamoto Ivory, Japan's largest ivory dealer, changed its name to the Sunamoto Co.

Esmund Bradley Martin, the world's leading expert on the trade, traveled around the carving factories in the East and found thousands of carvers out of work. The largest factory in China, the Beijing Ivory Carving Factory, had reduced its carving staff from 600 to 6. Another Chinese factory Esmund visited had employed 400 carvers at his previous visit. Now he found just one man left, making ear picks out of slivers of ivory. In Hong Kong, the story was similar. More than 1,200 carvers were out of work. Five hundred had signed on for a government scheme to learn how to carve cow bone.

Back in Africa, the poachers and middlemen were also out of jobs. Elephant poaching had virtually stopped in Kenya and Tanzania. The latest aerial count in the Selous Game Reserve had found not a single fresh carcass. On a similar count in Tsavo, only four carcasses had been seen. Little killing was reported in Zaire. Poaching was greatly reduced in Zambia. "There is little evidence that ivory is being sold in Africa at any price," concluded a WWF report.

Richard Leakey was now already talking about a world after the ivory ban. He was considering the possibility of allowing hunting again in Kenya. He was musing about raising $200 million to build roads, fences, museums and airstrips and buy equipment for the parks. "There's no point spending $20 million when you need $200 million," he said.

I left him smiling and walked over to my car. It was early afternoon, so I decided to drive down the road toward the Aruba lodge and dam. This was still good country for elephants. The road was twenty miles long and I drove slowly through the dust. I passed a gerenuk standing on its hind legs and curling its tongue around some vicious-looking thorns. A couple of wildebeests wandered across the track. For a while, I stopped to watch a pair of lilac-breasted rollers swoop for insects.

Aruba was like an abandoned film set. The lodge was empty and boarded up. A wind was whipping across the dam, plucking up tufts of water and blowing sand and grass across the earth. I shielded my eyes and looked into the lowering sun for signs of elephants coming down to drink. There was nothing. So I climbed back into my car and drove a little quicker, needing to be back at Voi by dusk.

Halfway along, I saw a herd of elephants. They were thirty or forty yards from the road, in the trees at the end of a patch of half-open scrub. I stopped and looked at them out of the window. They seemed old and lazy and slow. They were moving gradually in my direction and I waited for them. They came forward eating. When the leading female was about fifteen yards away, she suddenly realized I was there. The poachers may have been defeated, but this cow had not forgotten what men had done. She kicked up a terrible fuss. Her trunk and ears shot out. She trumpeted and began to charge.

Stirred suddenly from my own somnolence, I grabbed for

the keys, turned on the ignition and shoved the gear stick desperately into first. The cow was almost on me when the car shot forward and I roared away. My hands were gripping the steering wheel. My foot was down hard on the accelerator. My eyes were watching the road ahead. But for one second I flicked a look at the mirror. My acceleration had churned up a cloud of dust. But the elephant seemed to be just a couple of feet behind the car. Her head filled the whole mirror. Her ears were out, her trunk was up, and her whole face seemed contorted with fury.

Chapter Six

ORPHANS OF THE SAVANNA

Thick purple cloud hung over Uganda. The aircraft flew along a narrow corridor between the belly of the cloud and the dark shadow of the earth, like a shark cruising shallow waters. Every now and again, pale wisps of vapor trailed down like jellyfish arms and wrapped us in blindness.

My fellow passengers were a small, chirpy Dutchman named Luke and a tall, pale Englishwoman named Melanie. Both were traveling alone. Uganda was not yet a tourist spot and it attracted mostly oddball travelers: loners, war groupies, escapers, avoiders, eccentrics. I put Luke down as a lonely avoider. Melanie was a bit of a war groupie. I turned away from Luke's bright empty conversation, pressed my nose to the window and wondered what I was.

The plastic of the window was cold. The earth below seemed to glow green in the darkness. An hour into the journey, the pilot waved his hand to our right. A gap had broken in the clouds and we could see a ridge of mountains.

The peaks were streaked with icy sweat and furled with silk ribbons of mist. These were the Ruwenzoris, the Mountains of the Moon.

Somewhere up ahead lay my destination, the Ruwenzori National Park. In 1970, this park had contained more than four thousand elephants. But by 1982, after a dozen years of poaching by Idi Amin's soldiers and the Tanzanian army which invaded Uganda and overthrew Amin, fewer than two hundred elephants had remained. However, at this point, the slaughter had stopped. While across the rest of the continent the ivory killing had continued, the circumstances here—the end of Amin's rule, the withdrawal of the Tanzanian army, the remoteness of the park—conspired to leave these few remaining Ruwenzori elephants in peace.

As a result, these elephants had become a sort of test case. The consequences of the killing across Africa was not merely numerical. The constant shooting and harassment all over the continent had disrupted the society of many of those elephants which had managed to survive. Poachers usually took first the larger animals with the bigger tusks, leaving the infants and adolescents to fend for themselves. The infants generally died. In many places, such as the Ruwenzori Park, the surviving elephants were mostly adolescents without proper herd structures or matriarchs to lead them.

How then, in the Ruwenzori Park, eight years after the killing had stopped, were these elephants doing? Were they still psychologically traumatized? Were they breeding? Had they lost the wisdom and culture of their race? For some time, a young Ugandan woman named Eve Abe had been trying to find answers to these questions. She lived at Mweya, the park headquarters, and it was to visit her that I was now flying over western Uganda.

Looking out of the window again, I saw the silvery glimmer of Lake Edward leaking over the horizon. It seemed to lie not in a dip but on top of the land, like a pool of liquid mercury. We flew out over the waters, sinking downward. Then we turned back toward the Mweya headland. The plane bounced, looped and finally came down softly. I climbed out into the cool, damp air. It was almost a disappointment to have arrived: the journey through the skies had been so dramatic.

While the pilot was pulling out the luggage, an African in rumpled brown trousers came forward and wordlessly handed me a note. It was from Eve. She had been delayed in Kampala, and would not be back until the following day. A couple of porters from the lodge, dressed in frayed purple and grey uniforms, had also come down to meet the plane. We handed them our bags and followed them down a gravelly path.

I checked into the lodge and had a look around. A pair of huge curved elephant tusks stood at the entrance to the restaurant. An old map hung outside on the porch. It was dotted with illustrations of animals. Many were elephants. The name of the lake on the map was a mess of crossings-out. Lake Edward had been changed to Lake Idi Amin Dada and then, more recently, the original name had been restored. Also hanging on the wall was a blackboard recording sightings the previous day. It read: ONE LONELY ELEPHANT ON THE PENINSULA.

I walked through onto the porch. The lodge was perched on a high bluff surrounded by lawn. There were cacti and pink and red flowers in the garden. On one side, a rocky slope ran down to the thick reedbeds beside the Kasinga Channel. On the other, the land fell away more gently toward the lake. There was no sign of the mountains. It was growing late now and the lake and sky were both the color of a vivid bruise: blue, purple and yellow. While I stood looking out, a fork of lightning noiselessly split the skies and a moment later the thunder came, slapping like a wave against the lake.

Supper, with Melanie and Luke, was translucent fish or chicken with rice. The talk was footloose. Neither Luke nor Melanie had a real home. Luke was a salesman, hawking chemicals around Africa, on the road ten months of the year. He was forty, unmarried, monotonously cheerful. Melanie was a freelance journalist, living out of a backpack.

"What are you writing here?" I asked.

"A travel piece about the park," Melanie said.

I looked around. All the other tables were empty. The lodge needed some publicity.

In the morning, we all went for a ride along the Kasinga Channel. The launch was like a miniature Thames cruiser: round-bottomed with a roof on poles. The captain, an old man with a face like a rumpled rug, poked at the engine until it clattered into life and began to snort black fumes.

The noise drowned Luke's incessant chatter but did not seem to disturb the wildlife. The launch was a familiar monster. Herons and storks ignored us from the shallows. Smaller birds clung sideways to the thick reeds, swaying in the breeze. Moaning down the lake, we edged toward a group of hippos lazing like blubbery icebergs in the water, only their absurd little ears, piggy eyes and nostrils above the surface.

The captain eased the boat to within a few feet and then suddenly revved the engine and charged. Most of the hippos ducked under the water. A couple near the bank heaved themselves up onto the dry land. They had seen this trick before. Standing there, they seemed like cartoon cows inflated with air. Their tiny trotters poked out of swollen bellies. I half-expected them to float away in the wind.

When the ride was over, I wandered down below the lodge to the staff village. The housing quarters stood in a series of long, low concrete blocks. Off-duty rangers lazed against the walls, catching the morning sunshine. Women washed clothes at the pumps. Half a dozen ragged children stopped playing and directed me to the head ranger's house. Fred Bawane was a morose man with yellow eyes, a big nose and sideburns that led into droopy jowls. I was reminded of A. A. Milne's Eeyore.

"I joined the park staff in April 1972," he said, slow and sad. "The park was very nice. We had a good number of hippos and four thousand elephants. We also had many tourists. So many. For holidays sometimes you had to book two years in advance at the lodge. You could have any food you wanted. You could have wine and beer and whatever you wanted."

His yellow eyes softened at the memory.

"After 1973, the tourists stopped coming. And in early 1974, we started having problems with poaching by Amin's soldiers. They were just killing whatever elephants they saw. Even myself, I was arrested by them. They wanted to kill me, but I escaped."

"How did that happen?"

"We were on patrol and we found four soldiers who had killed two elephants. We went to arrest them, but instead they arrested me. They tied me up and put me in their Land Rover. But on the way to the prison, they stopped at some shops. They beat me badly and I pretended to be dead. Then they bought beer, and when they were drunk, I escaped."

"Did nobody else ever try to stop them?" I asked.

"Who would stop them?" Bawane said, chopping his left hand with his right forefinger to make the point. "The warden ran away. The manager of the lodge was arrested. He was taken when he stopped the soldiers stealing the big tusks in the lodge. We never saw the manager again, but his actions saved the ivory."

He paused, scratching at these unpleasant thoughts.

"There were two research officers also," he said. "They

were educated and the soldiers did not like them. So one evening the soldiers got drunk and took the two officers outside and shot them."

Bawane's face became even more gloomy. There was something in his countenance that made me want to apologize for the misfortune, as Africans do whenever they see or hear of tragedies or accidents.

"I'm sorry," I finally said.

Bawane nodded appreciatively and carried on.

"Even then it wasn't finished. After Amin, the Tanzanian army came here in 1979 on the way to Kampala."

That year, in his last great folly, Amin had invaded Tanzania. The Tanzanians had fought back and carried the war into Uganda, where they eventually overthrew Amin.

"The Tanzanians were even worse than Amin's men," Bawane continued. "They shot everything. Hippos, birds, elephants. They even threw a hand grenade at a herd of elephants. By this time, we were very few here. Just twenty out of one hundred and fifty rangers. When we tried to stop them, they killed two rangers."

"But you stayed?"

"I stayed."

"Why?"

"I had no money," he said. "I did not know anywhere else. This was my home. If I was to be killed anywhere, let it be here."

His cheeks spread in a cheerless smile.

In the afternoon, I sat on the porch with a pot of tea, reading and keeping an eye on the road. It was a Saturday, and several vehicles arrived with new guests for the lodge. But no Eve. When it grew dark, I switched from tea to beer. I was about to give up and head inside for supper when a pair of distant lights appeared at the end of the peninsula. I watched them flicker along like courting fireflies. When they drew close, I walked up to the gate.

The vehicle's lights dimmed: reassurance for the armed guards. A small woman was at the wheel. Her face and clothes were covered in red dust.

"Eve?" I said.

She breathed in sharply. I stood back, thinking I had been too forward. Then the woman laughed and said she was Eve. Later I realized this intake of breath was her way, the way of her Acholi tribe, of showing assent.

When Eve had washed, we went into the dining room for supper. There was fish or chicken on the menu. While Eve was giving her order to the waiter, I studied her face. Her features were smooth and understated. Her wideset eyes were gentle gashes above her oval cheeks. Her nose was a soft ripple. Her hair was cropped to her head. She was like an ebony carving—dark and smooth, capturing only the essentials.

"Was everything all right in Kampala?" I asked.

"Yes, fine," she said. "I received an urgent message, but it was just a form to renew my passport." She had been away forty-eight hours, half of it taken up by the journey. A phone call could have sorted out the matter, but there were no phones in Mweya.

The waiter arrived with our plates of scrawny chicken and hot rice. We ate in silence. Eve was ravenous. When we had finished, we had coffee and I asked about the elephants.

"You've been to Amboseli?" Eve said.

"Yes."

"So you have seen what a happy elephant society looks like. Well, here they have more food. The eating is better. But the elephants are less happy. They are still living under the shadow of all the killing."

The Ruwenzori population had grown a little since 1982.

There were now 240 elephants in the park. Sixty of them lived south of the Kasinga Channel. The other 180 lived to the north. These in the north were Eve's study elephants.

"The elephants left over by the poachers were not much of a society," Eve said. "A few matriarchs did survive and they have managed to hold their families together. We do have some herds that are still intact. But many of the other elephants came from herds that had been destroyed. They were lonely adolescents without any family. Now most of them are young adults. But they still don't have proper herds. Lots of them are disturbed. I call them the orphans."

Eve yawned. It was growing late.

"I will show you them tomorrow," she said.

Eve drove off and I followed my torchlight to my room. A gecko was suckered splay-footed to the ceiling. I watched its heart beating inside its thin pale pink skin and its eyes turning in their sockets. Then I turned off the light.

The dawn light floated in through the window. The morning was cold and dewy. I dressed and sat outside until Eve drew up in her Suzuki. We stopped at the gate to pick up a guard with a gun and then headed down the track toward the northern region of the park. Euphorbia candelabra stood in the short grass like overcrowded cactus candlesticks. To the north, the Ruwenzoris were a smudged shadow of cloud. We drove off the road, leaving a dark trail in the silver damp of the grass.

"I haven't been around for a few days, so I don't know where the elephants are," Eve said. "They could be anywhere."

We drove up and down the hills. I watched out for signs of movement among the trees and bushes and grey rocks.

"We are looking for a big herd," Eve said. "In Amboseli, you see the separate herds in different places, but here I usually find all the northern elephants together."

"Why is that?" I asked.

"I think it makes them feel better. They had such bad times. Now they want to stick together for reassurance and security. Elephants sometimes do that. Even though it is eight years since the poaching ended, they still need comfort. Elephants have good memories."

We bumped up to a rise and Eve surveyed the ground with her binoculars. A few Ugandan kob were grazing in the damp grass, but no elephants.

"Staying together is also good for the orphans," Eve said. "The matriarchs won't let the orphans join their herds. They don't like the orphans to get too close. But they allow them to hang out on the edges. That way at least some of the benefit of the matriarchs rubs off on the orphans."

Eve stopped the vehicle again and we looked around. There was still no sign of elephants.

"What do you do if you can't find them?" I asked.

"Sometimes I drive around for a few days. Sometimes I get a ride in a plane and find them that way."

"I think the plane that brought me down is still here," I said. "Perhaps we could persuade the pilot to take us up for a few minutes."

"I know this pilot," Eve said. "We could try."

Eve turned the car and began heading back.

A couple of miles from the lodge, we came to a crossroads. The lodge was to the left. On the track to the right was a pile of steaming elephant dung.

"Probably two of the bulls," Eve said. "When they are not with the females, they often hang out round here."

We followed a pair of large round prints. They led to a cluster of ruined, shuttered shacks. In the good times, this had been a thriving little village—a few houses, some shops, a restaurant, a bar, a little guesthouse. Now the peeling, faded blue paint was pockmarked with automatic gunfire. Half a dozen scrawny chickens pecked in the dust. A couple of women sat on the steps and watched us.

The elephant tracks had peeled off to the right. We could see movement in the trees on the hill beyond the village. We climbed out of the Jeep and pushed our way through the high weeds between two of the shacks. The ranger walked behind us, his gun over his shoulder.

On the other side, we had a clear view up the hill. One bull was a couple of hundred yards away. The other was farther up the slope. Eve began to walk toward them.

"Stop," the ranger said. "They can smell us."

He stared nervously toward the bulls.

"It's all right," Eve said. "I know these elephants."

"If it's coming, you just run," the ranger grunted. He planted his feet on the ground and refused to go any farther.

We walked on, picking our way through the thick, low bush. The ground was soft and slippery underfoot.

"That's Julian," Eve said, stopping. "He's got a chopped trunk. Probably caught in a snare."

I looked through the binoculars. Julian's trunk was clearly a foot or so short. It had none of the usual handlike dexterity at its end. But the elephant was still curling it around the vegetation and pulling leaves and twigs into his mouth.

"The other bull is M5. He hasn't got a name yet. He is very cheeky. Maybe I'll call him after you."

"Thanks a lot," I said.

The bulls moved slowly up into the woods. We found the ranger back at the car, chewing a piece of gum. He ignored us. We climbed into the vehicle and drove back to the lodge.

It was still early enough for breakfast. We sat on the porch beside the people I had seen arriving in their cars

the previous day: a group of diplomats, half a dozen backpackers, an African family, and a young white couple who
were playing with the lodge's pet duiker, an endearingly ugly
little creature.

After breakfast, Eve went off to see about the plane. I
walked to the edge of the garden and looked down toward
the channel. A herd of buffalo were nosing their way into
the water on the far side. The duiker had now left the couple
and sidled over to where I was standing. It rubbed its head
against my bare legs and I leaned down to stroke it. The
creature's horns were short and stubby. Duikers usually had
longer horns. Somewhere in the back of my mind, it regis-
tered that someone must have sawn the rest of these horns
off.

I turned idly back to the buffalo. Suddenly, something like
a hammer smashed into my shins. I wrenched my head down
and saw the duiker backing away from me. For a moment I
was utterly bemused. Had something attacked both me and
the duiker? Had I been bitten by a snake? Was this what it
was like to be shot? After all, this was Uganda—and I had
been told a bullet feels like a hammer blow. I stared down
at my shin, expecting to see splinters of bone and blood
pouring out. The leg looked fine. Then I noticed the duiker,
crouching low and pawing at the grass like an angry bull, an
expression of pure derangement in its bambi eyes.

I stepped back and the duiker came at me again. I was still
so startled that all I could manage was a feeble leap into the
air. The beast caught me on the ankle with the rock-hard
stumps of its horns. I yelped in pain, and as soon as I regained
my balance, I began to retreat more seriously. This time,
when the duiker charged, scuttling low to the ground, its
head and shoulders almost at earth level, I was ready. I fended
off its forehead with the top of my foot, kicking out like a

soccer player volleying a dipping cross. The duiker backed off too now, shaking its head like a boxer hit for the first time.

"What *is* that horrible man doing?"

The voice, high and strident, came from the porch behind me. I glanced quickly around. Everyone was watching. There was another twenty feet to the porch, but there was no way I could now turn and run from this midget antelope. I had to keep walking backward. I straightened up and tried to look nonchalant. When the duiker came again, in its fast crabbing jab, I lashed out harder with my foot. The beast dodged, I missed, and it cracked me viciously on the shin. I screeched. The pain was agonizing. The shin was already beginning to swell.

Indignation drifted from the porch behind me.

"Quite extraordinary."

"Is that man mad? What is he doing to that poor sweet little creature."

"Animal brutality. You wouldn't have thought a man like this would want to come to a national park."

Finally, I reached the safety of the raised porch. I grabbed a chair and turned toward the little monster like a lion tamer. For a moment, I entertained the thought of spearing the duiker with one of the chair's rusting metal legs. Then I remembered another duiker on another day. The shadows of the rain forest. A misunderstood question. My executioner's nod. The sudden snap of the animal's back legs. Perhaps this was duikerdom's revenge. I pushed the duiker off, and eventually it lost interest, stumbling stupidly away.

"What have you been doing?" Eve asked, coming up behind. "The plane's ready. Shall we go?"

Eve strode off and I hobbled after her.

"What's up with the duiker at the lodge?" I called.

"Oh, the duiker," Eve said, stopping to wait for me. "It's

a bit mad. It's always attacking people. That's why they had to cut off the horns. It's best to leave it alone."

"Thanks for telling me."

I climbed painfully into the plane. We took off and spotted the elephants almost immediately. They were grazing in the thick bush along the edge of the channel, hidden from the road by the trees. We had probably driven within a couple of hundred yards of them. Now we could see at least fifty of the big-backed creatures, spread out through the forest.

"I think they are all there," Eve said.

The pilot turned around to land. Eve and I took the Jeep and drove down the road. The sun was high overhead. Hard shadows edged the bright light. We drove into the bush where we had seen the elephants. There were noises of eating and shaking bushes all around. We stopped on the edge of a clearing. Four elephants were feeding on the other side. I watched one methodically twirling its trunk around the branches of the bushes and pulling the vegetation into its mouth. Even while it was chewing, its trunk was eeling out again, slithering around to find the next succulent mouthful.

"You see this elephant," Eve said, pointing to another beast. I looked. It was an adult, but without tusks. "There are a lot of tuskless elephants here. They were the ones that survived. Now I think this population will have lots of tuskless genes. We are breeding a population that can survive poaching better."

"Natural selection," I said.

"Yes," Eve said. "Oh, look. Over there."

A large elephant was coming slowly toward us. She was old and saggy. The line of her head and back dipped and rose like a roller-coaster track. She had long, slender tusks.

"That's Lady Irene. She's the matriarch of the whole park. She's my favorite elephant. She's such a good old lady. That's why I called her Irene."

"Irene?"

"My mother is called Irene. She is also a matriarch. She has seventeen children."

Eve's father had been a wealthy farmer and a trustee of the Ugandan national parks. He had fled with his family during Amin's time. The children were now spread out around the world—doctors, lawyers, scientists, academics. Eve was the only one of the seventeen left in Uganda.

"Lady Irene is so clever," Eve whispered. "She's always in charge. I've even seen two young bulls fighting and Lady Irene chase them both away, telling them off. She is really the matriarch for the whole park."

We watched the old lady wander over to a thicket and begin to feed. There was something serene about her. She seemed to know everything an elephant needed to know. She had seen it all. She had lived through the worst that life could offer and survived. Nothing would ever surprise her again.

Another elephant had now come into the clearing. She sidled uneasily over toward Lady Irene.

"Who's that?" I asked.

"That's Good Girl. She is one of the orphans. She wanders from one family to another. She's always hanging around at the edge of herds. All these orphans are a bit confused. One of them, Camelia, thinks she's a male. You usually see her with the bulls. It's like I was telling you, this is a different kind of population from Amboseli."

"In what other ways?"

"For a start, they don't talk so much here. In Amboseli the elephants are always rumbling and trumpeting. They are very expressive. Here they are much more quiet. They are like people who are depressed. There is also much less greeting. If elephants have been apart, they don't seem to mind. And then there's playing. In Amboseli, even the adults are always playing. Cynthia Moss calls it 'being silly.' Here, I hardly see even the calves playing."

"What about death?" I asked. "In Amboseli the elephants seem to have a concept of death. They are fascinated with elephant bones. Is that the same here?"

"No. I've never seen it. We have lots of bones, you can imagine, from all the killing. But the elephants here just ignore the bones."

"Why do you think that is?"

"I don't know. Perhaps they don't know who the dead elephants were. Perhaps there are too many. I can't really say."

We drove through to a clearing. There were more elephants around now. A small female walked ahead of her calf. The little elephant scuttled to catch up, squeaking in alarm.

"There seem to be quite a lot of calves," I said.

"Yes. In fact, another reason why the elephants stay together is for breeding. Here in the north we have only two mature bulls. There are more in the south and two of them sometimes swim across the channel. But that is not many bulls for one hundred females. And female elephants only come into estrus for a few days. If the females are all together, it is easier for the bulls to find the estrus females. That way they don't miss many opportunities to breed."

"So are the elephants breeding well?"

"They are having lots of calves, but there is a high mortality rate among the calves. Particularly when the mothers are orphans. In the last few months, three of the orphans have lost their calves."

"How?"

"I don't know. It's probably neglect. The orphans don't know how to be mothers. They haven't had any practice with other calves and they don't get any help from older

females. One day you see them with their calf. The next day
the calf is missing. You assume they are dead, though we
did find one calf wandering about on its own. We took it
back to Mweya. You didn't see it?"

"No," I said.

Eve grew quiet. Her eyes dimmed. She seemed to be thinking about something.

"Are you all right?" I said.

"I was thinking about the trouble these orphans cause with
their babies."

"What?"

"A few weeks ago, one baby died in the middle of the
main road out of Mweya. The orphan mother stayed with
the body and blocked the road. Whenever a car came along,
the cow charged it. So the warden went with some soldiers
to deal with the problem. When they arrived, the cow was
not there. The warden told the soldiers to climb out and
move the carcass away from the road. While they were doing
this, the cow returned."

As Eve spoke, an elephant came out from the bush behind
us and walked heavily just a few feet past the car.

"So what happened?" I asked.

"The cow grabbed one of the soldiers and threw him into
the bushes. Another of the soldiers started firing. There was
a lot of confusion. The elephant was killed, but so was the
warden. He was a good man. I lost two friends."

Life was not without problems for the Ruwenzori elephants. But their society had not fallen apart. The elephants
all lived together, for security, comfort and breeding efficiency. A few matriarchs had survived and they now formed
the foundations of the future elephant society. They passed
on their wisdom and taught the younger elephants about herd
life. There was even a logic to the orphans doing less well.

Slowly, the herd elephants would come to dominate. Then the society would be on its way to normality.

We sat in the car while the herd moved past us again. Eventually, the last elephant disappeared into the bush. Eve switched on the engine. We drove back to the road and headed home to the lodge.

Later, I went to look for the orphaned calf Eve had spoken about. It lived in the rangers' quarter and I found it picking at a pile of rubbish. It was a funny-looking creature. Its head seemed too big and its body was covered in long, thick black hairs. It reached out its trunk and felt my pockets and my hands. I had nothing to give it, so it turned away and resumed its search in the rubbish.

I stood back and watched the calf. It was a sad creature, far too young to be away from its mother and herd. The rubbish it was eating would probably kill it. And if it returned to the bush, it would be easy prey for lions. Out here, without proper care, it had little chance. But not all orphaned calves in Africa were so unfortunate. Back in Nairobi, where I was now heading, was a place for elephants like this: Daphne Sheldrick's animal orphanage.

T h e   h o u r   b e f o r e   d a w n   was the hour of the hollow men in Nairobi. I drove through a ceaseless flow of silent shadows: wrapped in ragged clothes against the cold, striding out from the hidden shanty towns toward the seven o'clock opening of the factories and workshops in the industrial district.

Toward the edge of town, the ghosts thinned and then vanished. A single red wound of morning sliced the black sky. I turned off the main road and skirted the edge of Nairobi National Park until I came to a small gate. A sleepy guard lifted the barrier and I drove past. A dirt track led through the darkness up to Daphne Sheldrick's house.

As I climbed out of my car, two grey shapes loomed out of the morning shadows. They were rhinos, Sam and Amboseli. Though they were only half-grown, they were already huge. Their bellies and haunches had the heft of ships' ballast: they made buffaloes seem like delicate ballerinas. I stepped back and let them through. They trundled past, snorting at the morning with their hot grassy breath.

When they had gone, I walked past their empty stockade and headed over to the stables where the other orphans slept. A man in a long green doctor's coat was opening the upper section of a stable door. I whispered hello, and he beckoned me over. A musty, horsey smell washed out from inside. I peered into the shadows. Two small elephant calves had just woken and they came over to the door, reaching out with their stubby trunks, folding and unfolding their ears like butterfly wings, rumbling and rubbing against the wooden slats.

"These are Ndume and Dika," the man whispered.

We moved on. He opened another door and the grey light slipped inside to reveal three more figures curled up together on the hay beneath a pile of brown blankets. The bedding stirred at the intrusion and a mêlée of limbs and heads emerged: wrinkled grey, furry black and white, smooth brown.

"The baby zebra is Magwa and the elephant calf is Tyaa," the keeper said as the beasts emerged. "And this is Moses."

Moses rubbed his eyes. He had a pleasant squashed face and a striped knitted hat on his head. He had spent the night in the stable. Tyaa was the youngest elephant, the newest arrival, and she still needed human company day and night.

"Jambo, Moses," I said.

"Mzuri."

We moved on to open the other stables. Soon we had

released six elephant calves, as well as Magwa the zebra. The animals milled hungrily around the narrow spaces between the buildings, rumbling, squeaking and shoving. One elephant reversed rapidly into another. Two began a pushing match. Magwa stood calmly in the middle, kicking out with his hooves whenever an elephant came too close.

"Dika, *hakuna*," shouted a keeper. "Dika, enough."

"Malaika!" scolded Moses. "Ajok!"

The calves ignored the keepers. Ajok, a tiny male, scarcely bigger than Tyaa, slid his trunk down my arm and pulled at my pen. I stroked his warm prickly hide. He rumbled and tried to reach into my pocket.

"Malaika, *hapana*, no!"

Malaika was raiding the haystack, pulling at chunks of cut grass, tossing some of them over her head and stuffing other bits into her mouth. The keepers marched over and tugged her away. She was the oldest of the calves and already a big creature, but once she realized the keepers were serious, she gave in meekly.

Slowly, order was restored. The keepers gathered the elephants together for their trip into the bush. The orphans spent most of the day in the park, learning important elephant lessons such as which plants to eat, which animals to avoid, how to drink and where to find shade. Ajok was still busy with my pen, but when he realized the others were ready to go, he let out a squeak and dashed over, his ears flat against his head and his trunk flapping in the air. The elephants now set off, one behind the other, their heads nodding from side to side.

Only Tyaa remained. To keep her warm, Moses tied a pair of blankets and a knitted woolen bedspread, matching his own hat, around her back. With her baby wrinkles and the long black hairs on her chin, she looked like a bright-eyed old lady in a homemade shawl. She wandered over to

investigate the others' sleeping quarters. She nosed around
in the hay, sniffing and tasting a pile of dung. Then she bent
her back legs in an ungainly squat and urinated. Moses collected the wet hay and wiped her behind with a cloth.

I sat and watched her and after a while she came over to
explore me. The morning light had crept over the stables
now, and as she poked at me with her trunk, I took a good
look at her too. She was a shrunken version of an adult
elephant: scarcely two feet high and several sizes too small
for her skin. She had skinny legs and a hanging belly. Her
trunk was short, squat, and useless: more like a fat maggot
than the powerful snake it would become.

She sniffed at me and peered out of the side of her head.
Her little eye sat in a field of grey-brown wrinkles, ringed
by long flirty eyelashes. The eye itself was white at the edges,
then brown, and finally a dark washed-out blue in the middle.
I ran my hand over her skin: it was warm, rough and bristly,
like a giant's unshaven chin. The ears were colder and
smoother, like thin tanned leather.

On her head, I came across a knotted piece of cloth buried
in the skin. I touched it gently, looking at the wound.

"Be careful with that," a voice said.

I turned around. Daphne Sheldrick had come up silently
from behind. She was holding a huge bottle full of warm
milk for Tyaa. She was a striking middle-aged woman with
eyes as hard and bright as a pair of blue diamonds. There
was a gash of red lipstick on her mouth. She gave the bottle
to Moses and he began to feed the calf.

"The cloth is to keep the wound open so it can drain,"
Daphne said. "We have to turn it every day and squirt water
in to keep it clean. When she first came, the wound was
infected and swollen. It was full of rubbish. When we lanced
it, we pulled out dirt and pebbles."

Tyaa had arrived only ten days previously. She was just a

few days old. She had been chased out of a farmer's field with her mother and their small herd. In the confusion, Tyaa had fallen in the ditch and been abandoned by her mother. She had been found the next day and the local game warden had given her some cow's milk and driven her down to Nairobi in the back of a truck. When she arrived, she was weak, hungry and frightened. But now she was feeding well and playing with the other calves. She had now spent almost as much time with her human parents as she had with her real mother—who was still alive, somewhere out in the bush.

"She's doing well," Daphne said. "We're feeding her on demand, day and night. She should make it."

Tyaa could not have fallen into better hands. Daphne had been looking after orphaned animals for fifty years, ever since she had adopted a baby duiker named Bushy at the age of three.

Daphne was born in 1935 and grew up on the family farm at Gilgil. Her father, Brian Jenkins, was a keen hunter and her brother, Peter, shot his first leopard at the age of fourteen. Daphne still remembered the excitement of the hunt. Those were the days of wildlife profusion. During the war, Brian Jenkins personally shot 50,000 head of buffalo, zebra, wildebeest and gazelle for the British troops. When Peter Jenkins grew up, he joined the wildlife department and became warden of Meru National Park. Daphne became a warden's wife.

She first married Bill Woodley, at the age of eighteen, and went to live at Voi, park headquarters of Tsavo East. When that marriage ended, Daphne went back home to the family farm. But she soon returned to Tsavo, to marry David Sheldrick and move into the warden's house at Voi. Daphne remained in Tsavo until David Sheldrick was removed from his post in 1976. Her two decades in the park were the stuff of adventure dreams. There were battles against poachers, journeys through the wilderness, nights listening to the hyenas howl and the lions roar. The men did the fighting and the guarding and the shooting of rogue animals. Daphne's job was to bring up the children and look after the procession of orphaned wild animals brought back by the menfolk.

In her time in Tsavo, Daphne raised a menagerie of creatures. There were rhinos, warthogs, zebras, elands, kudus, impalas, buffaloes, ground hornbills, civet cats, mongooses, porcupines and other creatures. But her favorites were always the baby elephants. These were invariably found standing over the carcasses of their poached mothers, suffering from thirst and heat exhaustion, and frequently sunburn. David Sheldrick or Bill Woodley or one of the rangers would coax them into a truck and bring them home. Once healed and fed, and over the trauma of the loss of their mothers, these elephants became the most mischievous, intelligent, endearing creatures imaginable. They turned on taps, raided food stores and occupied most of Daphne's time.

Daphne's very first elephant orphan was a male named Sampson. Daphne hired Africans as keepers and every day they would take Sampson out into the bush to learn about the wild. As other elephants arrived at Voi—and orphans of other species—they joined Sampson on his daily walks. Mornings in Tsavo soon became an extraordinary sight, as the orphaned elephants, rhinos, elands, kudus and others all trooped out in a long line into the bush.

Sampson spent his childhood at Voi, but as he grew older, he began to make contact with wild elephants. It was relatively easy for a bull elephant to return to the wild. Apart from men, an adolescent like Sampson had no enemies. And feeding was easy. One of the problems George and Joy Adamson had met in returning Elsa the lioness to the wild was teaching her to hunt. Sampson had no such troubles. His food grew on trees and bushes, and he had had years to learn which leaves and branches and fruits were best to eat. When he reached puberty, Sampson left Voi to take his place among the male society of Tsavo elephants.

This process, though, was more difficult for female elephants. Another of the early orphans was Eleanor, who had been found in northern Kenya and used in the film *Born Free* before she arrived at Voi. Like Sampson, Eleanor also made contact with wild elephants. But the female herds were tight organizations. It was not easy to break into a herd. And as she grew older, Eleanor settled for being the matriarch of the Tsavo orphans. Sometimes she would stay out in the bush for days. But she would always return to Voi. This was her home, her territory. Out in the bush, she was an outsider. At Voi, she was queen of the orphans. Thirty years later, she would still be living at Voi, taking in new orphaned animals.

The healthiest and happiest of elephant calves were still a handful, even with Eleanor's help. But not all the calves were healthy and happy. The calves that were already a year old when they arrived were partially weaned and able to survive away from their mothers. These calves might still be miserable when they were found, but they adapted very well to human care and company. Elephant society was so similar to human society that Daphne instinctively understood what was needed of her as a substitute mother. But those calves that arrived at Voi before their first birthdays were far more delicate. Over the years in Tsavo, Daphne took in more than a dozen of these tiny infants. Some lived a few months. But not one of them survived to return to the bush.

One such calf was Aisha, who became a special favorite. Daphne fed her cow's milk and smothered her with care and affection. Every night, she hung one of her dresses in Aisha's stables so that the smell would keep her company. When Aisha had diarrhea, she gave her antibiotics. Though Daphne kept her alive for six months, Aisha's health was always fragile. And when Daphne had to leave Tsavo for a few days, Aisha became desperate. She stopped eating, weakened and died.

Another youngster was Gulliver, "one of those delicate little creatures which were almost beyond hope and which I always dreaded having to look after," as Daphne later wrote. "My heart sank when he arrived." Eleanor was half-grown by this time and she quickly adopted the calf. She was helped by another older calf, Sobo, who became besotted with the baby. "The more we saw of them the more we realised that these gentle giants are not so very different from ourselves in their relationships with each other. Never was Gulliver left unattended even for a moment."

But without his mother's milk, Gulliver too failed to grow healthy. All Daphne's attempts to find a suitable diet had failed. Eventually, Gulliver gave up "the struggle and died by Eleanor's side, in the dead of night." Sobo was distraught. "While we prepared Gulliver's grave, Sobo stood beside his lifeless form and when we laid him gently in the ground, she came up and touched him lovingly with her trunk, reaching down in a last farewell. Even when the grave had been filled with the damp red earth of Tsavo, Sobo stood beside it for a long while before slowly turning and walking away."

For Daphne, Gulliver's death had been the last straw. She was ready to give up on these infant elephants. The next one that came along would be put down. The heartbreak was too much. But Sobo was not willing to forget. Every evening after that, when the orphans came back from the bush, Sobo would break away from the group and walk over to Gulliver's grave. One evening, watching Sobo, Daphne realized that she had no choice. She was duty-bound to continue trying to "unravel the mystery of how to hand-rear a very tiny elephant calf. Then Gulliver and many others would not have to perish, but enjoy a second chance."

Daphne and I left Tyaa and walked over to the porch for breakfast. We ate sweet porridge surrounded by a jungle of rambling green ivy, overflowing earthenware plant pots and elephant jawbones stained the color of clay. In front of us, the plains of the national park fell brightly away in the soft morning sun toward the distant knobbly backbone of White Grass Ridge.

"Did you ever manage to save one of the baby calves while you were still in Tsavo?" I asked.

"No," Daphne said. "Though I was getting close to the right combination of care and food. It was heartbreaking. Every time I saw one of these tiny calves, I would despair. But I learned from their deaths. I learned from every death."

When her husband died, Daphne left Eleanor and the other orphans with the park staff and came to live in this house on the edge of Nairobi National Park. Her first orphans here were buffaloes and warthogs. There were no elephants in the park. But eventually, two calves were picked up in other parts of Kenya, and brought down to Nairobi.

Their names were Olmeg and Oljori. They were both just a few weeks old, weak, sick and harrowed by the separation from their mothers. Olmeg had also been badly sunburned while standing over his mother's body. Daphne covered him with cream and suntan lotion. For the next few weeks, whenever Olmeg went outside, he had to be accompanied by a keeper with an umbrella.

Daphne now began to put into practice the lessons she had learned in Tsavo. She knew that the elephants should not be allowed to become too attached to any one person—in case that person had to leave. So she hired several keepers. They all dressed in the same green coats. But none spent too much time with either of the calves, though one or other of the keepers did sleep with the calves at night. Daphne had worked out that a smelly piece of clothing was not enough. Elephant calves were with their mothers night and day, and the replacement mothers had to give them the same twenty-four-hour care.

Daphne had also concluded that cow's milk was no good for the elephant calves. It was too rich and fatty. She could not get hold of large amounts of elephant milk, but analysis showed that powdered cow's milk was close enough. Daphne mixed the powdered milk with rice water and added other nutrients, like salt, calcium and vitamin C. This proved to be an ideal feed. Oljori quickly took to his bottle and began to improve. But Olmeg was in bad shape. He seemed to want to feed, but somehow was not happy. Then Daphne tried feeding him in the shade of a canvas tent. Olmeg was delighted. This felt like the shadow of his mother's belly. He began to feed and never looked back.

"They were such smart little elephants," Daphne remembered. "Olmeg developed a passion for Weetabix. If anyone even said the word, he would run around and try to knock over the Weetabix bin. So we took to spelling out the word, but he soon rumbled that."

Finally, a year passed. Olmeg and Oljori were beyond the danger point. Daphne had solved the secret of how to raise a baby elephant. All the years of sorrow had been worthwhile. When the two elephants were a little older, Daphne arranged for them to go down with their keepers to Tsavo. There they became part of Eleanor's herd. Every day, they and their keepers trooped off into the bush behind the now mature matriarch. One day, there was an accident. Oljori fell off a rock and broke his spine. He had to be put down. But Olmeg was still alive and living at Voi with Eleanor.

"It will take several more years before Olmeg becomes a proper wild elephant," Daphne said. "But I don't doubt that when he reaches puberty he will go off into the park permanently and join the other bulls. And then I think his time here in Nairobi will be just a treasured memory."

After Olmeg and Oljori, other calves followed. There were still lessons to be learned. One calf died from too high a dosage of antibiotics. Another succumbed to pneumonia, and from then on Daphne had taken to wrapping the young calves in blankets whenever it was cold. When Ndume arrived, he had been unconscious from thirst and hunger and had only been saved with a saline drip. Most of the calves were in shock when they were brought to the orphanage. It was a terrible trauma to lose their mothers and then be bundled into a car or aircraft and flown to a strange environment full of frightening two-legged animals.

"Elephants are very sensitive creatures," Daphne said. "They mourn very deeply. Sometimes you think there is no way a calf is going to survive. But they are also very resilient. I have learned so much from them—how bravely they accept tragedy, how silently they mourn, and then with what fortitude they get on with living."

Soon Ndume and Malaika, the oldest calves, would go down to join Eleanor in Tsavo. There, if all went well, they would begin the process of loosening their human ties and forging bonds again with wild elephants. One day, even Tyaa might make it down to Tsavo to join the wild herds. Humans had orphaned all these elephants and decimated Tsavo's population. In a small way, Daphne was reversing this process and helping to restock the park with a new generation of elephants.

When breakfast was over, I went to look for Tyaa. A family of warthogs had strolled in from the park. They stood and stared as I walked past. With their warts, coarse hair and tusks curved up on either side of their faces like military mustaches, they looked like pig-faced colonels.

Ajok had come back from the park with his keeper before the older calves, and he and Tyaa were playing in the bushes near the house. I followed a track and found the calves in a little clearing. They had an overinflated inner tube and were clumsily clambering over it. Ajok tumbled over and Tyaa stood with her front legs on the circle of the tube, her knitted bedspread still wrapped over her back. The two keepers watched the infants lovingly.

"Did you ever think you'd get a job looking after baby elephants," I asked.

"No, we did not. Never." They both laughed.

"How is it?"

"Oh, it's good. We like it so much."

"Why?"

"It's good to save the elephants. I like them."

Bored with the tire, Ajok came up and tried to shove me into a bush with his forehead. Then he curled his little trunk around my hand and pulled it into his mouth. The inside was soft and wet and warm. I stood there in the bush, shaded from the sun, and let him suckle for a while.

Exactly a decade earlier, in November 1980, another group of three orphaned elephants set foot for the first time on the red soil of Tsavo. These elephants had nothing to do with Daphne Sheldrick. Their names were Tshombe, Durga and Owalla. They were fifteen years old and almost fully grown. They had just arrived, by sea, from New York.

Tshombe, the only bull, died soon after arriving in Tsavo and was buried on the edge of the park. But Durga and Owalla survived their return to Africa. And while they did not stay in Kenya, they went on to play a part in another orphan success story in the bush of Pilanesberg National Park in the South African "homeland" of Bophuthatswana.

On the elephants' trail, I flew into Johannesburg and rented a car to drive to Pilanesberg. After East Africa, the gleaming modern world of Johannesburg scarcely seemed like the same continent. The road westward from the center of town ran through interminable sparsely populated suburbs of white-washed bungalows and concrete pavements. The shops all sold car parts, linen clothes or Big Burgers. Only the depth of the sky and the richness of the light were reassurance that I was still in Africa.

The city gradually thinned and finally gave way to the flat grey country of the Transvaal. Lines of wire blocked off windswept fields. Gas stations stood in empty concrete lots. Towns sprawled up like thick dabs of makeup on the face of the land. Roodepoort. Randfontein. Krugersdorp. The names and the architecture—square, uniform, practical—told a story of Afrikanerdom: material prosperity and cultural aridity.

At Rustenburg, I turned north off the main road and a few miles later crossed the "border" into Bophuthatswana. Suddenly, the road was old and cracked. Shacks made of scrap wood, beaten metal, sheet plastic and corrugated iron stood at its edges. Children scrabbled in the dust. Africans with ridged faces and bright clothes sat on the shoulder, staring and laughing. I drove on until I passed the belching cones of a massive power station, and turned left onto a dirt track that led toward the gate of Pilanesberg National Park.

A guard sold me a ticket and asked where I was from. "England," he said. "That is good."

Here despite the dismantling of apartheid, it was easier for a white to be liked by Africans as an outsider. I smiled too and drove on to the tourist center. There was a new hotel, shops and a restaurant. I went inside and ordered breakfast.

Twenty years earlier, neither this lodge nor the park itself had existed. The two hundred square kilometers that were now park had been livestock grazing land like the surrounding country. The best blocks of land were owned by white farmers and the rest was settled by blacks. There were several villages, a few shops, a couple of schools, a church, a magistrate's court and telephone lines. The land was not entirely tame, but it was not very wild either. The only large wild animals were a few leopards and some shy antelopes living in the rocky hills in the center. Many other species had once grazed and hunted here, but they had disappeared long ago.

Then, a few years back, when Bophuthatswana became "independent," the new government decided to create a national park for the homeland. A massive pleasure complex —Sun City, southern Africa's miniature Las Vegas, complete with casinos, strip shows and golf courses—was already being constructed nearby. Pilanesberg park would make an added attraction. The plan was put into action with South African efficiency. The people and livestock in the park area were resettled. Buildings, telephone lines, cattle dips and fences were removed or buried. Imported species of trees, such as the blue gum and poplar, were located and destroyed. New water holes were created. A strong new fence—to keep people out and animals in—was constructed around the entire area.

When the park was ready, more than six thousand wild animals were trucked in. They had been purchased from parks and private game ranches all over South Africa. There were hippos, cheetahs, buffaloes, giraffes, zebras, elands, wildebeests, gemsboks, springboks, waterbucks, sables, roans, kudus, impalas and both species of African rhino—though no lions. And in 1979, five adolescent elephants were trucked up from Addo National Park in Natal and released into the Pilanesberg. These were the first elephants to set foot in this region for more than 150 years.

I finished breakfast and drove up to park headquarters to meet an Afrikaner warden named Kroos Herbst. It was Saturday and a lone car stood outside the building. I walked in and wandered down the corridor. Eventually, I saw an open door and poked my head into the room.

"Ach," Herbst said. "You must be the journalist."

He was a sturdy thick-necked man with silver hair. His small son was playing in the office and Herbst told him to run off for a while.

We talked about the unique status of the park, and I asked how the animals had settled down.

"It's quite a success story," he said. "The animals have done so well that we've been able to capture some of them and sell them. We've also done a bit of hunting. There are so many impala we've even had to cull them. The elephants have also just started breeding. We are very pleased. The first four calves have been born over the last year."

Herbst nodded seriously.

"Of course, it hasn't always been so good with the elephants," he said.

Of the first five adolescents from Addo, three had died. Another broke out of the park and began to walk south back to Addo. Seventy miles from Pilanesberg, the elephant ran into an elderly farmer and killed him. The elephant was spared, but he was returned to Addo.

"The last Addo elephant is still here," Herbst said. "But he's a bit crazy. He doesn't stay with the other elephants. He lives with a group of rhinos. He thinks he's a rhino. We've even seen him trying to mate a female rhino."

"What did the rhino think?"

"She didn't seem to mind."

After the Addo elephant escape, a stronger fence was built. Two years later, a second batch of elephants arrived. There were eighteen calves, all orphans from the Kruger cull. They were an unhappy bunch. They had suffered the same traumas as Daphne's calves but had not been given the same individual treatment and care as the Nairobi orphans. Three of them died in their *bomas*. The rest did not take well to being released. They milled aimlessly around the *bomas* for a while before wandering disconsolately off into the park.

"But then of course we had a bit of luck," Herbst said. "These American elephants arrived."

I left Herbst's office and drove off into the park. The land was hard and rocky. Various types of acacia trees—umbrella thorn, tamboti and buffalo thorn—stood in the gravelly soil. The tar and dirt roads were smooth and flat. There were not many cars on the road, but the ones I saw all seemed to be sedans driven by middle-aged couples.

I also saw a good number of animals: giraffes, zebras, sables and a family of hippos dozing in the waters of Mankwe Lake. Beyond the lake, I came across a white rhino bull sleeping on a patch of red soil. But there was no sign of elephants. Herbst had said I would be lucky to see any. The elephant herds were still wary of people and they spent most of their time away from the roads, in the hills in the center of the park.

So instead, as I drove, I thought about the American elephants. As it happened, Durga, Owalla and Tshombe had all been born in South Africa. They were Kruger orphans, from the cull. They had been captured in 1965 and shipped out to a dealer in the United States who had sold them to a circus couple named Morgan and Eloise, who trained lions, bears and elephants on a ranch in the Rocky Mountains.

Morgan and Eloise already had six Asian elephants. To help with the three African calves, they hired a keen young man named Randall Moore. Morgan and Eloise were determined to disprove the old adage that African elephants could not be trained for the circus, and Moore was soon teaching Tshombe, Durga and Owalla many performing tricks. They learned to stand on their back legs, to sit, to skip and to dance a plodding waltz. Eventually, the three elephants, half-grown by this time, went on to perform their tricks in circus rings throughout the western states of America.

After a while, Moore left the circus to go back to college. But then Eloise and Morgan were both killed by their Asian elephants. Eloise was speared and tossed across the ring in the middle of a show in Quebec, while Morgan was trampled on by one of the bulls. Moore was then asked to assume responsibility for the elephants. Prompted by an idea he had formed while on holiday in Kenya, he decided to return them to Africa.

Fourteen years after the three elephants had set sail from Africa, Moore loaded them onto a ship to make the return journey. After several weeks at sea, the ship docked in Mombasa. A few days later, after a short truck journey up to Tsavo, Durga, Owalla and Tshombe stepped out of their containers and back onto the soil of Africa. It did not take long for them to adapt to their new surroundings. They seemed instinctively to appreciate the African bush. They swam in pools, crossed rivers, happily ate the local vegetation, and carried Moore past a pride of wild lions.

They also met wild elephants on several occasions. Durga and Owalla grew particularly excited when a couple of wild bulls came over to investigate them. The circus elephants even came across the bones of wild elephants and spent several minutes turning them over, looking at them and sniffing them.

But then two disasters struck. First Tshombe caught salmonella and died. Then the Kenyan authorities—apparently because they objected to South African–born elephants staying in Kenya—decided that Durga and Owalla would have to leave. Moore was forced to reload the elephants onto a ship at Mombasa. Temporarily frustrated, he was still determined to find an African home for his two creatures. The ship docked for a few days at Durban and here Moore learned about Pilanesberg. Quick negotiations were made, but the South Africans insisted that the elephants would have to return to the United States for a year's quarantine before they could come into South Africa.

Twelve months and two more sea voyages later, Durga and Owalla were finally winched off the ship and into the country of their birth. The Sun City complex, which had funded the trip, gave them a glittering welcome: with dancing girls, a Tswana choir, banners and a feast. Up in Pilanesberg, Moore kept his elephants in the *boma* for a while. Then he began to introduce them to the park. He rode with them all day across the savannas and through the hills. As in Tsavo, they quickly took to the country. They were still given fodder, but they began to rely more and more on natural feed.

It was now several months since the fifteen surviving calves from Kruger had been released. They were living in four small groups. The circus elephants' first contact with the calves was through their dung, which the two cows sniffed excitedly. Then the cows spotted some of the calves from a distance and rumbled to them. But there was still no direct contact. After a while, Moore left Durga and Owalla to wander through the park on their own. One morning, he found them grazing beside three of the calves. Durga and Owalla were pulling down high branches for the youngsters to eat.

When Moore approached, the calves huddled behind Durga. She wrapped her trunk around one of them and gently rumbled.

The elephants' family instincts were clearly strong. From then on, the three calves and the two adults were inseparable. Slowly, the other calves began to join up with this new family group. After four months, the herd had swollen to eleven. By the end of a year, all the elephants—except the disturbed Addo bull—were living as a single herd. Durga and Owalla had even given up returning to the *boma* for fodder. A pair of circus elephants from America had been returned to the wild and become surrogate mothers to a herd of lonely orphans.

His job done, Moore left Pilanesberg, and it was another four years before he returned. It was not hard to track down the elephants. The calves were now half-grown and Durga and Owalla were the matriarchs. Moore approached his two old friends carefully, but when Owalla saw him, she walked up to him and brushed his hand with her trunk. Moore gave her an order. "Trunk up and foot," he said. The elephant lifted her front foot into the air and saluted with her trunk as she had learned to as a calf.

I had now finished my circuit through the park and was heading slowly back toward the gate when I saw a pile of fresh elephant dung in the road. I stopped and peered down at the flat dirt. There were clear elephant prints leading up a small sidetrack. I turned off and drove a hundred yards. Then I saw an elephant browsing above the road in the scrub.

I stopped and peered upward. The hillside was a mottled coppery color. The elephant was walking slowly along the gradient, pulling at the bushes as it went. The dry vegetation cracked gently in the still air.

The Kruger orphans were now in their early-to-mid teens. The first cows had given birth and the older bulls were beginning to break away from the herd. This must have been one of those young bulls. Although Herbst had said the elephants were still shy, this bull seemed unworried by my presence. He strolled slowly along, unfurling his trunk and swinging his haunches as if his kind had never been away from these hills.

Chapter Seven

ELEPHANT FARM

The ivory ban was not the end of the elephant's troubles. It rescued the species from the immediate threat of annihilation by the ivory poachers. But it left elephants still facing the same long-term problem as the rest of Africa's wildlife: the mounting human pressure on wild habitats.

When the first great wave of elephant poaching had ended in the early years of the twentieth century, Africa contained only 100 million people. Ample space remained for elephants. But by the time the ivory trade was banned in 1989, Africa's human population had reached 450 million. People were taking over more and more of the land. Some large parks where there had been heavy poaching, like Tsavo, or Selous in Tanzania, did have room for elephant expansion. But in other areas, farmers and cattle herders had moved onto land as the elephants had disappeared or diminished in number.

In Kenya, cultivated fields nudged at the edges of smaller parks like the Aberdare and the Masai Mara. Farmers were always complaining about elephants raiding their crops. And Kenya's newspapers were full of letters decrying the land given over to elephants and other wild animals. Why should elephants be allowed to eat farmers' food? What was the point of elephants anyway? Why maintain national parks? Why not simply hand these areas over to farmers? Wouldn't this be of greater benefit to a developing nation?

These were the questions that had lain behind the idea of sustainable utilization, the philosophy of making animals pay their way, in the first place. They were still pertinent. And contrary to popular opinion in the West, the ivory ban did not render them invalid. The ban was not a victory for the purely esthetic approach to wildlife. It was simply a recognition that one aspect of sustainable utilization, the ivory trade, was uncontrollable. Both African governments and the people who lived around wildlife areas still needed economic reasons to justify the continued existence of animals and wilderness areas. Sustainable utilization was still the answer.

The CITES vote had therefore left open the possibility of renewed ivory trading by countries which managed their elephants well. It also lent its approval to the controlled sport hunting of elephants, containing a clause that allowed trophy tusks to cross international borders. And, of course, it still encouraged the broad industry of tourism.

Many of the most innovative schemes for wildlife use, both hunting and tourism, were found in Zimbabwe. So from South Africa, I flew up to Harare.

The empty road ran through a monotonous landscape of mopane and acacia scrubland. Cattle warning signs stood on the burned shoulders. Occasionally, I saw cows beside the barbed-wire fences. The names on the gates completed the story: Heyman, Odendaal, J. P. Meyer. This was rich white cattle land.

But as I entered the region of Chiredzi, in the southeastern corner of Zimbabwe, the clues began to change. There were still animal warning signs beside the roads, but the silhouettes were now of antelopes rather than cattle. And on one stretch of road, the antelopes were replaced by outlines of another beast: one leg held aloft, big ears, trunk waving in the air like a flag.

I had an appointment with a farmer named Clive Stockil. I followed the directions and drove past a towering field of sugarcane up to the farm buildings. I found Clive standing outside his warehouse, swapping jokes with his workers in Shona. He came over and shook my hand. Then he called out a few suggestions to the men and we headed over to his office.

Clive looked like a Rhodesian cowboy. His head was large and bullish. Orange hair retreated in a widow's peak from his sunburned forehead. More orange hair began above his lip and spread out across his cheeks into muttonchops and sideburns. Only his eyes were a different color: a startling pale blue.

He dressed like a cowboy too. His short-sleeved shirt was unbuttoned to his chest, revealing more curly red hair. His ample stomach and stocky thighs bulged out from a tight pair of denim shorts. A knife hung from his belt. The belt buckle said COLT FIREARMS. His socks were pulled up and folded over just below the knees. He had a cowboy hat on his head.

But Clive was almost a stranger to his appearance. He had little of the siege mentality branded on white Rhodesian minds during the years of isolation and sanctions under Ian Smith's rule. He was gentle, thoughtful and ready to laugh at himself. When he talked, unlike others of his kind, the words came out as conversation and not oration.

Clive had the sensitivity of a man who had experienced misfortune, in the way that troubles sometimes force men from complacent cultures to reassess their worlds. He had certainly had his share of bad luck. He had been born with a withered arm. And some years back, his family ranch, tens of thousands of acres hacked out of the wilderness by his father, had been traded away in a deal that went bad. The loss had devastated the old man and Clive's inheritance was reduced to just a few hundred acres.

I looked out of the window. The farm sloped away. It was no longer rambling cattle country but dense arable fields, glimmering green and gold in the sun. Clive and his father had made the most of the little that was left, irrigating the soil and growing sugarcane and other crops.

"When did your father start the farm?" I asked.

"Just after the war," Clive said. "Dad was born up by Fort Victoria, halfway to Harare. But he wanted wild land, where he could get away from people and have room for his cattle. It didn't get much wilder than down here. In 1945, there were no white settlers at all. The African population was sparse. The land was practically untouched."

Old Mr. Stockil had gone to see the army major in charge of land grants and been allowed to choose ten thousand acres anywhere he liked on the lowveld. The only condition was that he work the land himself. He had cut his way down through the bush. There were no roads this far south, no towns and little water. Mr. Stockil had even had to bring in his own work force. But before long, he was raising cattle and had built the house we were sitting in. Clive was born here in 1951.

"The nearest white family was several hours' walk away,"

Clive said. "I grew up playing with the sons of the farm workers and the local hunting kids. I spoke Shona and Shangaan more than I spoke English. I ran around hunting and watching all the wild animals."

This part of the lowveld had been one of the best wildlife regions in Africa, crammed with elephant, rhino, buffalo, zebra, wildebeest, lion and leopard. But over the years, more and more white ranchers followed Mr. Stockil. Soon there were herds of cattle everywhere. And the wildlife was steadily driven out.

"The general ranch policy was to shoot wild animals on sight," Clive said. "I can remember on a neighbor's ranch just south of here they were especially keen on shooting zebra. They thought zebra were responsible for the grass shortage. In the 1950s, a government conservation officer came down here and told the farmers to get rid of the buffalo and zebra and impala and elephants. He said they couldn't expect to farm their land successfully in a zoo."

Not all the ranchers took this advice. Some, like Clive's father, enjoyed having wild animals on their land. They were forced to shoot lions to protect their cattle. And in the early days, they also had to shoot zebra and buffalo to feed their families and workers. But they tried to keep many of their wild animals. Driving across the land and seeing herds of impala or zebra grazing happily in the grass was part of the joy of this region of Africa, part of the reason for wanting to be here in the first place.

Clive inherited this fierce love of wildlife. And wandering through the bush as a child with the boys from the Shangaan hunting tribe, he came to see wild animals with a hunter's respect rather than a farmer's antagonism. As he grew older, Clive also began to see cattle as unhappy intruders.

"This is not rich, fertile land," Clive said. "The rainfall is poor and the vegetation is brittle. The soil is easily damaged. And cattle are the worst culprits."

He turned to the window and pointed out.

"There's a big ranch over there," he said. "Down by the river. Until sixteen or seventeen years ago, it was untouched land. Full of wildlife. Then they brought in cattle. The livestock stayed near the river at first and quickly overgrazed the land. Within ten years, the riverine strip was bare, ruined, a dust bowl. So they dug boreholes in the interior to bring up water for the livestock to drink, and moved the cattle there. Pretty soon this land also began to deteriorate."

He paused and licked his red mustache.

"In the meantime, the wildlife had moved back down to the river. And there the land quickly recovered."

"It actually recovered?"

"Yes. Nature has made its own balance. The land and the animals help each other. Elephants keep the woodland from growing too thick and at the same time disperse the acacia seeds. The bulk grazers like buffalo, zebra, wildebeest and hippo weed out the coarser grasses and allow finer, richer grass to come through. The wildlife and the vegetation have a symbiotic relationship. They thrive on each other. Cattle destroy the productivity of the land. But the wildlife nurture it."

As a result, Clive had come to believe that the conservation officer who had advised his parents' generation had been wrong. Ranchers like his father had allowed wild animals to graze alongside their cattle and had benefited from the resulting healthier vegetation. The best way to farm on this land, Clive decided, *was* in a zoo.

As time passed, Clive and a few other ranchers began to consider the next logical step. What about getting rid of the alien cattle altogether? What about farming only the wild animals? Clive had recently managed to buy 60,000 acres of cattle land. It was not in good shape. But Clive was planning to revive both this land and the family fortunes by moving out the cattle and returning the ranch to its original inhabitants, the wildlife.

"How do you switch to wildlife?" I said.

"Well, there's still some game left on these ranches," he said. "There's leopard and impala. And once you get rid of the cattle, other animals miraculously reappear. They seem to be able to smell the fresh grass and they jump in over the fences. They come in from the wilder ranches and the areas that are still wilderness. Then you can buy in other animals. You can buy anything in Zimbabwe. I can bring in giraffe, buffalo, elephant. Anything. In fact, some of us have already brought in a herd of black rhino."

Clive's new ranch lay in the middle of fifteen ranches, covering 850,000 acres. Clive had persuaded his new neighbors to join together and purchase thirty black rhinos. The ranchers had knocked down their internal fences and were building a strong outer fence around the entire area. The rhinos—almost 1 percent of Africa's entire black rhino population—could roam safely through the ranches among the cattle.

"Isn't all this rather expensive," I said.

"It's not cheap," Clive said. "But we expect to get the money back. We're not doing it out of the goodness of our hearts. I can't afford simply to buy land and turn it into a zoo. I'm turning to wildlife because I think I can make more profit from wild animals than cattle."

A cattle rancher did just one thing. He raised and sold his cattle. But a game rancher had wider options. He too could raise and sell his game meat. But he could also sell live animals to other ranches. He could bring in paying hunters. And he could build camps and lodges and start attracting tourists. Tourism was one of Africa's fastest-growing businesses.

Millions of Western and Japanese tourists had already been on first safaris in Africa. Many wanted to come back and experience something more special—like camping, walking and horseback riding on a private game ranch.

"It can work," Clive said. "I've only just got started. But old Ray Sparrow over on the Lonestar Ranch has already got rid of all his cattle. He now has only wildlife. He's doing well. You should go and see him."

I spent the night in a little motel on the banks of the Chiredzi River. Spiders the size of crabs scuttled across the walls. The only other guests were three Japanese engineers. I sat alone at one table in the dining room. They sat at another table, slurping soup and jabbering in a language that sounded like some kind of verbal sword fight.

Clive had arranged for me to visit Ray Sparrow the next afternoon. As the Lonestar Ranch lay near the entrance to the Gonarezhou Game Reserve, I decided to head over to the park in the morning and have a look around. The Gonarezhou had been closed for the past three years because of trouble with poaching and attacks on park rangers. Even now, it was officially open only to Zimbabweans. But at the gate I gave a Harare address and the guard waved me through with a smile.

It was a chill day, and I drove along a pale sandy track through a brittle white landscape. There were signs of elephants everywhere: piles of dung, footprints in the dust, torn tree limbs and branches, even raw patches on the baobabs where elephants had stripped the bark. But I saw none of the creatures themselves.

A couple of miles from the gate, I did find some old half-buried elephant bones. Another year and they would have disappeared completely. They were already peppered with beetle holes, and grass was growing over them like skin healing a wound. I tugged at the end of a splinter that stuck out of the grass, and half a jawbone came away in my hand.

The bone was large and full of teeth, each one the size of a child's fist. Elephants die naturally when the last of their seven sets of teeth wears down and they starve to death. These teeth were craggy and still fit for chewing. This elephant had not died of old age. I looked around. Nothing was moving. The only sound was the shrill rasp of cicadas, buzzing like the engines of a fleet of model airplanes.

I drove on. Crumbling and fading stone signs pointed down tracks that were rough and overgrown with neglect. For a few hundred yards, a set of lion tracks padded along in the sand. I stopped the car and squatted down beside a print. It was shaped like a clover with four dots of dew ahead of it. I bent over and sniffed. There was a faint smell of lion, a fuggy, slightly uriney tang.

There were no other cars in the park. The only animals I saw were impalas, scratching at the earth and peering nervously out from the bush with wide, wet brown eyes. As I approached one herd, they suddenly took off, racing one by one across the road in front of me. Some leaped low and flat against the ground, their legs stretched out ahead and behind like vaulting ballet dancers. Others pronked high in the air, drawing in their front legs like begging dogs.

The sun was the color of ice in the mint-blue sky when the track arrived at a bank over the Runde River. The sandy bed was a quarter of a mile wide. The only water lay in stagnant brown pools on the far side. I clambered down and walked out onto the sand. A little way from the bank, the vista opened out to the south. In the distance were the grand Chilogi cliffs. I stood and looked in awe at the bands of red and black rock rising dramatically out of the plains, like Arthur Conan Doyle's Lost World. Then I remembered the lion prints and walked back to the car.

I sat with my back to a wheel and ate my sandwiches. The Gonarezhou was one of the great elephant parks of Africa. But in recent years, it had suffered from heavy poaching. Between 1987 and 1989, 1,000 elephants and 150 black rhinos had been shot. This was the reason the park had been closed. The Zimbabwean authorities blamed Renamo, the brutal rebel movement from neighboring Mozambique, whose western border ran along the eastern edge of the park. But people I had talked to in Harare privately accused the Zimbabwean army of the slaughter. The killing had begun *after* the army sealed off the park. This was an old Rhodesian army trick. Cry enemy dangers. Seal off an area. Carry out your own atrocities in private. Then blame the enemy.

I thought about some of Clive's ideas. He argued that private ranches could provide the safest havens for wildlife. In the national parks, the animals depended on the honesty and integrity of badly paid park staff. But private game ranches farmed the animals for their own profit, so there would be greater incentive to protect the stock.

"It's like cattle," Clive had said. "No one has ever had to worry about conserving cattle in Africa because they have a value. It's the same in England. A farmer will get up in the night to help a cow through a birth. He loves his cows because they are his living. I want to give wildlife the same value."

In the distance, a pair of eagles wheeled and jousted above the cliffs. I climbed back into the car and wound slowly out of the park. A few miles from the gate, I found the entrance to the Lonestar Ranch. Ray Sparrow's driveway was four miles long. Bumping down the track, I saw a family of warthogs, a small herd of wildebeests and some kudus—more game than I'd seen in the Gonarezhou all day.

A farmhand directed me to the ranch shop. Ray Sparrow was serving behind the counter. This was the only shop within thirty miles, and a vast array of goods sat on the shelves: gob-stoppers, Surf, VapoRub, clothes, batteries, baby goods, sugar, tea, medicines.

"Ah, my good chap," Mr. Sparrow said. "You've come just at the right time. I'm closing up."

His voice was stentorian, his tone Victorian. He served the last customer and came through a flap in the counter. He looked like Dr. Livingstone. He had a strong-boned face and a bushy white beard. He was wearing a khaki shirt, a khaki jacket, khaki shorts, knee-length socks and a khaki topee, which he slung onto his head. He walked along twirling a fine wooden walking stick, with a pair of runty dogs at his heels.

"Come along," he said. "It'll be dark soon."

The dogs followed us into the car and we drove up a track and parked on a gravel terrace shaded by trees. We walked up steps carved into a rock and came out onto the top of an enormous dam wall. A circular stone building stood on the grass at the side. This was the dining room for a new lodge. The view from the tables was glorious. The lake wound away for miles. Steep woodland ran down to the edge. In the setting sun, the waters were the color of wine.

"That's the biggest private dam in southern Africa," Mr. Sparrow said proudly. "Three and a half billion gallons. Built the whole thing myself."

He knocked his walking stick against his foot.

"I've got seventy-three thousand acres here that was nothing but wilderness," Mr. Sparrow said. "I came down here after the war. My family have always liked the wild areas. My grandfather went up to Kenya. He had a farm in Eldoret."

One of the dogs began to yap.

"Quiet," he scolded. "He was killed by a train."

"Your grandfather?"

"Yes."

"How?"

"His Model T Ford got trapped on a railway line."

"But the trains only ran at ten miles per hour back then."

"Hummm," Mr. Sparrow said, twirling his stick. "He was very old at the time."

Ray Sparrow had come down to these parts a few months after Clive's father. His interest was cattle, but like old Mr. Stockil, he had refused to run the wildlife off his land.

"I was the butt of the other ranchers' jokes for keeping the animals," he said. "I stopped going to ranch meetings because there was so much anger. Some of those fellows believed that if a buffalo even walked through your herds all the cows would drop dead of foot-and-mouth disease. Of course, now we are realizing that it's the cattle that give foot-and-mouth to the wildlife, and not the other way round."

"When did you get rid of your cattle?" I asked.

"Five years ago. Sold all my stock. Now we're building these lodges round the ranch. This one here. A couple more. We also have some tented camps."

"What animals have you got on the ranch?"

"Ooh, everything. Rhino, giraffe, buffalo, kudu, cheetah, leopard, lion. I used to shoot lion. Never liked it, but I had to. Now I don't, I encourage them to come in. That gives me great pleasure, I can tell you. And then we've got thirty-nine jumbos."

"Elephants?"

"Oh, yes. When it's warm, you can stand up here and watch the jumbos and buffalo come down to drink."

I looked down at the lake. It was growing late. The sun had sunk behind the hills. The sky was a grainy grey. The lake was turning a deep inky black.

"I have to go back to the house now," Mr. Sparrow said. "I'm expected for supper with my son. You come back tomorrow and I'll tell you about the jumbos."

I d r o v e   u p   t o   Mr. Sparrow's house just as breakfast was finishing. The whole family was seated in a broad circle on the porch, but the first to greet me was Korty, the family's pet vulture. It was an ugly creature with a bald red and blue head. It flapped rapidly over, lunging out with its huge talons and vicious curved beak.

"Get out of here, Korty."

Ray Sparrow jumped up, brandishing a hippo-hide whip. The vulture backed off, its bald head turning even redder, annoyed that it had been denied a slice of Englishman.

Mr. Sparrow collected his hat and stick and we walked over to his Landcruiser. Most of the Lonestar Ranch was similar landscape to the Gonarezhou: dry, flat mopane and acacia woodland broken by occasional *kopjes*, rocky islands that rose above the trees. We followed a track to one of these *kopjes* and Mr. Sparrow clambered up the rocks. At seventy, he was quick and agile: the stick was just for show.

The rocks rose above the uppermost canopy of the trees. We stood at the summit and looked down upon the world. It was like being on a mountaintop above a solid green mass of cloud. The foliage stretched in every direction, broken only by the occasional peaks of other *kopjes*.

"How far does your land go?" I asked.

"See that line of shadows on the trees? In the distance. Beyond the mopane and the ironwood." Mr. Sparrow pointed toward the horizon. "Up to that, it's all mine. Those mountains beyond are in Mozambique. Just look at all those trees. Wonderful, aren't they. Mahogany, terminalia, brachystegia. Oh, there are dozens out here. And so many plants. I'm sure there are still plants in these regions that have yet to be identified."

His voice rose and fell like an orator.

"Sometimes up here," he said, "I can look out on the bush and imagine that it's still like it was. Without the roads and the people and the telephones and the airport."

I hummed my agreement. I was happy up here. The sun was growing stronger and the warmth was delicious.

"So tell me about your elephants," I said.

"The ellies," Mr. Sparrow said. "Well, they all came here as calves. Brought them here myself."

They were orphans from culls carried out in Zimbabwean parks like Hwange. The Sparrows took the calves in as a money-spinning sideline. They helped to capture them at the culls, brought them back to the Lonestar and arranged for them to be transported to buyers in Africa and outside.

"I can't say I ever liked those culls," he said. "The shooters would go in and blot the herd. We'd stand by and every time a calf came into sight, they'd ask if we wanted it. If we said yes, we went in and got it. If we said no, they'd shoot it. It was tragic, a yes or a no for a life."

"How did you catch them?"

"Ropes. By hand, with ropes. Then we put them in a truck and brought them back here. It was always traumatic for the ellies, so we put them in boxes together. Ellies are happier if they've got company. When they arrived, we made sure they had sound too, for company. Kept the radio on all the time. We had a lot of ellies, man. Eighty-seven was the most we ever had here at one time."

"And you just decided to keep a few?"

"No, not really. We didn't mean to keep any. We'd put them in *bomas* for the first few weeks and then let them roam around the ranch with keepers. But then a contract fell through, some fifteen or sixteen years ago. We were left with twenty-three calves. We couldn't get rid of them. After a while, they were too big to sell. So they just stayed. Now they're breeding. We've had fourteen calves to date."

While he was talking, a series of short, loud barks were rising up from the trees below.

"Impala rut," Mr. Sparrow said. "It's nearly over. It's been very rampant this year. I enjoy the rut, I do."

We listened for a moment. The barking grew fiercer.

"You can watch a ram gather half a dozen does," Mr. Sparrow resumed. "He puts them in a corner and fights off another ram. While he's doing it, another young buck comes in and services all the does. Oh, yes, that's a bit of fun."

"Do you still take in calves from culls?" I asked.

"We haven't done so for a few years. Last time we did, the herd came into the *bomas* and stole two of the calves."

"Your herd came in? The former orphans?"

"That's right. Elephants are very sentimental. Perhaps these ones remembered their own childhoods. They broke into the *bomas* and pulled the two calves away. We heard the fuss and got in there with lassos and tried to stop them. I got a rope around one calf's feet, but the other ellies made such a fuss that I was glad to let the rope go slack. In the end, we just watched the herd take away the two calves."

I tried to imagine the scene. Ray Sparrow tossing his lasso around. Elephants trumpeting and rumbling. Dust and chaos. The two calves running off like jailbreakers.

"What will you do with your elephants?" I asked eventually.

"Oh, just leave them. They're happy."

"You won't cull them?"

"Man, that's a long way away. We could support a hundred elephants on the ranch. It will be a good few years before we have that many. I won't be around then. But in the end, I suppose you have to watch out. Elephants are very destructive. They will happily pull down a hundred-year-old tree just to get at a few fronds at the top. They can turn forest into a Flanders field. If they are limited to one area, they just eat and eat."

"Have you ever shot an elephant?"

"Oh, yes, I have done. But I never liked it, I can tell you that. I never liked it. Felt like shooting a man to me. These days I don't like shooting anything. On this ranch, we try to catch and sell as many of our surplus animals as we can."

"Do you have hunting?"

"At the moment, yes. It helps to pay for building the lodges. But if we can make enough money from tourism without hunting, so much the better. I don't want killing. All over the world, everything is being pilfered, desecrated, ruined. The trees, the birds, the animals, the rocks."

He ran his hand across his white beard.

"I want to use lions to cull," he said. "They can keep the numbers of the game down. They are a lot crueler than us, but at least they are more natural."

We stayed a little longer, bathing in the sunshine. Then we picked our way down the rocks and drove farther along the tracks through the woodland. In a quiet, shady spot, Mr. Sparrow stopped.

"Come along, I have something to show you," he said. "We don't have a weapon if we meet a lion. But I suppose that's OK."

He strode ahead through the grass, his topee on his head, his stick twirling in his hand. He began to whistle. After a few bars, I realized it was "Auld Lang Syne."

"Have you ever been to England?" I asked.

"Just once, a few years ago. I was delivering an elephant. Once was enough, I can tell you. I stopped to ask a man directions and he just kept on walking. Didn't even say a word. Not a friendly folk over there."

He stopped in the lemon-colored grass in front of a tree. "Look at that. Brachystegia are wonderful. In September the leaves drop off and then new ones come through. They are every shade from pink to maroon. It's incredible, you just stop and gape. The trees around here. I love the trees."

We strolled up to a small outcrop of grey rock. A snake wiggled across just ahead of us. I stopped short, but the old man carried on, still whistling.

"Striped sand snake," he said after a moment. "Mildly venomous. Very fast. Don't worry. It's the mambas you have to watch out for. These hills have some of the biggest mambas in the world. They are very aggressive. Probably the most aggressive snakes in the world after the spitting cobra. We've lost a few men to mambas. If one bites you, that's tickets."

We were now walking round the base of the *kopje*. An overhang protected rounded walls of rock.

"Bushman paintings," Mr. Sparrow said, stopping and pointing at the rock with his stick.

I peered into the shadows. There were sketches all over the walls of the rock: figures in various shades of ocher against the yellow and grey stain of the stone.

I looked at a group of men running with bows in their hands. The drawing was simple but full of life. A few clear lines caught the movement of the men, their heavy curved thighs and calves at full stretch. Some of the animals were depicted in greater detail. There were three giraffes with hair on their necks and tiny horns on their heads. The necks were long and curved. They were running with characteristic ungainliness.

I moved further around the rock and found the portrait of a herd of ocher elephants. A mother was reaching out with her trunk to draw back a calf. A tuskless adolescent stood beside her. Another adult had huge tusks and ears sticking straight up out of its head. In the background were the faded images of more men, carrying spears and bows, hunting the elephants.

In Amboseli, some months earlier, I had looked out on a scene not so different from these rock paintings.

I had stopped my vehicle to watch a herd of elephants advance across a pan. They came forward in a typical line, plodding rhythmically over the dry earth, trunks swinging from side to side like marching men's arms. Halfway across, they suddenly halted. Their trunks leaped into the air. They huddled close together and tasted their surroundings. With their short-sighted eyes, the elephants could not see what they had smelled. But my eyes were better. I watched a pair of Masai—tall, slender men, carrying long spears—advancing toward the herd.

The elephants wavered for a few minutes, trying to locate the source of the scent. Then their thirst overcame them. They lowered their trunks and continued to trudge toward a small watering hole surrounded by high green reeds. The Masai carried on walking too, heading directly toward the elephants. Before long, their heavy fatty odor drifted over to the elephants again. The animals halted and sniffed the air. This time the scent was stronger. The elephants turned as one and pounded away, splashing white dust into the air.

The Masai watched the elephants flee. Then they changed their direction and began to walk toward the watering hole. A few minutes later, another pair of Masai came over the horizon, followed by a herd of cattle. This particular water hole lay on the edge of the park, and the Masai were allowed to bring their cattle down here to drink. I sat and watched for a while. The men were dressed in togalike red *shukas*.

Their slenderness and the ocher paint they wore made them look just like the stick men in the bush paintings. While the cattle were drinking, one of the men took off his clothes and began to pour water over his head, gleaming wetly in the bright sunlight.

I understood exactly what the Masai had done. They had frightened the elephants away so that they could bring in their cattle to drink first. It had been enough simply to let the elephants catch their scent. The elephants knew from other occasions that the Masai would attack them with spears if necessary. The bull I had watched Dr. Jonjo treat was a casualty of one of these attacks. The Masai did not usually spear the elephants for their ivory. They had little interest in the tusks. They used their spears out of resentment. The elephants had been given their land, their watering holes, their wealth—while they had received nothing in return.

Later I went to see a young Kenyan named Kadza Kangwane who was studying the relationship between the elephants and the Masai. Kadza was staying at Cynthia Moss's camp and we sat in the dining tent, surrounded by all the elephant jawbones that Cynthia and Joyce Poole had collected. Kadza had an owlish face, khaki skin and a plummy English accent.

"The Masai haven't always been so antagonistic toward the elephants and the other wildlife," she explained. "It's us who've alienated them by trying to segregate them."

Traditionally, the Masai had lived peacefully among the wildlife. The young men had hunted lions and rhinos from time to time as a rite of passage, but most animals had been left alone. The Masai were proud of all these wild creatures.

"The Masai say that as God created man and animals, we should be together," Kadza said. "Animals and the Masai share their world. Masai boys kill lions to become men, and when they die, their bodies are coated in fat and left out for the hyenas. The Masai even say that if a man sees an elephant birth and collects the placenta, he will become very rich."

The elephant also had a special place in Masai mythology. The first elephant was created out of a Masai woman. It was the woman's marriage day. Her husband's friends came to fetch her. Masai law said that a woman leaving her home to become married should not look back. But the bride-to-be could not resist one final glance. She turned around and was instantly transformed into an elephant.

"There's another thing," said Kadza. "If a Masai sees a human skull in the bush, he will put flowers in all the orifices. He will only do the same for one animal, the elephant. So you see, the Masai like and respect elephants. I don't think they take great pleasure in spearing them. They do it because they feel they have no alternative. They are trapped. These are their lands and they cannot use their old watering holes."

"So what can be done?" I asked.

"The Masai can be taken into account, that's what can be done," Kadza said, her eyes flaring at the injustice. "Amboseli makes loads of money from tourism. Some of the money should be shared with the Masai. A Masai has got to be able to look at an elephant and say, 'This animal is drinking water that my cattle want, but I don't mind because I'm going to get a hundred shillings a month compensation.' "

The cash and jobs Kenya made from tourism were quite enough reason for the government to maintain Amboseli and other parks as wildlife areas. But the authorities were beginning to accept what Kadza suggested: that it was not good enough simply to put the money into the national coffers. The local people must also benefit. As long as the Masai saw wild animals as a threat, they would continue to spear them. But if they benefited from the animals, then they would appreciate their value. They would stop killing them and might even start to look on them with a protective eye.

Under Richard Leakey, the Kenya Wildlife Service was beginning to put such benefit schemes into action. A percentage of park revenue was being directed to the local people. Schools and clinics were being built with "elephant" and "lion" money. Cash had also been set aside to sink boreholes and make new water holes for Masai cattle in the areas outside Amboseli.

In the Amboseli region, there was also a possible bonus to such a scheme. The core area of Amboseli had too many elephants. They were destroying the woodland and reducing natural diversity. In southern Africa, the solution would simply have been to cull the excess elephants. But the Kenyan authorities had never liked culling. And the Amboseli elephants were particularly precious. They had been studied for longer than any elephants in Africa. Each individual was known. Its history was recorded. It would have been a scientific tragedy to cull some of the park elephants.

There were also other objections, as Cynthia Moss had explained to me. "When you know what I know about elephants, you see culling as unethical," Cynthia had said. "In principle, I don't object to hunting. Elephants have always been hunted by men. That is natural. But shooting whole herds is above and beyond the realm of cruelty. The elephants that survive the culling are terrorized. I have no doubt that they know what's going on. They communicate to each other."

Cynthia was so horrified by the idea of culling that she suggested it would be better to kill all the Amboseli elephants at once rather than regularly cull to keep down the numbers.

"They could decide that Amboseli shouldn't hold more than fifty elephants," she said. "So they'd kill off six hundred and then cull a few more every five years. The elephants would be in a constant state of fear. That's not conservation. It's playing some kind of aberrant God."

The overpopulation of elephants in Amboseli was still a dilemma. But involving the Masai more in the wildlife could provide a solution. Boreholes were being sunk outside the park to provide water for cattle herds like the one I had seen. Some of these holes could also be used by the elephants. At present, the elephants were keeping to the park. But if they felt welcome, they would quickly spread out again to regions fringing the park. The Masai would have to share their water with elephants, and other animals. But if organized properly, the Masai could begin to attract tourists onto their communal land. Amboseli was already overcrowded with tourists. If tour guides could camp on Masai land outside the park and see elephants and other wildlife, they would be happy to pay fees directly to the Masai.

This would benefit everyone. It would relieve the park of excess tourists and excess elephants. It would provide more income for the Masai. And it would give the elephants a wider range. If it worked, it would be an example of imaginative sustainable utilization at its best.

One evening in Zimbabwe I went to dinner with the Stockils. Clive's wife was a fluttery, birdlike woman. She served dinner on trays in the living room. We ate while watching a spaghetti-eating contest on television. The contestants stuffed great twirls of the pasta into their mouths.

I talked about Amboseli. Clive found it difficult to accept the Kenyan dislike of culling. He loved wildlife too, but he had a hunter's attitude. Nature was cruel. Animals were killed all the time. It was part of the way of things in Africa.

"But isn't culling playing God?" I asked.

"Of course it is," Clive said. "But as soon as you put a fence or road onto the land, you are playing God. You are changing the habitat, altering nature. It would be best to leave nature untouched. But once you have touched the land, you have to take responsibility. Nature can't adapt quick enough, so you have to help her. When elephants roamed freely across the continent, they could move on before they destroyed one area. But once you have fenced them into a limited area, they have no choice but to eat until they've eaten every tree and blade of grass in sight. Then they and lots of other animals all die anyway."

"That's a very extreme example," I said. "Some biologists say that nature will balance itself out, even when it's been distorted. In somewhere like Kruger, the authorities are not giving nature a chance. They are just freezing nature in one part of its cycle. Maybe rises and falls in the numbers of elephants and other animals are natural. Maybe they are healthy."

Clive shrugged. It was a difficult question. The point was that no one really knew how best to manage a restricted area of wilderness. Even David Western's studies in Amboseli were only twenty years old. Cycles of woodland and plant might run for hundreds of years—though it was true that if an island park, a wilderness area surrounded by cultivated land, lost an entire species, it might never be able to recover those animals.

"You were talking about giving elephants a value to the Masai and extending the range of the Amboseli elephants," Clive said, changing the subject. "Well, I've been involved in a similar scheme here, using hunting. The revenues from hunting a few elephants every year have been directed to the local people. As a result, we've changed attitudes towards elephants."

This had begun a decade earlier with the Shangaan, the

hunting tribe Clive had run around with as a boy. The Shangaan lived mostly in South Africa and Mozambique. But a small group, a few thousand, had settled many years before in this part of Zimbabwe. Their lands had originally been the area that became the Gonarezhou. When the park was created, they had been forced to move out. They were very unhappy about this and had continued to hunt in the park. At independence, the Shangaan celebrated. They associated their removal from the park with the white men. They assumed that independence meant the returning of the land to the black man. They expected to get their homeland back. When this failed to happen, they grew angry. Protest poaching increased.

The warden of the Gonarezhou went to talk to the Shangaan. The way he saw it, the Shangaan were ruining a national resource. The way the Shangaan saw it, they had been driven out of their ancestral home and been forced to take up farming. And when an elephant from the park raided their crops, they weren't even allowed to shoot it. Both sides were furious. The warden was also unable to speak Shangaan. So Clive was called in to translate and mediate. He listened to both sides and came up with a solution.

"I suggested a compromise," he said. "The Gonarezhou was full of elephants. They kept overflowing onto the Shangaan land. What if the Shangaan were allowed to hunt a few of these elephants each year? Not the ones in the park, simply the ones that strayed out of the park. And better still, what if they were allowed to sell rights to these elephants to foreign sport hunters for large sums of money? I managed to get the Shangaan and the wildlife department in Harare to agree. The first year, I brought in two American clients and shot two elephants."

"And did it work?"

"Very well," Clive said. "In fact, I'm going over to Mahenya, the Shangaan area, at the weekend. Why don't you come and have a look?"

Mahenya District lay along the Mozambique border, an hour-and-a-half drive from Clive's house. We set off early in the morning, keeping the windows shut against the cold air. On the way, Clive told me more about the elephant-hunting scheme.

"The first year, I brought in two American hunting clients," he said. "I'll show you my camp later. It was a big occasion. I hired staff and trackers from the local villages, and when we shot the first elephant, there was a great celebration. The Shangaan love elephant meat, and it had been a long time since they had killed an elephant and felt safe enough to hang around and eat the whole thing."

We were now crossing the Sabi River. A dozen soldiers lounged at the checkpost and waved us through.

"Carry on," I said.

"OK. So the chief of the nearest village takes charge of the carcass," Clive said. "We remove the tusks for the client and then the villagers start in on the meat. If it's organized, the chief presides over everything and makes sure the elephant is cut up in an orderly fashion. The chunks of meat are spread out on the ground and each villager comes up to receive his share."

"But it's not always orderly?"

"No. Sometimes it gets out of hand. It boils up into a frenzy. You've got the carcass ringed by men, shoulder to shoulder, with their families lined up behind their backs. Each man's got an ax or a machete and is swinging into the carcass as quickly as he can and passing the meat back over his shoulder to his wife. The more he cuts, the more he gets."

"It sounds pretty dangerous," I said.

Clive laughed and licked his mustache.

"It is. I remember seeing one guy disappear into the interior of the elephant to get the heart and liver. Another guy was chopping away at the ribs and his ax went right through and hit the guy inside on the head."

I winced.

"Just imagine it," Clive continued. "People are losing fingers, getting sliced to bits. Another time, this guy got badly cut over the eye. Blood was streaming down and he couldn't see properly. He was losing cutting efficiency. So he ran off and grabbed a burning stick from a fire. He held the stick to his head, cauterized the wound and then went back to work."

We had arrived at the edge of Mahenya and we stopped at the first village for Clive to talk to some of the elders. They were skinny men with handsome bony faces, dressed in ragged Western clothes: torn pinstripe jackets, plastic shoes and Michael Jackson T-shirts. The conversation seemed agitated.

"What was all that about?" I asked when Clive climbed back in and we carried on.

"A land mine exploded further down the road yesterday. A truck was blown up, the driver was killed."

We drove on until we reached an army camp. There were trenches and sandbags everywhere. The Zimbabwean army was unofficially at war with the Renamo rebels across the border in Mozambique. We asked about the land mine—it was on the road we were planning to take—but the soldiers simply shrugged. It wasn't our business.

We drove on.

"Shouldn't we be looking out for signs of disturbed earth?" I said a little nervously.

Clive laughed.

"No point," he said. "If there's a mine, you wouldn't see it."

"That's a comfort."

A little later, we passed the truck lying on its side at the edge of the road. The area where the front right-hand wheel had hit the mine was a mangled mess of blood-covered metal. Clive drove straight past and we continued without mishap until we reached the main village in the heart of Mahenya. It was strung out over a wide area. Clive stopped to show me a grinding mill—a much treasured possession for the village farmers, who had previously had to pay extortionate rates to private mill owners.

"Paid for with twenty-five hundred pounds of hunting money," Clive said.

Next we passed a clinic—three smart blue buildings. The elephant-hunting scheme had also contributed to this. Finally, we came to the school. The news of our arrival had spread quickly, and within a few minutes the school principal arrived. He was a shy man with a smooth, shiny face. We shook hands and he proudly showed me around the school. It was a simple few blocks, but lovingly laid out. The trees and plants in the gardens were all neatly labeled. The classrooms had desks and chairs and blackboards, proud possessions in rural Africa. The schoolchildren's drawings and essays decorated the walls. In the principal's office hung handwritten adages like A HEALTHY BODY MAKES A HEALTHY MIND and LEADERSHIP REQUIRES HUMILITY. The hunting scheme had contributed £6,500 to this school.

We said goodbye to the principal and walked off through the village. The people all knew Clive and the men came up to greet him. Clive pointed out one grizzly, grumpy middle-aged man who had a finger missing.

"That's John Puzi," Clive whispered as we walked away. "I'll tell you about him later."

For now, Clive wanted to show me his hunting camp. We

had brought a picnic and we could eat it there. We walked back to the car and drove down through the trees. Several times we saw elephant dung on the pale sand.

"Lots of elephants," I said.

Clive nodded.

"There are," he said. "I flew a count last year. Saw two hundred and fifty on Mahenya land. Ten years ago, I doubt we'd have seen more than a dozen."

"So the scheme has been a success."

"Absolutely. As soon as we had shot the first elephant and the Shangaan had tasted the meat and seen the money, they realized that it was worth keeping elephants around. Before, if an elephant came within five hundred yards of their fields, they'd be out there chasing it away or shooting it. Now it's the village closest to where the hunters shoot the elephant that gets the meat. So everybody wants elephants on their land, at least during the hunting season."

We turned off the main track and cut down a narrow sandy path. Grass grew high between the two track lines.

"Over the past decade, the Shangaan elders have set aside more and more land for wildlife. Almost one hundred square miles of Shangaan communal land now belongs to the elephants. That includes the land we are on now. A few years ago this was full of cattle. We've extended the elephants' range."

"And reduced poaching?"

"Completely. Before we started the scheme in Mahenya, the park authorities did a sweep around this part of the Gonarezhou. Antipoaching units spent ten days and nights at this end of the park. They caught eighty-one poachers. After the scheme had started, they tried exactly the same thing. They found only ten people in the park."

The vehicle rocked around a bend and we pulled up in an open patch of sand shaded by the massive canopies of a couple of trees. The day had warmed up and this was a cool, peaceful spot in the heat. A guard stayed permanently at the camp, looking after the tents, chairs and tables. The guard began to set out the picnic, and I pushed through the grass on the far side of the camp and came out onto the bank above the Sabi River. On the far side was the Gonarezhou. The world buzzed with the sounds of insects and the distant rustle of the bush.

"So tell me about your friend with the missing finger," I said when we had sat down to eat.

"John Puzi," Clive said. "He lost his finger in a gun battle with rangers in the park."

"So he's a poacher."

"Was. He's retired. But Puzi was only ever a sidekick. His partner, the master elephant poacher, is Shadreck."

"Shadreck?"

"Shadreck is another Shangaan," Clive said. "He was born in Mozambique around 1940 and moved over the border to live in Mahenya during the 1960s. He soon acquired a gun and began to hunt elephants in the Gonarezhou. In his time, he claims to have killed over a hundred elephants in the park."

Efforts to catch him proved fruitless. To the villagers, he was a hero of sorts—brave enough to take from the white man the animals that rightfully belonged to the Shangaan. They protected Shadreck when he was at home. And when he was in the bush, he always seemed to outsmart the rangers.

"There was a ranger here in the 1970s called Charlie Mackie," Clive said. "Once, Charlie was tracking Shadreck and he stopped for a call of nature. Charlie was squatting in the bush when Shadreck suddenly appeared, catching Charlie with his pants down. Shadreck pointed his gun at him and said, 'Don't move, my friend.' Then he vanished into the grass."

Clive laughed, his red face even redder with amusement.

"During the civil war in this country, the warden here was a man named Ron Thompson," Clive continued. "He was asked by the army to set up an informer base, to try to find out what was happening with the rebel units—Mugabe's and Nkomo's lot—over the border in Mozambique. Shadreck was always moving back and forth across the border. He knew everything that was going on. Thompson had this bright idea."

"To use him as an informer?"

"Right. Thompson sent a message to Shadreck offering him an amnesty in return for some informing. Shadreck replied with a message saying he needed proof that he could trust the warden. Shadreck suggested he should be allowed to shoot an elephant in the park and take away the tusks."

"And the warden agreed?" I could already see where the story was going.

"Yup. Shadreck met Thompson in the park. They found an elephant and Shadreck shot it. He took the tusks and promised to send Thompson information."

"And they never heard from him again?"

Clive nodded through his laughter.

Shadreck evaded all attempts to catch him until the hunting scheme began. Then Clive asked the Shangaan elders if they would help to snare Shadreck. Things had suddenly changed. The poacher was now a threat to the Shangaan's own livelihood. When Shadreck next appeared in Mahenya, the elders passed a message through Clive to the park authorities. The notorious outlaw was picked up. It was almost too easy.

"Shadreck was proud of his achievements," Clive said. "He considered himself a master elephant killer. He said, 'Put a weapon in my hands and I'll track down and kill any elephant anywhere. I'll shoot it at night, in the day.' He took us round the Gonarezhou and showed us carcasses of elephants he'd killed."

Shadreck was convicted of poaching and given a five-year sentence. He served a little over two years and was released. For a while, he disappeared into Mozambique. The way Clive had heard it, he was first hired by a Mozambican ivory dealer to shoot elephants in the Gorongosa National Park. The businessman provided Shadreck with a gun and gave him £100 for a large tusk. Shadreck shot fifty-two bulls in three weeks.

Then Shadreck was hired by the government army to shoot game for them for food. They gave him a gun and he went out to hunt, keeping the ivory for himself and handing over meat to the soldiers. Then the Renamo rebels got hold of him. He was feeding the enemy, so they threatened to kill him. Shadreck wriggled out of the situation by offering to hunt for Renamo instead, using the government gun.

"For a while, he was hunting for both sides," Clive said. "At the same time, he was marketing ivory and rhino horn through Zimbabwe. Eventually, the army found out what he was doing. They tracked him down to a village which they anyway suspected of supporting the rebels. One night, they raided the village. Thirty-nine people were massacred."

Clive poured some coffee from the flask.

"Everyone thought Shadreck was finally dead. Then, all of a sudden, he creeps out of the woodwork. Somehow he survived. But now he's completely blown his cover in Mozambique. Everyone is out to get him. So he comes back to Zimbabwe. He was all right over here, he'd served his sentence. I met him and tried to persuade him to get a job with the national parks and bury his past. He'd have been very useful. He said he was very keen. He promised to come and see me. Then he disappeared."

A few months later, one of the Shangaan elders sent a message to Clive. Shadreck was back to his old ways. The park authorities set up a trap again and Shadreck was caught once more with rhino horn and ivory. This should have been

the end of Shadreck. By this time, the Zimbabwean government had introduced a minimum fifteen-year prison sentence
for trading rhino horn. Shadreck had been caught red-
handed. But Shadreck was not a poor man. And he was not
without influence: one of his cousins was married to the head
of the Zimbabwean central bank. Shadreck spent a year in
remand in Harare. He was never tried, and one day he appeared back in Mahenya, a free man.

"Two months ago our scouts were patrolling inside the
rhino conservancy," Clive said. "On our ranches. And
they see two guys sitting under a tree eating sugarcane. They
went up to talk to them and the two guys took off. They
were in such a hurry they left their backpacks under the tree,
and inside the backpacks were two shiny new AK-47s. A
week later, one of the men was tracked down. He was also
a Mozambican Shangaan. He said his companion's name was
Shadreck. But Shadreck was nowhere to be found. The police
still haven't caught him."

Clive grinned delightedly. He would not have been happy
if Shadreck had killed any of his rhinos. But he could not
help but admire Shadreck's skill, his nerve, his cheek.

"All right, so Shadreck is still around," Clive said. "But
life is very difficult for him. He can't go back to Mahenya.
He's always on the run. He's been in jail twice. He's smart,
but I don't think he's taken a single elephant in Zimbabwe
for years. It's the hunting scheme that's done that."

The following afternoon, I drove out to Se-
nuka, Clive's new ranch. This had never been a family ranch
like the Lonestar. There was one small house near the gate,
for the manager. It was empty now. I looked around. There
was no sign of Clive. So I sat on the porch to wait, reading
old English magazines.

The last of the cattle were still on the ranch. They were moving through the bush not far away. I could hear their continual lowing and mewing and groaning. After a while, the cattle appeared: low-slung, ugly creatures, shuffling along in mushrooms of dust lit up by the afternoon sun.

Clive arrived shortly afterward. He had been driving around the ranch and had seen three black rhinos browsing on the thorns.

"Pity you missed it," Clive said. He was full of pride. "Climb in, I want to go over to the lodge."

I jumped in. There had been cattle here for eighteen years, and the land seemed barren and dusty. There were low barbed-wire fences everywhere and huge patches of bare soil.

The lodge was being built on a rocky hillside: a simple affair of a few permanent tents, and a stone dining room. Clive beckoned me up onto some boulders. I clambered after him. There was a natural hole at the top of the *kopje*, as though someone had plucked out one of the large rocks. Clive had already begun to cement up the holes and was going to make this into a bathing pool.

We stood on the top and looked out on the ranch.

"I've already got bookings for bird safaris," Clive said. "As soon as I get rid of the cattle, I can start bringing more animals in. We've already got the rhinos, and other animals have begun to come in from the other ranches and outside. They can smell the fresh grass. Lots of eland have already turned up."

We climbed down and drove farther into the ranch.

"All this fencing is coming down in the next couple of weeks," Clive said. "Then there'll be no fencing at all, thank God. Just look at this place. Twenty years ago it was virgin bush. Now it's been well and truly stuffed up by the cattle."

Clive stopped the Jeep and we climbed out. We were standing over a broad, deep gully. The soil at the edges was crumbling. There was no grass to bind the earth. The end of the gully was like a deep handprint, clawing into the land.

"This place is on the verge of being turned into a desert," Clive said. "The whole ranch has been overgrazed. There is nothing to keep the topsoil in place, so when it rains, the water runs down even the slightest slopes in great sheets. It digs into the ground and creates these deep gullies. The soil all ends up in the Indian Ocean. Then the next time it rains, the gullies get deeper and wider. Pretty soon, ten percent of your ranch is destroyed. Then twenty percent. Then a third."

The gully beneath us was half-full of old bits of wood. Clive had been collecting the fence posts and using them to fill in the hole.

"It is still reversible, but I'm going to have to fill in every one of these holes," he said. "You've got to ensure you have a good soil base. That's the first thing. Without good soil, you can't grow anything—grass, trees, cattle, even rats."

"How long will it take to recover?"

"Several years. You've got to have several seasons for the full mix of grasses to come back. At the moment, this land can support some animals but not all. If I brought in sable, it would be useless. They couldn't survive."

"You are going to bring in animals?"

"Yes, sure. Some are here, others will come, and others I'll have to buy in."

The animals varied in price. Sable were up to £3,000 each. Giraffe were a little more and elephant calves closer to £4,000.

"Are you going to get elephants?" I asked.

"Eventually, I'd like to. The last elephants were shot on this ranch in 1957—two or three hundred of them—but their bones are still here. So in a way, elephants have not completely left these lands. If I reintroduce some, they'll find the bones. They'll still have a sense of their own species' existence here."

The sun was hanging just above the horizon now. It was huge and a deep, dirty orange.

"This place is an ecological disaster," Clive said. "It's practically ruined. But I'm determined to reverse that process, to encourage the growth of all the indigenous plants and the return of all the indigenous animals. It's the biggest challenge of my life."

He smiled happily and licked his mustache.

Chapter Eight

KING LEOPOLD'S
DREAM

O f all the grandiose im-
perial ventures of the nineteenth century—Cecil Rhodes in
southern Africa, James Brooke in Sarawak, Queen Victoria's
India—the most extraordinary was probably that of King
Leopold II of Belgium.

As a young prince, Leopold had traveled widely in the
tropics. He had visited Egypt and the Near East. Then he
had journeyed to China, India and Ceylon. Leopold was particularly impressed by the grandeur of British rule in India.
And when he returned to ascend the Belgian throne in 1865,
he had decided what he wanted: a tropical empire. But Belgium was not as ambitious as its king. The Belgian government's main concern was to settle its internal dispute between
Flemings and Walloons. So after a few frustrating years, Leopold decided to go it alone. He had his own money. He
would create his own empire.

For a while, Leopold considered New Guinea. But these
were the great years of African exploration. In 1858, John

Hanning Speke discovered Lake Victoria. In 1864, Sir Samuel White Baker found Lake Albert. In 1867, Dr. David Livingstone began his exploration of the Congo. And in 1871, Livingstone was found at Ujiji by Henry Morton Stanley. By the mid-1870s, Leopold had settled his imperial dreams on Africa, and in particular the Congo basin.

In 1878, Leopold arranged a meeting with Stanley. The journalist-turned-explorer had just returned from a second long journey across Africa. He too was obsessed with the Congo. But he had not been able to interest Britain in his ideas. He was therefore ripe for Leopold's money and flattery. In 1879, Stanley agreed to return to the Congo as Leopold's agent. For the next five years, Stanley traveled up and down the Congo, building trade stations, signing treaties with more than four hundred African chiefs and generally establishing Leopold's interest in the region. When the Berlin Conference was held in 1884 and 1885, Africa was sliced up between six European overlords. Five were nations: Britain, France, Germany, Portugal and Italy. The sixth, and possessor of the largest slice of all, the million square miles of the Congo Free State, seventy-five times the size of Belgium, was King Leopold.

Leopold was a man of his time. He had energy, vision, wit and courage. But he was also blinkered, greedy and brutal. He had great plans for his new fiefdom. He would bring to the Congo the three C's: Christianity, Civilization and Commerce. In return, the Congo would provide him with glory and wealth. But these plans were fraught with difficulties. Early on, Leopold ran out of money. At first he mortgaged the liveries of his palace servants. Then he was forced to sell off trade concessions to huge tracts of the Congo Free State to private businessmen.

These concessions, rich in rubber, gold and ivory, became virtual fiefdoms. They had no proper policing and no law other than the law of profit. The concession owners were free to run their lands as they liked. And many ran them with appalling brutality. Entire villages and regions were virtually enslaved. Tens of thousands of Africans were murdered or mutilated. Eventually, the stories from the Congo proved too much. The Belgian government became embarrassed and in 1908 it finally felt forced to take over the running of the Congo Free State from Leopold.

The king was heartbroken and he died less than two months later. But not all King Leopold's dreams died with him. And more than eighty years after his death, one of these dreams—a dream of elephants—was still surviving in a corner of what was now Zaire, at a place called Garamba National Park.

The pilot was a stocky American from somewhere wide and flat and Middle American, like Kansas or Nebraska. He had a thick neck, blue veins on his nose and a bushy mustache. A line of sweat had darkened his shirt against his spine. He was also wearing a crash helmet. Now he began to say a prayer.

"Dear Lord," he said loudly, for all our benefit, "please guide our takeoff and bring us safely through our journey. We put our faith in you. Amen."

I was sitting in the third row of the Cessna. I peered forward at the pilot, but all I could see was the edge of his mustache and spidery wrinkles spreading out from his eyes beneath the crash helmet. I wanted to reach forward and tap him on the shoulder. "No," I wanted to say. "It's your job. You're the pilot. You bring us safely through the journey. And while we're at it, what about crash helmets for the rest of us?"

But I said nothing. These American missionaries might be

a bit odd, but they ran the only flights from Nairobi into eastern Zaire, and the way by road was long and slow and often closed. So I looked out of the window in silence while the plane drifted into the air and turned eastward away from Nairobi. The sounds of the engine became a gentle vibrating hum and the continent passed slowly by below: the Rift Valley, the patchwork fields of western Kenya, the huge sea of Lake Victoria, western Uganda, and finally the glistening waters of Lake Mobutu Sese Seko, once Lake Albert.

The Zaire border lay halfway across the lake. From the western shoreline, grooved green hills rose sharply up toward the belly of the plane. Then the hills flattened into a high plateau, and out of the land rose the unimpressive sandy streets and dull iron roofs of Bunia. Two Zairian officials came out to meet the plane. One was a tall, stooped man with long arms and red eyes. The other was a dwarf, who greeted me with a ringing laugh. The tall man took my arm and asked what present I had to give him. The dwarf carried my bags, and when I had safely negotiated customs and passport control, I gave him a cheap ball-point pen. He grinned happily and put the pen in his shirt pocket.

I had two days to wait in Bunia before catching another flight on my way north to Garamba National Park. The only place to stay was the mission guesthouse and I rode into town with another guest. His name was Alistair Simpson. He was short and bearded. He looked like a gremlin and had the manner of a door-to-door brush salesman.

"Are you saved?" he quizzed me.

"I don't think so," I said.

"I've just come from Kinshasa," he said. "I preached in front of tens of thousands of people. More than three thousand were brought to Christ."

"How do you know?"

"The Lord's will is clear."

"Oh."

When we reached the guesthouse, the evangelist and I were told we would be sharing a room. Alistair's eyes glittered evilly.

"You'll be saved by morning," he promised.

Everyone ate lunch together. The table was covered in a plastic red-checked cloth. Our hosts were an Irish couple named Eric and Anne. They could have been brother and sister. Both were chubby, curly-haired, and had round, red, blotchy faces. They prayed and then served up meatloaf, mashed potatoes, vegetables and bread. Alistair spooned huge portions onto his plate and shoveled the food unceremoniously into his mouth.

"The Lord provides," he said through the meatloaf.

Eric and Anne had been in this part of Zaire for fifteen years. Before Bunia, they had spent a decade deep in the forest, running a mission school. They didn't want to sound ungrateful, they said. The mission guesthouse was a nice place. But they missed the people and bush and wildlife.

"You'd have loved it out there," Eric said in his high, chirpy voice. "We used to see elephants all the time."

"But not round here?"

"You don't see many in this area. There are too many truck drivers. They all carry guns to feed themselves along the way. They shoot chimps, rats, monkeys, elephant, anything they can get their hands on. They'll eat anything."

"The Lord provides," Alistair muttered again. I watched him take another huge slab of meatloaf.

"Monkey fingers and toes are a great speciality," Eric said. "And cats and dogs." He looked around and whispered. "I'm surprised the pet cats and dogs have survived here."

In the afternoon, Alistair sat on the porch reading the Bible and I went out to have a wander around Bunia. This was where old Mr. Johnson, the missionary from Bujumbura, had first settled in the 1940s. It was a sleepy, uncrowded town. The streets were wide and dusty. Little seemed to be happening. The odd fruit salesman dozed over a pile of dusty oranges. Soldiers lazed in the shade. Occasionally, a truck or Jeep swayed past, avoiding the potholes and the little islands of Tarmac left over from times of smoother roads.

Eric had suggested I visit a missionary named Herb Cook. I found his house down a quiet lane. It was a typical colonial affair, with a porch and thick, cool cement walls. Once it would have belonged to a Belgian *colon* or a Portuguese trader. Now it was inhabited by American missionaries.

"Come on in," said Cook.

He was a thicker-featured George Bush. His wife looked like a housewife from a 1950s vacuum-cleaner advertisement. They couldn't have been more American. But Herb had never lived in the United States. He had been born here in the Congo, almost half a century back, and had lived here all his life.

"Back then, this part of Africa was somewhere," he said. "My folks arrived in 1938. They settled in Aba, two hundred miles north of here. There was a Cadillac showroom in Bunia and a Chevy showroom in Aba. You could walk in off the street and buy a new American car. And if they didn't have the one you wanted, it would be sent up the river from Kinshasa. You'd have it in a couple of weeks."

The Belgian government had come late and reluctantly to colonialism. But once it had picked up King Leopold's pieces, it had taken its duties seriously. This part of the Congo had been an important crossroads. One arm of the Nile ran into Lake Albert. Next-door Uganda had been a prosperous trading colony. Traffic had flowed up the Congo River from Kinshasa. The Belgians had built roads and communication lines. Bunia and Aba had been thriving cosmopolitan towns, populated by Belgians, Greeks, Portuguese, Lebanese and

Indians, as well as Africans. The shops had been full of French cheeses, Greek olives, Italian salamis and German dessert wines.

"You wouldn't believe it now," Herb said. "But the streets in Aba and Bunia were paved. The road to the mission station where I lived in Aba was lined with trees and flowers. The town was beautiful. There was a public swimming pool and folks from Adi, fifty miles away, would drive in on Saturday mornings to spend the day by the pool. In the evening, they'd drive home. Now Aba to Adi is a twelve-hour drive."

The civil war that followed independence in 1960 had driven away most of the Belgians and other foreigners. The new government of Zaire was based in Kinshasa. It might as well have been on another planet. Kinshasa was twelve hundred miles away in West Africa. In the early chaos after independence, the country's communication network collapsed. Roads were reclaimed by the forests and swamps. Other than by air—and there were no commercial flights—the fastest way of traveling between the east and the west was along the Zaire River. Steamships ran from Kinshasa to Kisangani in only ten days. But Kisangani was four hundred miles—well over a week's journey—from Bunia.

The government paid little attention to the east. The telephone system quickly gave out. Power stations stopped working. Trade dried up. Shops closed. Banks were abandoned. Money for schoolteachers failed to arrive. Nor could eastern Zaire rely on its East African neighbors. To the north was southern Sudan and to the west Uganda, both crumbling under their own civil chaos. Cut off, ignored, without finance, eastern Zaire was like Britain after the Romans—tumbling back into a dark age.

But the infrastructure of the region had not completely collapsed. The Kinshasa government's failure to take over from the colonial rulers had left a void, and into this void had stepped the missionaries. There were now several thousand missionaries, mostly American, spread out across eastern Zaire: in Bunia, Aba, Nyankunde, Ipulu, Baku, Watsa, Isiro and dozens of other towns and settlements. With funds from the American Bible Belt, the missionaries had set up a sort of parallel administration. They ran the best clinics and the only modern hospital, with three hundred beds, a dozen foreign doctors and a first-class operating theater. They trained teachers and set up schools. They had the only reliable radio communication system. Their dozen planes served as a local transport network, carrying passengers and emergency medical cases. These planes were also the only reliable postal service in the region. And in return, all the Zairians had to do was say they believed in the Lord.

That night, after supper, Alistair was waiting for me when I went to bed.

"Who made all this?" he asked. "Who made the beauty of Africa?"

"Who made God?" I replied.

"Ha! The lost soul."

An hour later, with Alistair still on the hard sell, I gave in. "All right," I agreed. "I'm saved."

Alistair grunted in delight. I lay awake wondering whether the conversion of the Zairians was any more sincere than mine. But Alistair was unworried. He was soon soundly asleep, the sheets tucked under his chin, snoring like a pig.

On his travels around India and Ceylon, before becoming king of Belgium, Leopold had been greatly impressed by trained elephants. Years later, when he began to turn his dreams of empire into reality, the king remembered these beasts. With their sturdy limbs, powerful trunks and quick minds, they were just the thing to help carve out a working African colony.

In 1878, the year he hired Stanley, Leopold also signed up another Englishman. Frederick Carter was the kind of man upon whom the British Empire was built. He had been an officer in the Indian army and a consul in Baghdad. He was honest, brave and not overly intelligent. A sketch of him in a Belgian memoir from the 1880s, *Les Belges dans L'Afrique Centrale*, showed a steadfast face with deep-set eyes, hair parted in the middle and a jowly beard.

Leopold's idea was initially to bring a few Indian elephants to Central Africa. He would then see how these elephants fared. If they did well, more could be recruited. Eventually, they might be used to help train up a native African herd. Carter was therefore dispatched to India to procure the elephants. A year later, on June 1, 1879, he arrived off the coast of East Africa on board the ship *Chinsura*. With him were thirteen Indian mahouts and four mature elephants: two bulls named Sundergrund and Naderbux, and two females, Sosankali and Pulmulla.

The elephants were winched ashore in front of a huge crowd. The mahouts were dressed in their finest bright silks, adorned with knives and jewels. Carter, also in silk and turban, was dubbed the "white sheik." "Not in the memory of the Negro had one dreamed of anything so extraordinary," *Les Belges dans L'Afrique Centrale* recorded. "They watched the elephants lift one leg in front of another, dance, and move and stop at the slightest sign from their conductors. All the people stared at this unbelievable spectacle and for years to come they would speak of these prodigious elephants."

This was the effect for which Leopold had hoped. His elephants would be not merely pack animals but the giant mounts of the new imperial masters. For the next four weeks, Carter set about organizing his party. On July 2, 1879, the caravan departed, to the applause of the crowd, the noise of drums and tambourines and the firing of guns. As well as his four elephants and thirteen mahouts, Carter had hired ten Zanzibari elephant hands, eight guards with guns, four personal servants and seventy-one porters.

The first leg of the expedition proceeded without trouble. The elephants seemed to adapt easily to the mountains, the thick bush and the tsetse fly. In scarcely more than a month, the party covered two hundred miles and arrived at the settlement of Mwapwa. Here Carter ordered a halt for several days. But before the party could set off again, disaster struck. Sundergrund succumbed to an attack of apoplexy and died.

The Indian mahouts had disliked Africa from the first day. Their unhappiness now intensified. They complained about the food, the drink, the land and the people. They told Carter they wanted to return to the coast and catch the next ship back to India. Carter insisted they continue. But when a few days later Naderbux also fell ill, apparently with rheumatic fever, the mahouts refused to tend him.

"He lay on the floor, dead in appearance but still breathing, his mouth open, his skin cold, his eyes dull," recorded *Les Belges*. "His breath was like the wind from a forge. Carter lay down by his side to study his heartbeat. It was like watching a mechanic at work. The poor beast was in pain, so Carter shot him dead. He went back to camp as if he had committed a crime."

Down to two elephants, Carter pushed on. The vegetation was now dense, harsh scrub and the thorns and branches continually tore at the human and animal members of the party. Fifty men preceded the elephants, carving out the route through the bush. For fifteen days, the party saw no sign of any other humans. On October 28, they finally arrived at the town of Tabora, five hundred miles from the coast and two-thirds of the way to Lake Tanganyika, their goal.

From Tabora, the march was even slower and more laborious. The mahouts were little help, and halfway to the lake, Sosankali fell ill. Carter removed her baggage and for a while she recovered. Then the rains came and the journey continued through cold, marshy country. On December 14, the party reached a hill above Lake Tanganyika. Below them lay the town of Karema. Here, within sight of success, Sosankali lay down and died. The following day, Carter rode into town on top of Pulmulla, the matriarch and the last of his Indian elephants.

Carter was undaunted. "The elephant is definitely the animal you need in Africa," he wrote in a letter to a friend named Captain Foot. "I sincerely hope that someone will take charge of organising savage elephants to domesticate and use. I would be happy to do this myself so long as I am sent some already trained elephants and two men well trained in training them. I am returning to Zanzibar to await new orders. I have intentions of trying a new way back."

Carter and the mahouts remained at Karema for several weeks. They built Pulmulla a shelter and arranged for six of the African elephant hands to remain with her. The elephant was in good health when they finally left. But she did not remain well for long. Pining for her Indian mahouts, she soon sickened and eventually she died of "a broken heart."

Unaware of this final tragedy, Carter was well on his way back to the coast. On June 24, 1880, he arrived at a village named Pimboué. His party of porters, mahouts and a few soldiers set up camp just outside the village. That night, by chance, Pimboué was raided. The attackers were a tribe known as the Rougas Rougas. They were heavily armed with guns, sold to them by ivory traders. In the night, they won a brutal victory against the villagers. And in the morning, drunk on alcohol and blood, they turned on the elephant party.

Carter and his men had no chance against the hundreds of armed Rougas Rougas. Some tried to flee and were cut down. Others made their stand with Carter. Only one man escaped, Carter's retainer, a Swahili Arab named Mohammed. He made it back to the coast with Carter's notebooks and the story of Carter's end. The bravest of the men had gathered around their leader and fought off the Rougas Rougas. But one by one they had fallen wounded or dead. Carter was the last man to fall.

"It was a terrible scene, like the combat of ancient heroes," *Les Belges* recorded. "His wounds bleeding, fatally injured, lying on the ground, this man took up his gun. Seventeen times he fired and seventeen men fell to the ground. When his rifle was empty, he defended himself with his revolver. But at last, several shots hit him and his head fell back and his eyes closed forever. Like ferocious beasts, the Rougas Rougas fell upon his corpse and cruelly mutilated it."

Carter's death brought Leopold's elephant scheme to a halt. For the next two decades, the king was busy dealing with the financial and administrative problems of the Congo Free State. But Leopold had not forgotten about elephants. And when he heard about a couple of Belgian missionaries who had successfully tamed and raised an orphaned elephant calf, he decided to start again. But this time there was no need for Indian elephants. African elephants could be captured and trained from scratch.

At Bunia airstrip, the customs-official dwarf grinned and lent me the pen I had given him. I filled in the departure slip and he pocketed the pen again. In the aircraft, the pilot said a prayer and we took off into the wind, skimming northward beneath the low clouds, a couple of hundred feet above the earth.

Once we had left Bunia behind, the land was virtually empty of people. Occasional clusters of brown huts blended into the rocks, bushes and grassy fields. When we flew over, adults looked up and children ran around waving. Then the pale colors of the rocky plains abruptly ended and we were flying above dense forest. This was the northeastern corner of the Central African rain forest. A thousand miles to the west, through virtually unbroken vegetation, was Bayanga.

For a while, we flew over what looked like the heads of a million broccoli stems. But this was only a tiny corner of the forest, and after less than an hour, the tree line ended as suddenly as it had begun. Now the landscape was violent and outlandish. Huge outcrops of rock rose like great stone limbs out of the earth. I saw knees, elbows, rumps and skulls—like a fossilized man a mile long, half-buried in the ground. It felt as though we were moving farther and farther away from anything familiar.

But eventually, a few dirt tracks began to cut through the land. The rocks turned to fields. Huts appeared. And then a grassy airstrip spread out ahead of us and we landed on the outskirts of Aba. Dark puffing rain clouds were whipping toward us from the south and the pilot was eager to be gone. He swapped mail sacks with a couple of Italian missionaries who had come down to meet us, then jumped back into the plane and rose up into the darkening air.

I stood in the grass looking back at the clouds and scanning the sky to the west for another plane. Eventually, I heard a drone and a pale shape dropped rapidly and landed. A short, stocky man with ginger hair and a red face jumped out. He was wearing shorts and a khaki shirt.

"I'm Fraser Smith," he said, and shook my hand. "We'd better get going."

The first raindrops had begun to fall: large, slow, plunking balls that splashed onto my outstretched hand. We clambered into the plane and headed west, away from the edge of the storm. Soon the sky and earth were looking less gloomy. A few minutes later, we were over Garamba National Park. It was a land of high grass plains, rolling beneath us across the earth. Fraser flipped the plane down toward grey shapes moving shoulder-high through the blades. These were elephants, scattered across the plains in small groups. There seemed to be hundreds of them. Then the Dungu River appeared, a bright brown thread in the carpet of grass, and we came down.

Fraser said nothing. We climbed into his waiting Land Rover and drove a few hundred yards to Nagero, the headquarters of the park. He stopped beside a hut.

"We've had this one cleaned up for you," he said. "If you'd like to come to supper, I'll pick you up at dusk. See you later."

He drove off. I threw my bags into the hut and walked outside to stretch my legs. Nagero was spread out along the unruly southern bank of the Dungu River. Half a dozen identical thatched huts stood in the thick grass. On the other side of a broad dirt boulevard, lined with high trees, lay the park offices, warehouses and workshops. At the far end were the smaller mud huts and ragged allotments of the staff village.

Trees and high grass lined the riverbank. I walked down a path and found a gap in the vegetation. The river flowed past beneath. The Dungu was the southern border of the park. The two thousand square miles of Garamba stretched away northward to the border with southern Sudan. This park was a World Heritage site. Almost 300 species of birds and 140 species of mammals, including 4,000 elephants,

30,000 buffaloes and 3,000 hippos, lived here. Garamba was also home to the last twenty-five northern white rhinos in the world. But it was probably the most remote park in Africa. The nearest town or telephone or shop was a week's drive away. Apart from the occasional missionary family or overland truck, few visitors ever came to Garamba. When I signed the park guest book, I saw I was the first guest for more than three months.

I walked back to my hut and sat on the porch watching the birds in the trees and the park staff wandering back and forth. Even Bunia seemed a lifetime away. The rolling of the world brought in the dusk. The day blackened like photosensitive paper in a dark room. The graininess dissolved into night. The first mosquitoes began to whine, so I crept under my net and lay there until Fraser's headlights swept across my open door.

The Smith's house lay a mile down the river. Kes Smith was taut and skinny. Her face was drawn and weather-beaten. Her skin seemed to have been pulled tightly across her face. There was a wariness in her eyes.

"A drink?" Kes said.

"Thanks."

I sat uneasily on a couch at the end of the main room. The house was one long wooden structure. The beds lay behind a partition and the kitchen and living room stretched down to where I was sitting. In front of me the house was half-open to the night and the river below. Suddenly, two children tumbled out of the bedroom and came over to investigate me. They had white hair and angelic faces and were wearing pyjamas. Chyulu was five and named after a range of hills in Kenya. Dungu, the boy, named after the river, was two. Their presence warmed the atmosphere. Kes and Fraser came over and we finally started talking.

"How was your journey?" Kes asked.

"The journey was fine. Staying at Bunia was a bit odd."

"Umm," Kes said. "Yes, I've stayed at the guesthouse."

On instructions from Nairobi, I had brought some chocolates, and I handed them over.

"Mummy, chocolate," Dungu said.

I was suddenly very popular, especially with Dungu and Chyulu. Fraser smiled and Kes's features softened into prettiness. Outsiders did not come here very often. It had taken a little while to weaken the defensive walls.

Over supper—homemade bread and rich stew—Kes and Fraser told me their story. They had come to Garamba seven years earlier. Fraser was born in Botswana and schooled in South Africa. He had worked on various wildlife projects, including Pilanesberg in South Africa. He had been hired by the Zairian government, with WWF money, to oversee the refurbishment of Garamba Park. Kes was an English biologist. She had come out to Africa to study wildlife and never gone home. Her work here was studying and monitoring the park's unique population of northern white rhinos.

When they first arrived, Kes and Fraser had chosen this quiet spot a little away from the main camp to set up their tents. It was a simple existence. Their only communication with the outside world was through their radio, and the aircraft, when it was working. But when Kes was expecting Chyulu, Fraser had built the house. It was still a simple, homemade affair. The kids bathed in a pair of plastic tubs on the floor. The kitchen implements hung on nails on the wall. One large cupboard held all the sacks of sugar and flour. Early on, the entire wall facing the river had been open. Wild animals used to wander in from the park. For a few months, an orphaned baby hippo had taken to sleeping under the kitchen table. But there were also other animals around.

When Dungu and Chyulu had gone to bed, Kes and Fraser told me about the incident of the man-eating lion.

"It was during the preparations for the fiftieth anniversary of the founding of the park," Kes said. "My mother had come to stay. We were cooking supper when Fraser came in, grabbed his gun, said nothing and went out."

"They were building a monument along the river, down by the hippo pools," Fraser continued. "A couple of masons and some rangers were camping out there. That evening, two of the men ran into Nagero and said that one of the masons had been eaten. The warden grabbed his gun. I came back here and got my rifle and a flashlight, and we drove down to the pool. When we got there, the lion was already dead. Kamate—you'll meet Kamate—had got there before us. Holding a torch, he'd found the lion and shot it. The lion turned out to be old and sick. It must have waited in the bushes, and when the mason walked away from the fire, it pounced. The poor fellow was dead and already half-eaten."

After this, Fraser had built up the house wall. I looked at the wooden planks. They reached about three feet up. The rest of the way to the roof was open to the night. The defenses would not have been able to keep out a sick kitten, let alone a lion or a leopard.

But life had been too busy to worry about the house. Fraser had been occupied with the park. He had brought in machinery and vehicles, rehabilitated the tourist huts and helped to arrange the patrolling of the park. He had also fixed up ways of crossing the river into the park. There was no bridge, so Fraser had mended the pontoon, a floating wooden raft on ropes, and built a ford for dry-season crossing. Kes was also kept busy by the children and by the white rhinos. She carried out regular counts and monitored the rhinos' feeding and breeding patterns. Their number was slowly growing.

But this was not all. Kes and Fraser also had another project, one they considered vital for the future of the park. This was the rehabilitation of King Leopold's dream.

The man King Leopold appointed to establish his training school for elephants was a Belgian army commandant named Jules Laplume. It was 2,100 years since Hannibal had taken an army of African elephants across the Alps and more than 1,400 years since the last record of working elephants in Africa: a pair of bulls pulling a chariot at Axum, in Abyssinia. But in 1900, Laplume traveled to Api in northern Zaire to set about reviving the art of training wild African elephants.

Laplume's initial job was to capture some calves. For his first season, he used the traditional Indian method of driving the elephants into enclosures called *keddahs*. This did not prove a great success. In India, the mahouts used tame elephants to separate the calves and drive away the wild adults. Laplume had no trained elephants, and every time he seemed to end up with either whole herds or no elephants in his *keddahs*. When he did finally manage to separate one cow and calf and shoot the cow, the calf soon died of shock.

The following year, Laplume changed tactics. When the rains ended, he took his gun and a party of Africans with ropes out into the bush. The Africans' job was to run down the calves and lasso them with ropes. If any adults caused trouble, Laplume was there to shoot them. This coarse method proved far more successful. By September 1902, Laplume had captured eight calves between the ages of one and four.

Laplume now had to start training these calves. He had no experience and only books about Indian methods to go by. When Leopold died in 1908, Laplume was still struggling. But the Belgian government offered to continue funding the

project, and by 1914 Laplume had a total of thirty-three elephants at Api. Then came the First World War. Laplume
was captured by the Germans and spent the entire war in a
prison camp. But in 1918, he was freed and returned to Api.
Soon after, he was given a grant by the new king, Albert.
He used the money to bring over seven Indian mahouts to
teach his men the correct methods for both catching and
training the elephants. The mahouts stayed for eight months.

A few years later, in 1925, Captain Keith Caldwell, a British game warden from Kenya, visited Api. He wrote that the
"Indians were dissatisfied with their quarters, their food, their
clothes, their pay and everything else they could think of,
and made themselves a perpetual nuisance. They treated the
elephant calves very harshly and two soon died from the
'dressage des Hindous.' " But in the eight months the mahouts stayed, they did teach Laplume and his elephant handlers, or cornacs, the basic elephant tricks. By the time they
left, the elephants would lie down, pick up objects, push
down trees and obey various other commands.

Impressed by Api, Caldwell reported that the African cornacs were much more gentle than the Indians had been. "The
head cornac chants a song and the remainder beat time with
their branches on the young elephants and join in the chorus.
This lasts for about ten minutes and the whole time it is going
on the elephants are fed with small pieces of manioc, sweet
potato or pineapple. The chant is very catchy and the whole
performance rather striking." Caldwell did, however, see the
graves of twelve cornacs killed by their elephants.

The elephant school was now on firm footing. But the
surrounding areas were severely depleted of wild elephants.
So in 1927, it was decided to move the school to an area of
greater elephant profusion. More than twenty trained elephants made the move, carrying the cornacs and many of the
school possessions on their backs. The new school was sited

at Gangala na Bodio, a small settlement on the edge of the Dungu River. Gangala was about to become one of the two headquarters of the new Garamba National Park, along with Nagero.

In 1936, Armand Denis, later to become the presenter of *On Safari*, the first television wildlife series, visited Gangala na Bodio. Denis found a civilized settlement. The guesthouse was "a fine building with three rooms, baths, quarters for the native boys, a place to keep a vehicle under cover and a broad verandah. . . . For once we were able to unpack our trunks, to spread ourselves in chests-of-drawers and wardrobes and to have a real bath." The commandant was now Raymond Lefebvre, another Belgian soldier, who ran the school like a military academy. At sunrise every morning, the Belgian flag was raised to a fanfare of trumpets and the "tubby native sergeant major, bare-footed, inspected the buttons, equipment and caps of the men." The cornacs then spent the day training their calves: tying their legs, forcing them to sit, teaching them to pick up objects with their trunks and eventually preparing them to accept a person sitting on their backs.

The highlight of Denis's visit was a day spent with the elephant catchers, the *chasseurs*, out in the field. The *chasseurs* were "Asandeh tribesmen, big powerful fellows, merry and full of courage, whose fathers and grandfathers were notorious man-eaters, and they proudly call themselves *Basolda na Mbongo*—elephant soldiers." When they approached an elephant herd, they "removed their uniform jackets and in this way became real warriors once more, like their fathers."

The methods had scarcely changed since Laplume's days. Three men carried rifles and nine had lassos. They approached the herd downwind and at a signal, all fired and shouted at once. The elephants immediately took off. "Then," Denis wrote, "we were treated to the wonderfully sporting spectacle of the Asandeh running after them. For a short distance, a hundred yards at most, elephants can keep up a speed of about 20 mph at a sharp amble, but then they slow down to something between 10 and 12 mph. These athletic young natives can soon overhaul the elephant calves which lag behind."

The *chasseurs* simply ran alongside the calves and slipped their ropes around the running elephants' legs. When a calf was lassoed like this, other men came over to help. More ropes were passed around the other legs and the calf was maneuvered toward a tree. The ropes were then tied around the tree trunk. The calf was now caught and adult elephants could be driven off with guns or shot. At the end of the day, each captured calf was tied between two trained elephants and led ceremoniously back to camp.

These methods could be dangerous. Denis recorded fifteen deaths among the *chasseurs* in the previous thirty years. But they were highly successful. As the years progressed, the elephant school grew larger and more efficient. By 1951, the school possessed more than a hundred trained elephants engaged in various local projects, including ploughing fields for farmers, pulling wagons and helping with logging.

In 1964, during the civil war in the Congo, Mike Hoare, the British mercenary, led an unit of mercenaries to Gangala na Bodio. Needing provisions, he asked the *conservateur* if he could borrow his elephants. "One by one a string of elephants emerged from the deep bush to stand silently on the sandy track leading down to the river, as though awaiting further orders," Hoare later wrote. The mercenaries rode the elephants into the park and shot three buffaloes from their backs.

I w o k e t o t h e sound of crashing leaves and creaking boughs. I threw on some clothes and went out into the watery early morning. A troop of black and white colobus monkeys were playing in the towering gero tree outside my hut. When they noticed me, they stopped and peered down, holding their heads on one side and twitching their noses. Their black faces were surrounded by creamy manes and their fluffy tails hung down like tempting bell ropes.

I was still standing below, looking up into the tree, when a smiling figure approached. This was Kamate, the man who had killed the man-eating lion. I looked him over. He was short and round. His face was boyish and friendly, though he must have been in his forties. He was dressed in a jean jacket, white shirt, pinstripe trousers and leather cowboy boots. On his head was a floppy hat.

"The elephants are ready," Kamate said in English. "I am the officer here in charge of the elephants. I have prepared them for you to ride."

I looked over to the park buildings and saw three elephants walking slowly around to the front. Sitting astride their backs were their cornacs. The elephants were Lwiru, Kukutu and Kilo. Along with Zombe—who, Kamate said, had decided to stay out in the bush feeding—these were the last of the trained elephants from King Leopold's elephant school.

We walked over. The elephants were all female. Lwiru, the leader, had long, slender tusks that almost reached to the ground. She knelt down and I scrambled onto her back. The seat was made of metal, wood and cane, and was held in place on top of a couple of blankets by ropes around the animal's belly. In India, the mahouts sat on the necks of the elephants, but here the cornacs perched high on the back, just in front of the seat.

Kamate climbed onto another elephant and Zombe's cornac joined his colleague on the third. Then, with a little prodding, we began to walk out of camp. When the river was low, the elephants would wade across and enter the park.

But at the moment, the waters were too high and fast-moving. The elephants could swim, but it made them nervous. So instead, we were heading down to the hippo pools where Kamate had shot the lion.

My cornac was a skinny old man named Dankangu. He spoke a few words of French. As we ambled along, he told me that he had been a cornac with these elephants since they were very young.

"How long ago was that?"

"Long," he said.

We left the camp behind and headed into a broad swampy area. The bright yellowy-green grass came up to the elephants' shoulders. The beasts squished through the mud and down into the water. Lwiru's steps were slow and deliberate, and as she walked, she pulled at tufts of moist grass with her trunk and stuffed them into her mouth.

The pale cloud cover was burning away under the sun and the sky was turning a warm, soft blue. Birds flitted from reed to reed. We walked slowly through the swamp and then out the other side. We were now on a broad grassy path, lined on either side with the high elephant grass, gleaming in the sun. We moved at the elephants' pace. When they wanted to stop and break off a succulent branch, we stopped. Dankangu muttered at Lwiru and hit her with his swish, but she paid little attention. When she was ready, we moved on.

Eventually, we came out by the hippo pools. This was a broad bend in the river where a large group of hippos spent their days in the slow water. They were there now, bunched together in the brown waters, only their brown nostrils, eyes and ears sticking up above the surface. From time to time, one of them would disappear completely, the water plopping as it closed over the empty surface. A minute or so later, there would be another plop and the hippo would resurface somewhere else, its eyes dripping water and glaring around.

Kamate waited on his elephant while I slid down and had a look around. The elephants took advantage of the stop to eat more seriously. Eventually, Kamate said it was time to go back. The cornacs wanted to look for Zombe.

We ambled back down the path, Lwiru farting and defecating along the way. I was idly looking down into the grass when I saw something gleam, like a lick of flame. At the same time, Lwiru caught a scent and reared sideways. The grass rustled and I saw the gleam again: the yellow and black haunches of a leopard stealing away from the path into the denser vegetation.

We found Zombe happily browsing in a thicket. The other elephants rumbled a greeting. Zombe's cornac walked over with his long stick and tried to persuade the elephant to let him climb onto her back. The words he used were a mixture of French and Bangala, the local language. There were even some Hindi words—such as *saba*, meaning "quiet." But Zombe was uninterested. She had decided to take the day off and there was nothing her cornac could do about it. In the end, we left her and swayed back to park headquarters.

When we had dismounted, Kamate and I went over to the bar. There were no drinks, no fridge and no barman. But there was a barrel of fresh water from the well. While we sat on the concrete porch, quenching our thirst and watching the river flow by, Kamate told me the story of how he had ended up in Garamba National Park, in charge of the trained elephants. In the late 1960s, as a young man, he had traveled across the border to Uganda to attend university. One holiday, he had found a job with Richard Chipperfield, from the circus family, who was out in Uganda catching animals. Kamate had got on well with Chipperfield, and when the catching was over he had accompanied him back to England, to work at Longleat and Woburn. He had stayed in England for seven years.

Out here in the bush, this story sounded so unlikely that skepticism must have shown in my eyes. Kamate looked a little hurt and told me to wait. He walked off to the staff village and returned with a pile of photographs.

The pictures were from another era. In one, a young man was standing in the back of a black-and-white-striped Land Rover. He had long blond hair and was naked to the waist. This was Richard Chipperfield. A young woman stood beside him. She was also blond, and was wearing a tiny short shirt and a pair of bell-bottomed trousers. They were Kings Road, circa 1970. Behind them, smiling bashfully, was young Kamate.

I now listened unquestioningly to Kamate's narrative. Chipperfield's catching technique was an updated version of the method used in the elephant school, he explained.

"We caught animals with a rope," Kamate said. "We drove beside an animal and then dangled the rope over its neck. We even caught elephant calves this way."

"What happened if the mother objected?"

"We had a piece of wood in front of the car. We could push them away with this."

He pulled out another photograph. The Jeep had a thick wooden bumper. A large elephant was standing in front of it. The animal must have just tried to lift up the Jeep and snapped one of its tusks. The tusk was caught by the picture in midair.

We looked through the rest of the photographs. Most were of Kamate as an elephant keeper. Here he was with elephants in Tanzania. Here again at Longleat and Woburn.

"This is the minister for wildlife for Uganda," he said. The photograph showed a podgy man in a grey suit standing a few feet from an elephant. "He was minister for wildlife and he was afraid of elephants," Kamate laughed.

"Why did you leave England?" I asked.

"My wife was sick, so I came home to Zaire."

"Is she OK now?"

"No, she is still sick, so I left her with my parents. I have a new wife now. I have five children with her."

"Oh."

"You take a picture of me now," Kamate said. "Then you can send it to me for my collection."

When Fraser finished working, he came over to the hut to collect me. There was no moon and the night was utterly black. Driving away, the headlights lit up the white ghost of a hippopotamus, grazing on the grass. The hippo lifted its head and its piggy eyes burned red in the lights. Then it lurched off, its huge belly and haunches swinging into the night.

Over supper, I asked Kes and Fraser about the elephants. In the years before and after independence, the numbers at the school had declined. The Belgians had lost interest and stopped catching new calves. Some of the elephants were killed during the civil war. By the time Mike Hoare turned up at Garamba in 1964, there were only fifteen trained elephants left. Later the numbers fell even further. When Kes and Fraser arrived at Garamba, there were only the four I had seen earlier in the day. Gangala na Bodio was even more run-down than Nagero, so the elephants were brought up here.

"They were very undisciplined," Kes said. "None of the old cornacs were left. The ones we have now were just junior hands when the school came to a halt. The elephants had been neglected. They would let people climb on their backs, but they wouldn't take instructions. We had to do a lot of work with the cornacs and the elephants to get them back into shape."

Garamba remained the only place in Africa where people could ride elephants through the bush, and Kes and Fraser saw elephant-back safaris as the best way to attract tourists to this remote spot. But the four elephants were already middle-aged. So together with the warden, the Smiths decided to catch some new young elephants while the older elephants were still alive and fit enough to help with the training.

The elephant catching was not without problems. The Smiths used a dart gun on the calves. But they could not simply shoot aggressive adults, as the Belgians had done. Nor was it possible to drive across country in Garamba, so the elephants had to be tracked on foot and there were some nasty moments when mothers decided to charge. But over several years, they managed to capture several young elephants without killing any adults.

The cornacs wanted nothing to do with these lively, aggressive youngsters. Fraser himself had worked for a time with Randall Moore in Pilanesberg and had picked up a little wisdom about trained elephants. But by this time, Kamate had also been hired. He had worked with elephants for years and he was put in charge of the new Garamba elephant school.

"We were starting from scratch without any money and pretty much in the dark," Kes said. "So we left it to Kamate. His techniques were, well, his own. He used ropes and a lot of force. In some ways, it was very depressing. There is nothing worse you can do to a baby elephant than take it away from its mother. But the calves did calm down and they slowly began to learn."

One of the captured calves died and two ran away, but another two, Rudi and Kwanza, stayed for nearly three years and became very tame and friendly. They learned to follow instructions, and while they were not old or large enough for adults to sit on their backs, they happily allowed Chyulu and African children to ride on them. Then news of these tame elephants reached Kinshasa. A government minister decided that it would be entertaining to have them at the zoo in the capital. The order could not be disputed. Rudi and Kwanza were sent off in a truck. The journey proved too much. Long before they reached Kinshasa, they were dead.

Since then, the scheme had faltered.

"Now we've got only one calf left," Kes said. "Lungunya."

"Where is she?"

"In a compound beyond the staff houses. Ask Kamate. He will take you to see her."

K a m a t e   a n d   I   w a l k e d   through the village. Fires smoked outside mud and thatch huts. The women smiled respectfully at Kamate. He was wearing his uniform: green beret, tight-fitting fatigues and high boots. He looked more like a park captain now, and less like a gigolo from Kinshasa.

Beyond the village, the path wound through ragged vegetable allotments. The fences around the cultivated plots were slung with tin cans to scare away the hippos, but there were still large trotter prints in the earth and bare patches in the carpet of vegetation where hippos had feasted. A little farther on, down by the river, was a fenced field, the elephant compound. Lungunya was browsing in one corner. A couple of trainee cornacs, young loose-limbed men with careless attitudes and ragged clothes, were lounging on the earth. As we approached, they climbed resentfully to their feet.

Kamate barked an order and they went over to Lungunya. The elephant backed away, but they caught hold of the rope around her neck and cajoled her into the training pen. This was a small area with a thick, high fence of tree trunks and heavy boughs. I walked up to Lungunya. She was about three years old, a skinny creature some four feet high. She had tiny tusks, a hairy face and frightened eyes.

Kamate gave more orders and the two handlers slipped a rope around Lungunya's back right leg. They tied the rope to the fence. Then they began to hit her with branches, shouting at her to sit down. Her eyes grew wild and full of panic. She squealed horribly and tugged at the rope. Several times, her trunk lunged toward the handlers like a boxer's fist. But each time, straining forward, she was held back by the rope. She squealed more, rumbling, farting and excreting.

I was standing in the corner, wincing at the scene. Kamate caught my expression and shouted louder at the men.

"I am not watching these boys," he said. "I am too busy. They are not doing their job. Before, she was sitting."

He told the men to stop and Lungunya soon calmed. The handlers now picked up leaves and grass, and the elephant sidled over to them and picked at the food. She was like a battered child, so desperate for affection that she was ready to take it even from those who beat her.

Kamate and I walked back through the vegetable garden and the village. Nearing the park buildings, I saw a man sweeping the ground. His feet were shackled together with a chain, like a convict.

"Who's that?" I asked.

"Haruna. He is a poacher."

"Why is he in chains?"

"He is very smart. If he was free, he would run all the way back to Sudan. We would not catch him."

"What was he poaching?"

"We can ask him."

We strolled over and talked to the guards. They were sitting in front of a tiny concrete building. In better times, this had been the generator room. Now it was the guardroom. I looked inside. The floor was grooved and uneven: built to hold the generator. Sometimes as many as a dozen poachers slept here. The guards called to Haruna and he shuffled over and stood in front of us. He was tall and wiry. A patchy beard sprang from a handsome, bony ebony face.

"Why are you here?" I asked through Kamate.

"He says he was arrested because he had a gun and he was shooting animals," Kamate translated. "At first, he did not admit this, but we beat it out of him."

"You beat it out of him?"

"Yes. We beat him. I told him that if he didn't tell the truth, we would beat him. He didn't talk, so we beat him. Then he started to talk."

I looked at Haruna. He was smiling shyly.

"What did you shoot?" I asked.

"Buffalo, bushpig, baboon."

"Any elephants?"

"Yes. Sometimes."

"For the ivory or the meat?"

"For both. We ate the meat and sold the ivory to a white man. He used to come every month in his aircraft."

"What did you catch him shooting?" I asked Kamate.

"Oh, everything. This man is a famous poacher. He has shot at our guards many times. We have always tried to catch him. Now he is caught, it is good."

"What will happen to him?"

"I think he will go to court in Isiro."

While we were talking, the guards had started chatting with Haruna. He was from Sudan and came south into the park to hunt. The guards were from Zaire. But they were all from the same world. All had grown up in small villages, farming and hunting for a living. They understood each other. If a guard lost his job, he would become a poacher. If a poacher was lucky, he might become a guard. I looked at them. They looked back at me and giggled.

"Ask him what he thinks about the trained elephants," I said to Kamate.

When Kamate spoke, Haruna giggled again. The guards also began to laugh. Their faces creased with amusement. They looked at me, looked at each other and roared.

"What are they laughing at?"

"Because they are happy," Kamate said.

The men laughed more. Soon I felt ridiculously happy and in a moment I was laughing too.

I t   w a s   m y   l a s t   day in Garamba and I was invited for a picnic in the park with the Smiths. The family rolled up in their Land Rover and we drove down to the river.

The Dungu was still running high. Its khaki waters bubbled and swirled along. The log raft, anchored to the bank, swayed gently. Fraser hooted his horn and half a dozen men wandered down from the village. They pulled the raft into place and laid planks from the muddy bank to the logs. Fraser drove the Jeep up onto the raft. We all followed and the men carefully pulled the raft across. I watched leaves and twigs circling past in the thick water. Then we drove off the raft and the men tugged themselves back over to the other side.

There were no proper roads in Garamba. The narrow track soon tunneled into the high grass. The golden walls were ten feet high. The passage was blind and uncomfortable. With the window open, blades flipped against the car and threw in a constant cloud of seeds, shavings and insects. And when we closed the window, the car rapidly became an oven.

Every now and again, we stopped to cool off and climb onto the roof for a look around. The fields rolled away in every direction. We could see isolated trees and small copses. But it was virtually impossible to spy what lived beneath the dancing tips of the blades of grass. It would, I thought, have been a different matter twelve feet up on an elephant's back.

After an hour or so, we came to a region where the grass had been burned. The park authorities were experimenting with burning different parts of the park—seeing how the new shoots attracted game. The burned areas had black soil peppered with fresh green grass. It was possible to look around now. We watched a herd of buffalo and, in the distance, saw a family of elephants weaving in and out at the edge of the long grass.

Finally, the track brought us out onto the banks of the Garamba River, thirty miles north of the Dungu. The picnic spot was an open patch of sand in the shade of a copse of trees overlooking a broad meander in the river. It was cool and lovely beneath the trees.

Unloading the car, I caught sight of the radiator grill. Driving through the park, parting the grass, the car must have brushed against tens of thousands of ears and blades. The grill was thick with broken grass, seeds and thousands of insects. The insects were buzzing and crawling and climbing over each other—orange beetles, green aphids, red ticks, brown cicadas, white ants, multicolored centipedes, whining flies and hundreds of thin-legged spiders.

Fraser built a fire and we cooked our food: leftover stew, toasted sandwiches and hot tea. Then we lay down on our backs in the shade and stared up at the branches of the tree and the placid milky afternoon sky.

"I went to see Lungunya yesterday," I said. "She didn't seem very happy."

"No," Kes agreed. "She's on her own. We really need to get her company. And we need to improve our training."

In some ways, Kes and Fraser would have liked to let the

four trained elephants grow old in peace—and not to have caught any more youngsters. They did not have King Leopold's desire to use the elephants to open up Zaire, to spread commerce, civilization and Christianity. In fact, the Smiths' dream was very different from Leopold's. They wanted to maintain the wilderness, to fend off civilization. But Garamba was no different from any other wilderness area in Africa. It had to find a way to justify its existence. And the trained elephants were Garamba's greatest asset.

"There was terrible elephant poaching here in the late 1970s and early 1980s," Kes said. "Before the rehabilitation program was set up, poachers came in from all sides and particularly south from Sudan. There are so many guns available up there. It's fallen off recently, specially since the ivory ban. But there is still a lot of hunting for meat. When we first arrived here, the rangers themselves simply saw the park as a larder. They were living off the wild animals. There were snares and traps all round park headquarters. You'd see very few animals round there."

"The locals also bribed the rangers to act as guides," Fraser added. "Sometimes with ludicrous results. A year or two back, a poacher in one of these bands shot a buffalo. The animal was only wounded and it charged and started goring the poacher. The ranger shot at the buffalo, but killed the poacher. The other people then beat up the ranger. He ended up in jail."

"What happened to the buffalo?"

"It ran off and survived."

The new park administration, helped by Fraser, had improved the lot of the rangers. They had better pay, good uniforms and enough food. Their morale was higher. They were now, on the whole, protecting animals more than shooting them. But this was only half the battle.

"In the end, the local people have to see the park as a

positive resource that benefits them," Kes said. "The best way to do that is to bring in tourists. Way up here, we're not going to get mass tourism, but if we can train more elephants, then maybe we can fly in wealthy tourists who will be willing to pay a lot of money to ride through the bush on elephants."

The idea was comparable to hunting, where the money from shooting a few animals helped to protect all the other wildlife. Here the domestication of a few elephants could pay for the security and wild habitats of several thousand others. The first attempts to restart King Leopold's scheme had not worked. But Fraser and Kes were determined to try again. They were applying to WWF for more money. They wanted to bring in elephant experts—perhaps even to hire some more mahouts from India to spend a few months at Garamba and train some young cornacs.

I brushed away a fly from my face. There was not yet an acute conservation problem here in Garamba. This part of Zaire was sparsely populated. If anything, over the previous few years, the land had been growing more wild. But it took twenty years to train an elephant. And within twenty years, development would probably reach even Garamba. There would be logging companies and cattle ranchers. And there would be more people, more mouths to feed. An elephant project started now could perhaps pre-empt such development. Elephants could be trained. A small lodge could be built. Tourism and development could be kept to a minimum. It would mean capturing more unhappy calves like Lungunya. But if the purity of the wilderness of Garamba could be saved, then perhaps it was a sacrifice worth making.

A hundred years earlier, King Leopold of Belgium had dreamed about harnessing Africa's own resources to build the continent's future. Africa was a very different place now, but in a way, as I saw it, a modern version of Leopold's dream was still valid. Africa was not one huge primitive safari park, for the benefit of Western vacationers. But nor could it suddenly transform itself into a modern world, another Europe or United States. It needed to combine the two contrasting influences, the new and the old, the airplane and the elephant, in an African dream of the future.

I stood up and walked down to the riverbank. The future seemed a distant place, at that moment as far away and utterly out of reach as London or New York. What it held, I could only dream about. But at least I was here now, standing in the stillness, able to look out on the land as it had been for tens of thousands of years, wild and open and uncompromised, the grass whispering in the breeze, the waters sliding intently onward, and a kingfisher hovering above the surface, wings beating and beating against the warm air, moving neither backward nor forward, neither up or down.